o

...ceptions of reality in
American poetry

CONCEPTIONS
OF REALITY
IN MODERN
AMERICAN
POETRY

CONCEPTIONS OF REALITY IN MODERN AMERICAN POETRY

BY L. S. DEMBO

UNIVERSITY OF CALIFORNIA PRESS
BERKELEY AND LOS ANGELES
1966

UNIVERSITY OF CALIFORNIA PRESS
BERKELEY AND LOS ANGELES, CALIFORNIA
CAMBRIDGE UNIVERSITY PRESS
LONDON, ENGLAND
© 1966 BY THE REGENTS OF
THE UNIVERSITY OF CALIFORNIA
LIBRARY OF CONGRESS CATALOG CARD NUMBER:
66-18470
PRINTED IN THE UNITED STATES OF AMERICA

TO MY PARENTS

PREFACE

I have tried in this work to bring to a focus some of the important literary and philosophic issues raised in twentieth-century American poetry. The poets I have selected are, either explicitly or implicitly, concerned with "objective reality" and the ways of knowing and revealing it; they are similarly concerned with the role of the poet himself and the relation of language to reality. It is my contention that despite great differences in temperament and idiom, these poets adhere to a common logic—one naturally imposed by the involvement of poetry with epistemology and ontology. I have further argued that the extension of this logic to the ethical realm, encompassing myth, history, and social life, underlies the complex long poem, or "neo-epic," that has become a characteristic phenomenon of modern American poetry. To study conceptions of reality in this poetry involves an inquiry into the relations between subject and object, between the poetic sensibility and the world that is to be revealed. Specifically to be dealt with are the problems of exotic perception when that world is one of "objects," and of psychological projection when that world is one of human affairs.

Since the emphasis of this study is formal rather than historical, I have discussed prototypes and forerunners not because I wish to establish sources, but simply to clarify current theory and practice. By the same token, I have not tried to make philosophic bases into philosophic superstructures—to engage in that kind of overelaboration in which a work whose logic seems broadly to adhere to that of a given philosophy is interpreted uniformly in light of that philosophy. Finally, I offer the thesis of this work as a possible perspective, hardly an all-embracing theory.

I am indebted to the following publishers for permission to quote from copyrighted material: Grove Press, for quotations from H.D.'s *Helen in Egypt*, copyright 1961, and

vii

Robert Duncan's *The Opening of the Field,* copyright 1960; Houghton Mifflin Company, for quotations from *The Complete Poetical Works of Amy Lowell,* copyright 1955; New Directions and MacGibbon and Kee, Ltd., for quotations from William Carlos Williams' *Collected Earlier Poems,* copyright 1938, 1951, *Collected Later Poems,* copyright 1944, 1948, 1950, 1963, *Paterson,* copyright 1946, 1948, 1949, 1951, 1958, and *Pictures from Brueghel,* copyright 1949, 1962; and from Ezra Pound's *Personae,* copyright 1926, 1954, and the *Cantos,* copyright 1940, 1948; Alfred A. Knopf, Inc., for quotations from Wallace Stevens' *The Necessary Angel,* copyright 1951, *Collected Poems,* copyright 1954, *Opus Posthumous,* copyright 1957; Harcourt, Brace and World, Inc., for quotations from E. E. Cummings' *Collected Poems, 1923–1954,* and T. S. Eliot's *Collected Poems, 1909–1962;* Liveright Publishing Corporation, for quotations from Hart Crane's *Collected Poems,* copyright 1961; Macmillan Company for quotations from Marianne Moore's *Collected Poems,* copyright 1951. I am equally indebted to Faber and Faber Ltd. for permission to quote from Wallace Stevens' *Collected Poems;* T. S. Eliot's *Collected Poems, 1909–1962;* Ezra Pound's *Personae* and the *Cantos;* and Marianne Moore's *Collected Poems.*

I am also grateful to Mrs. Jeri Weiss and Mrs. Christine Ashenbrenner who assisted me in research and proofreading and to the Central Stenographic Bureau of UCLA for preparation of the manuscript.

L. S. D.

Madison, Wisconsin
November, 1965

CONTENTS

1. INTRODUCTION

The preoccupation with "external reality" that underlies much of the theory and practice of the chief twentieth-century American poets is part of a tradition that began in England at least as early as Hazlitt and in France at least as early as Théophile Gautier and the Parnassians. Its principal thesis is that art must be directed toward the object and not the subject, that the artist must attain what Leconte de Lisle called *impassibilité*, in which one escapes the tyranny of "personal caprice and taste," the *angoisse du coeur et de ses voluptés*.[1] Accordingly, it involves the view that art is a medium for "knowing" the world in its "essentiality," for apprehending things as they are. Thus for Hazlitt, writes W. J. Bate, the artist seeks to "capture the fluid almost intangible nature or 'identity' of the object . . . and to disclose and present it in its unique individuality." This end is effected through "gusto," or "sympathetic identification." Strong emotion exists, but it is emotion "turned *outward* toward its object, to the external world, not on subjective emotion directed inward."[2] A crucial elaboration of this theory is, as one critic, Everett Knight, points out in connection with modern French literature, a post-Kantian attack on conceptualization itself as being hopelessly subjective, with the attendant view that essential reality is accessible, but only through artistic perception.[3] In such a theory, as one can readily deduce, "knowledge" becomes indistinguishable from aesthetic emotion. A recent version of this conception, I might add, is Alain Robbe-Grillet's absurdist rationale for the *nouveau roman*: here art must aim at describing the "slippery surface" of the real world, a world "without meaning, without soul, without values"; the *sens priviligé* of the artist is simply the eye for form, *le regard*.[4]

A characteristically "objectivist" vision of experience appears in the theories of Schopenhauer—particularly relevant

here because Schopenhauer was a principal influence on
Henri Bergson and Bergson on T. E. Hulme, aesthetician
of the Imagist movement, in which modern American poetry
had its beginning. We find in *The World as Will and Idea*,

> [If a man] ceases to consider the where, the when, the
> why, and the whither of things, and looks simply and
> solely at the *what*; if, further, he does not allow abstract
> thought, the concepts of reason, to take possession of his
> consciousness, but, instead of all this, gives the whole
> power of his mind to perception, sinks himself entirely
> in this, and lets his whole consciousness be filled with the
> quiet contemplation of the natural object actually present,
> whether a landscape, a tree, a mountain, a building, or
> whatever it may be; inasmuch as he *loses* himself in this
> object . . . then that which is so known is no longer the
> particular thing as such; but is the Idea, the eternal
> form . . . he who is sunk in this perception . . . is *pure,*
> will-less, painless, timeless *subject of knowledge*.[5]

Implicit here is the conception of two discontinuous realms
of experience, that of "will," emotion, reason, and action,
and that of nonemotion, passive contemplation, and "knowledge." Accordingly, Schopenhauer's ideal of perception involves a purification of all elements associated with normal
vision and response, particularly the "concepts of reason."
Such elements constitute the self or personality that must
be surrendered if true knowledge is to be acquired.

It is precisely the theory of discontinuity in Bergson's
thought, with its consequent dualisms, that appealed to
Hulme. In "Bergson's Theory of Art," Hulme asserts that
it is the function of the artist to penetrate the "veil" that
separates men from Nature, the "life-force," "the *élan vital*"
that permeates existence. On the one side of the veil lies
the realm of action, governed by the intellect, which classifies
and categorizes; it is a realm of "stock-types" and "plain
language" that conveys nothing more than approximations
of reality. On the other side lies the realm of knowledge,
governed by "intuition," wherein things are perceived in

their "individuality" and "freshness." Here language is not conventional but metaphorical. Hence art, the language of knowledge, is characterized by its "passionate desire for accuracy," and "aesthetic emotion" becomes the "excitement which is generated by direct communication." [6]

Hulme's well-known essay, "Modern Art and Its Philosophy," with its prophecy of a formalist revolution, is actually based on a theory of nature that is at the opposite extreme from Bergson's vitalism. Instead of "placing himself back within the object by a kind of sympathy," as the Bergsonian essay conceives it in the tradition of Hazlitt, the artist is now said to

> . . . create a certain abstract geometrical shape, which being durable and permanent shall be a refuge from the flux and impermanence of outside nature. The need which art satisfies here is not the delight in the forms of nature, but the exact contrary. In the reproduction of natural objects there is an attempt to purify them of their characteristically living qualities in order to make them necessary and immovable.[7]

It would seem that whereas the Bergsonian artist would seek to capture things in their particularity (or *haecceitas*), the formalist artist would seek to capture them in their universality (or *quidditas*). The common denominator of these two visions is the notion that some kind of "purification" is necessary—that subjectivity, in the one essay associated with reason as the wrong mode of universalizing (seeing in terms of "fixed types"), and in the other with reason as the wrong mode of particularizing (vivifying or personifying objects), must be transcended. But whether or not these positions are reconcilable is not the issue, and, in fact, their contrariness all the more points up the author's primary concern with the idea of discontinuous realms of experience and the need for perceptual or psychological purification to move from one realm to the other.

The desire to purify perception and response of conventional reason, sentiment, and even of conception itself—

to acquire knowledge of an essential reality and to reveal its nature (basically aesthetic)—appears in one form or another in all the poets to be discussed. Pronouncements of the Imagists, Williams' famous principle "No ideas but in things," Stevens' "The world must be measured by eye," Marianne Moore's ideal of seeing "the rock crystal thing," Crane's notion of poetic "surrender" to the object, and similar theories in the other poets, are symptomatic of an objectivist way of looking at experience in general and the function of poetry in particular.

The idealization of language, a marked feature of modern poetry, is a direct manifestation of objectivist logic. In *What Is Literature?*, Sartre asserts that the poet has, once and for all, "chosen the poetic attitude which considers words as things and not as signs." Signification has become "absorbed" into the "phrase-object" which is a mirror of the world.[8] Less approvingly, Allen Tate speaks of "that idolatrous dissolution of language from the grammar of a possible world, which results from the belief that language itself can be reality, or by incantation can create a reality: a superstition that comes in French from Lautréamont, Rimbaud, and Mallarmé to the Surrealists, and in English to Hart Crane, Wallace Stevens, and Dylan Thomas."[9] More simply, language has been regarded as a mode of revelation, a logos that has the essentiality of the object as a referent; as the expression of radical perception it is itself radical.

We cannot but agree with Tate that Mallarmé's poetry, for example, reflects a dissolution of language from the grammar of a possible world, but that is precisely Mallarmé's point. In a theory that shows the influence of Schopenhauer, language is the sole means by which man can transcend a world governed by Chance (*le Hasard*) and penetrate to an ultimate realm (*l'Absolu*), which, correspondingly, is experienced only through logos (*le Verbe*). The language of poetry seeks to approximate the language of the Absolute, but since it originates in the causal world, it is constantly subject to Chance. Expression of *le Verbe* in a poem is therefore no more certain than the casting of dice, and *un*

coup des dès jamais n'aboulira le Hasard. At once a poetic
and a metaphysic, this theory affected both the form of the
poem (dissolution of conventional grammar and syntax) and
the content, the subject often being the struggle of the poet
to attain transcendent perception.[10] Preoccupation with language as a determining force in human experience (rather
than simply as a medium of communication) and with the
need for some kind of purification has occurred, of course,
outside poetic theory and in such diverse thinkers as Friedrich
Schlegel and Ludwig Wittgenstein. It may or may not involve
a mystique of perception, but when it does, as in Mallarmé
and in modern poetry, one cannot deny that it has a coherent
metaphysical basis.

The idealization of language, based upon a perception-
mystique, is possible in poetic conceptions of historical,
social, and "cosmic" reality no less than of ontological reality.
The modern American neo-epics, which represent an extension of objectivist logic from the realm of aesthetic reality
to ethical reality, are all concerned in one way or another
with the subject of logos, as well as aspiring to be forms of
logos in themselves. In the latter instance, we find a mode
of presentation that is purportedly beyond normal logic and
reflective of a purified form of perception and response: the
ideogrammic method in Pound's *Cantos*, the Apollonian-
Dionysian dialectic in Crane's *Bridge*, the meditative-musical
progression in Eliot's *Four Quartets*, what we might call the
"field of action" technique in Williams' *Paterson*. All of
these anticonventional modes seek to transcend the rational
and chronological apprehension of history and to provide
a total illumination that can be provided only by the poem.
As for the subject, we discover, as has been observed by
Roy Harvey Pearce and modern critics in general, that the
poet has become his own hero.[11] An underlying theme of
the neo-epics is the poet's own quest for creativity through
the mastery of language, his struggle to purify "the dialect
of the tribe," wherein lies personal and social salvation.
Hence Williams writes that *Paterson* "is a search for the
redeeming language by which a man's premature death

might have been prevented"; Pound employs the Confucian theory of *cheng ming* in which the use of a so-called rectified terminology becomes a primary issue in the renovation of society. One hardly does more than state the obvious by pointing out that in Eliot the Christian struggle for apprehension of the Word is parallel to the personal poetic struggle for linguistic perfection. Crane's Bridge, apprehension and revelation of which is the object of a quest, is described as a "multitudinous Verb," the "white pervasive paradigm of Love," and is related to what is elsewhere called the "bright logic" of poetic speech that comes after suffering.[12]

It is problematic whether radical theories of perception do not in fact come full circle to a kind of subjectivism—whether there is not a blurring of the distinction between objective revelation and subjective transformation or re-creation of external reality. Anticonceptualism of the kind found in Schopenhauer or the existential writers explicitly resolves itself into a philosophical idealism in which the perceiver, through his consciousness, becomes the determining element of the world he perceives. (As in Stevens, the *idea* of the world becomes the world.) In Sartre's aesthetic ontology, both writer and reader "create" the work, and the world it projects, insofar as the fictional world created by one comes to life only in the consciousness of the other.

The attempt to extend perceptual realism from the ontological to the social and historical realms, as in the neo-epics, presents a similar problem. Here subjectivism takes an explicit psychological, no less than an implicit epistemological, form. To begin with, as we have seen, a major theme in the neo-epic is, almost invariably, poetic creativity itself. The dramatic basis of the poem is usually the endless pursuit of a goddess, a muse, a personification of beauty, or an embodiment of natural or divine forces, with whom union means self-realization. What is crucial is the state of mind of the speaker during the quest for an ideal that can be asserted or momentarily apprehended in an aesthetic moment, but never definitively realized. The very conception of a quest is, in a sense, the projection of a self-image and a certain frame of mind. For the quest requires a faith, a tragic optimism, which can withstand repeated failure and survive the suffering that comes with it. Indeed, to carry the logic a step farther, when placed in the context of a quest, suffering becomes meaningful, and the poet becomes a hero not for what he achieves but for what he endures; "For us," says Eliot in the *Quartets*, "there is only the trying." And this remark has its counterpart in Williams' *"La Vertue est toute dans l'effort,"* an adage relevant to the experience of Paterson.

If this kind of stoicism is a state of mind, it is one that involves ethical and, implicitly, epistemological or ontological problems. The poet in his quest passes through various forms of hell—personal, social, or theological—but he accepts hell in the name of paradise. Similarly, the goddess symbolism characteristic of the neo-epic usually pertains to a figure with both demonic and ideal manifestations. Crane's Pocahontas may appear as Magdalene, Pound's Helen-Aphrodite as Circe, and Williams' nameless goddess as a whore. The ability to see the one in the other, the ideal in the demonic, is the basis of the poet's vision. For Pound's speaker, whether he is sitting on the steps of the Dogana in Venice, walking the streets of Paris, observing a hell of usurers, or suffering incarceration in Pisa, what matters is that the ideal image of the goddess and all it signifies be retained in the mind; and, in fact, Canto 74 states that "the drama is wholly subjective." In the "Tunnel" section of *The Bridge* the poet, in despair over the metropolitan hell symbolized by the subway, still speaks of "some Word that will not die"—and it will not die because it is kept alive in his mind. Given these considerations, it is, again, problematic whether the neo-epic can be said to be realistic or idealistic; external reality requiring a special mode of perception becomes, in part, internal reality sustained by a particular sensibility. Or, perhaps to overstate the matter, social and

metaphysical vision becomes bound up with a form of solipsism.

I might add that the theme of poetic quest has profoundly influenced the form of the neo-epic, which, philo-
sophically, is capable of endless accretion. The *Cantos*, for
example, does not present a developing pattern of events
with a recognizable beginning, middle, and end; it views history as cyclical rather than progressive, and its adherence or
lack of adherence to chronology is of little thematic importance, since one epoch epitomizes another. Thus the Rock-
Drill and Thrones cantos really do not "advance" the argument of the Pisan cantos before them, just as the Pisan
cantos elaborate but do not advance the argument contained
in the first thirty, or for that matter the first ten, cantos.
That is to say, the ideal is sought, apprehended, and lost in
a series that logically can terminate only with the author's
inability to contemplate history. We find Williams adding
a fifth book to *Paterson* some years after the completion of
the main work, and, apparently still dissatisfied with the
"resolution" therein contained, beginning work on a sixth
book prior to his death. Accordingly, the cycle of despair and
faith that marks *The Bridge* is brought to a conclusion in a
literary but not a philosophical climax; the sequence ends
with a hymn celebrating the appearance of the Ideal expressed in the symbol of Brooklyn Bridge, but far from
representing the realization of what values the Bridge signifies beyond the merely aesthetic, the poem actually expresses nothing more than the ecstasy of the speaker. And
since the poem ends with a question, we can predict that
he will fall from his Dionysian pinnacle to an Apollonian
dejection, to continue the cycle. With its specifically Christian frame of reference, *Four Quartets* presents a vision in
which it is clear that what is available to the Moral Man is
not salvation, but recognition of the need for salvation, for
internal discipline, and for faith, qualities perpetually sought
by poets but finally attained only by saints. Not only does
"Burnt Norton," written as an independent poem, stand by

itself, but, in a sense, so does each of the remaining three
quartets, since each epitomizes the quest.

Whatever the complications to which their premises lead,
all the writers in this study believe that art is a special mode
for "knowing" a hidden, objective reality and expressing its
beauty—thus they can be called "aestheticists." In practice,
however, imagist poetry—that of Fletcher, the early H.D.,
and Amy Lowell—is not esoteric, for it is not really preoccupied with epistemology and ontology. I have therefore
reserved the term "objectivist" for those radical aestheticists
whose poetry is an esoteric manifestation of their concern
with esoteric perception, with "transconceptual" vision. I
have placed Williams, Stevens, and Marianne Moore in this
category. I have then gone on to discuss the generally aestheticist and specifically objectivist aspects of Cummings,
Crane, Pound, and Eliot, and two avant-garde poets, Charles
Olson and Robert Duncan.

2. IMAGISM AND
AESTHETIC MYSTICISM

The chief characteristic of the New Poetry, whatever its form, said Amy Lowell in 1916, is "externality! the regarding of the world as having an existence separate from oneself." "Introspection," she added, "is not the besetting sin of the new poets, as it was the poets of the nineties. Again all these groups of new poets seek life and vividness. They are all desperately sincere and to portray the world about them in its truth and beauty is their only aim." [1] Despite the vagueness of this assertion, one can detect in it a characteristically aestheticist set of values. The terms "life and vividness" explicitly recall Hulme as does Miss Lowell's comment elsewhere that the modern poet has a certain "zest in seeing things and recording them." Imagism, itself, she once defined as the technique of "picture-making without comment," a value that recalls not only Hulme, but the early aestheticist movement of *la poésie visible, l'école pittoresque*, which reached its high point (and, according to one historian, its conclusion) in the *Emaux et camées* of Théophile Gautier.[2]

While Amy Lowell's pronouncements scarcely reach the level of "speculations," they at least have a general descriptive value, just as her values broadly reflect those of the movement with which she associated herself. As she herself realized, Imagism was less a school than a "habit of mind." Holding to her narrow definition of Imagism as the technique of picture-making, she could argue with justification that sometimes one wrote imagistic poems, sometimes not, and, in fact, her own poetry indicates that, for the most part, she did not. On the other hand, as a "habit of mind," that is to say, as a set of assumptions and attitudes about objects, images, poetry, and the universe in general, Imagism represents, within broad limits, a coherent, pervasive, and consistent response.

In discussing the six articles of the manifesto set forth by Richard Aldington and Amy Lowell in the preface to the first Imagist anthology, Willard Thorp notes that the first three, concerned with common speech and exact usage, new rhythms, and freedom in choice of subject, are repeated in every new poetic movement.[3] The last three, concerned with presenting an image, producing a "hard and clear" poetry, and achieving "concentration," he argues, come to the heart of the whole matter and return us to the theories of Hulme. He might have added that the last two also return us to the ideals of Parnassus. For example, in his attempt to justify his Hellenic poems, Leconte de Lisle argues for a poetry that will free itself from *"mesquines impressions personelles, envahie par les néologismes arbitraire, morales et profanes, esclave des caprices et des goûts individuels."* [4] In seeking control and discipline—detachment from both self-sentiment and social action—the Parnassian aesthetic accordingly demanded a concrete style, *la nuance exacte.* Or, going back even farther, we are again reminded of Gautier's value of "sculptured poetry."

It is the third article that perhaps represents a novel emphasis, if not an original contribution to aestheticism, so long as the "presentation of an image" means something more than picture-making as such. We recall, for example, Ezra Pound's definition in "A few Don'ts by an Imagiste":

> An "Image" is that which presents an intellectual and emotional complex in an instant of time. I use the term "complex" rather in the technical sense employed by the new psychologists, such as Hart. . . .
>
> It is the presentation of such a "complex" instantaneously which gives that sense of sudden liberation; that sense of freedom from time limits and space limits; that sense of sudden growth, which we experience in the presence of the greatest works of art.[5]

The point I am making is that an image is, precisely, an Image. And, indeed, this whole definition, with its mention of "freedom," transcendence of time, and "growth," has a strongly Bergsonian cast. René Taupin has argued that the Imagists believe with De Gourmont that since sensation is the basis of everything, the poet must seek to strike the senses. "By the image, a fusion of two different things produced by a natural act of the spirit, the poet restores his sensation in tact." Such an image represented a synthesis in itself; "the image, a new word, a new vision risen from the basic sensation, is this sensation directly communicated." Taupin goes on to speak of the "accurate mystery" of Imagism, "born of the very precision of details." [6] To be noted here is the idea of the image as a new word and new vision in itself. The implication is that the image is not simply a vehicle for transcribing a sensation but represents part of the sensation itself—or, better, it is an idealized re-creation of a sensation, a "new vision," which has come to be a thing-in-itself.

On the other hand, one cannot forget that an image requires an object, and that a semimystical view of the image subsumes a similar view of the object and, indeed, of nature in general. For example, even after Imagism as a movement had long been dead, Richard Aldington could express a characteristic attitude:

> This brings me to two other elements of poetry about which I feel great diffidence in speaking—I mean reverence and the sense of mystery. By "reverence" I understand no false or affected humility, but an intimate and spontaneous conviction that what is not me, what is outside me, is far greater and more interesting than I am, although the only account I can give of it is how it appears to me and through me. By the sense of mystery I understand the experience of certain places and times when one's whole nature seems to be in touch with a presence, a genius loci, a potency. I won't go into the

psychology of this or even attempt to argue that it may not be a self-induced delusion. I shall only say that the experience seems to have occurred to many other people in many ages, and add that when I use the word "god" or "gods" or the name of some Hellenic deity, I am not indulging in a mythological flourish but refer to the actual experience of some "potency." [7]

Important here is that a given object is not a manifestation of the divine, but of itself—aesthetically—generates the sense of mystery in the mind of the sympathetic or empathetic beholder. Aldington's remarks, I might add, shed light on Pound's oft-quoted comment that he believes in the Greek deities and, correspondingly, on the mythic-aesthetic moments that recur throughout the *Cantos*. They are also relevant to the Hellenism of H.D. and recall the whole tradition of Hellenism and aestheticism that began with *le rêve hellenique*, associated in particular with Louis Ménard and Leconte de Lisle. As was mentioned in the preceding chapter, it was the opinion of one historian of the tradition in France, that Hellenism ultimately reduced itself to an attempt to create beauty in art. And one can draw the conclusion in general, I think, that in the association of Hellenism and aestheticism, the latter has a strong tendency to absorb the former, as, in fact, it has a strong tendency to absorb any other approach to experience with which it is associated in imagist poetry.

I hope I have not suggested that one can consider any object described in an imagist poem as, per se, a "potency." Impressionism or sensationalism is possible without mysticism; it is only in a larger context, when such impressions begin to be idealized as modes of superior "knowledge" in a vitalistic or nihilistic vision transcending mere hedonism, that a mystical light it cast over them. It is, I think, in the poetry of Leconte de Lisle that we find a prototype of the impressionistic experience at the mystical level, and we might, briefly, consider its particular complex of attitudes and feelings. The poem "Midi," which, following the style of Leconte de Lisle, presents an aesthetic moment and then discourses on it, is characteristic enough:

> Midi, roi des été, épandu sur la plaine,
> Tombe en nappes d'argent des hauteurs du ciel bleu.
> Tout se tait. L'air flamboie et brûle sans haleine;
> La terre est assoupie en sa robe de feu.

That this moment represents something more than mere sensual response to a tropical noon is made clear in the three concluding stanzas:

> Homme, si, le coeur plein de joie ou d'amertume,
> Tu passais vers midi dans les champs radieux,
> Fuis! la nature est vide et le soleil consume:
> Rien n'est vivant ici, rien n'est triste ou joyeux.
>
> Mais si, désabusé des larmes et du rire,
> Altéré de l'oubli de ce monde agité,
> Tu veux, ne sachant plus pardonner ou maudire,
> Goûter une suprême et morne volupté,
>
> Viens! Le soleil te parle en paroles sublimes;
> Dans la flamme implacable absorbe-toi sans fin;
> Et retourne à pas lents vers les cités infimes,
> Le coeur trempé sept fois dans le néant divin.[8]

The man who might come upon the scene with "joy" or "bitterness," not yet disillusioned with both tears and laughter, perhaps represents the romantic mind in particular against which Leconte de Lisle posed the ideal of poetic *impassibilité*. More generally, he represents the conventional human sensibility. For the Aesthetic Man, on the other hand, who has purified himself of all desire (who has stoically, in one sense, dehumanized himself and his mode of perception), the *midi* offers a "supreme, austere pleasure," a Sensation or aesthetic Knowledge to be experienced only by one who has yielded to the Divine Nothingness, or meaninglessness, of the natural world. The "sublime speech" of the sun signifies nothing beyond itself, either in a human or an eternal world, just as the man who apprehends it in a transconceptual response experiences nothing but the pure sensation of the *flamme implacable* into which he is absorbed.

If "Midi" is concerned with the sensual aspects of an encounter with Néant, then "L'Orbe d'Or," the aesthetic moment at sunset, is concerned with another element in the experience, that of "repose." Here, "coffee trees," "ripened sugar-cane," and sugar mills (the scene is, once more, Leconte de Lisle's native island of Réunion) exhale, under the sun's influence, an incense; and, as the evening star emerges,

> L'âme, qui contemple, et soi-même s'oublie
> Dans la splendide paix du silence divin,
> Sans regrets ni désirs, sachant que tout est vain,
> En un rêve éternel s'abîme ensevelie.[9]

Between the incense and the vision of the star, the poet experiences what Leconte de Lisle in another poem refers to as *muette ivresse*, the silent intoxication in which sensuosity and repose are fused in a total mystical-aesthetic experience that represents a contingent moment in a chaotic world. That natural objects can create such a *muette ivresse* indicates, to return to our original proposition, that they have the power of the genius loci, mentioned by Aldington, the innate potency of the god-in-the-object, the special influence of the thing-in-itself that contains eternity and reveals it to the purified perceiver.

The form of the experience that characterizes Leconte de Lisle recurs in John Gould Fletcher and to a great extent, as I hope to demonstrate later, in Hart Crane. Fletcher has sometimes been considered peripheral to the Imagist movement—and if Imagism is defined in the narrower sense of "picture-making without comment," the judgment is accurate enough. On the other hand, one can argue equally that Fletcher represents the imagist "sensibility" in its most mystical form. The crux of Fletcher's poetics and much of his poetry is a theory of empathy that ends in a vision of "interpenetration." In the preface to *Goblins and Pagodas*, for example, he describes the ways in which various poets would treat the same subject, that of a book lying on the desk. He argues that he himself would

> . . . link up my personality and the personality of the book and make each a part of the other. In this way I should strive to evoke a soul out of this piece of inanimate matter, a something characteristic and structural inherent in this organic form which is friendly to me and responds to my mood.
>
> This method is not new, although it has not often been used in Occidental countries. Professor Fenollosa, in his book on Chinese and Japanese art . . . calls this doctrine of the interpenetration of man and inanimate nature, the cardinal doctrine of Zen Buddhism.[10]

The appeal of "Zen Buddhism" for Fletcher was, perhaps, no more accidental than the appeal of Hindu mysticism for Leconte de Lisle. Thus Fletcher reveals the same impulse to escape from the self into the object in a mystical-aesthetic moment. "Irradiations," a poem that begins with a vague apprehension of nature and moves toward "interpenetration" of subject and object reaches a climax in which "the ultimate divine union seems about to be accomplished":

> You trees, now talk to me . . .
> You winds, now play with me . . .
> I now am yours and you are mine: it matters not
> What gods herein I see . . .
> We drink and pass the cup, immortally.

And finally the poet attains a state of full mystical identification:

> I am a wheeling swallow,
> Blue all over is my delight.
> I am a drowsy grass-blade
> In the greenest shadow.[11]

One can see in the process a mystification of eighteenth-century "sympathy" psychology, discussed previously in con-

nection with Hazlitt and Hulme. The belief, as Bate describes it, "in the importance of the artist's capacity to enter
totally into his subject" similarly lies behind "Wordsworth's
calm and meditative regard for nature . . . [the] subjectively
nostalgic and almost nihilistic expression in Byron's occasional identification of himself with the ocean, the storm,
and the mountains, or in Shelley's yearning to merge himself in the West Wind. . . ." [12] As in Leconte de Lisle,
sensuosity thus has a metaphysical and, ultimately, a moral,
significance. Fletcher argued that

> In the manuscript of "Irradiations" . . . were . . .
> paeans to dancing, glorifications of the color and intoxica-
> tion of sheer life to put all the grim and monotonous
> pessimism of my early poems to utter shame. . . .
> Nietzsche must have been right after all; only he who
> could learn how to dance . . . would be able to triumph
> over the future. Man's greatest victory over adverse cir-
> cumstances lay in the power to dance over tragedy.[13]

"The power to dance over tragedy"—the Dionysian response
that was to recur in Crane's *Bridge* and to be asserted as a
value in the final book of Williams' *Paterson*—represented
the characteristic aesthetic reductionism in which the mysti-
cal-sensationalistic moment, the moment of *ivresse*, was considered the final solution to all human problems. "Drench
me," says the poet in "Autumnal Clouds," "drown me,
darken me, make me drunken with the deep red torrents of
joy, / Till I forget all things in this world but this, / The
glory of God everlasting, the fire of passion and death." The
fire of "passion and death" is, in effect, the fire of Leconte
de Lisle's sun at noon that consumes the poet in *néant
divin*.

The actual sources of despair, the "things in this world"
of which the poet seeks forgetfulness, are those both traditional to the *mal-du-siècle* attitude and personal to Fletcher:
ennui, for example, as described in "The Empty Days":

> Along the street
> In the afternoon. . . .

> Passes his shadow gaunt as death. . . .
>   [the giver of empty days]
> But it is not death he sells but days,
> Long days, unchanged; gray, futile days.
> But no one buys from him any more,
> They would all rather have death instead.

To the speaker, in particular, he has given

> love that has failed and fallen
> Into a soulless, cloudless depth of blue despair. . . .
> A Dead-Sea husk of memory . . .
> The ashes of opportunity burnt out, of experience
>   shattered. . . .

Again, freedom is conceived of in mystical terms:

> Sea where the night has stalked weeping and raging
>   with passion,
> Into your dawn I fly;
> Out over the glittering, cold, inhuman distances,
> To the gate where the east displays
> Its immense beauty of violet-shrouded silence. . . .[14]

If a passage like this one is reminiscent of the experience presented in Crane's "Voyages," it also suggests the repose or "death" of "L'Orbe d'Or." The peace of the Sea of Nothingness coexists with the ecstasy associated with the Sun or Fire (as, indeed, it does in *The Bridge*):

> Oh, sun of mine, enter my burnt-out heart;
> Kindle the altar-fires
> Death-flaming in the stillness
> Of those black, polished walls.

Or, as we discover in a much later poem, the sight of rhododendrons "blazing" beneath the rain, a sight ignored by the crowd that passes before them, represents the vision of a thing-in-itself that converts an "empty day" into an ecstasy:

> No eye had part in it, but we who saw
> Ourselves torn free at last from space and time

> Kindled again to the old gleam of flame,
> Within its heart that held our very souls
> That day.   ("That Day")

But inevitably the vision, and all that the poet associates
with it in his personal life, fades back into the light of
common day:

> The rhododendrons shattered under rain;
> The flame that lit the distant hillside town
> Faded to brown . . .
> Our wills were broken and shed
> That day.   ("That Day")[15]

The power of the aesthetic experience to absorb other
experiences—the tendency toward aesthetic reductionism—
is similarly apparent in the pseudolove poems which spring,
ostensibly, from Fletcher's tempestuous affair with Daisy
Arbuthnot after a sexually apathetic youth. Here, love is
conceived of as the sharing of a vision of nature that fulfills
itself when the partners, mutually inspiring one another,
reach a state of transcendence:

> time and life were a dream—
> A dream of the light that woke in your eyes,
> A dream of the joy that sang in my heart;
> A dream of the autumnal garden.
> When the dusk came, our two souls flitted
> Outwards for ever and ever together:
> We did not heed the chill blue darkness,
> For the night had no more power over us.
>   ("The Walk in the Garden")[16]

Or else, in the consummation of love, the poet, as in "Irradiations," undergoes metamorphosis into a natural element. He conceives of his love for the lady as an "aster
flower" and himself as "the wind of the autumn night" that
she will breathe until the dawn. Such images are not so
much metaphors or analogues to an actual love affair, whatever it might have been, but rather they translate the experience into the central idiom of Fletcher's poetic life.

That love really meant mystical empathy with nature
and involved a kind of death is made clear in "Shadow on
the Prairie," a late poem in which the experience is strikingly
similar to the one that underlies Hart Crane's Pocahontas
symbolism in *The Bridge:*

> It seemed to him, the land
> Was a gigantic woman, sprawled asleep
> Beneath the sun; a river crawled to her hand,
> The nape of her neck was girdled with the deep
> Green of corn. . . .

The poet attempts to embrace this image:

> He strove to get closer; in his eyes was a crazy light;
> His throat was burning
> With the will to slow extinction, to unsummoned
>   night;
> To forget the dun towers, the vast and appalling
>   weight
> Of the great oil-town from which he had that day
>   come;
> And the sweet curves of her body brought peace from
>   too much debate—
> Mole-darkness under the sun.[17]

In this kind of mystical love or empathy poetry it is
clear that, for all the intended realism and externality
of approach, the true center of interest is not the object in
its essence but the feelings of the poet, not description but
expression. And this tendency in Fletcher is characteristic,
if we might digress for a moment to expand upon the problem. Consider, for example, Aldington's "Daybreak," in
which the dawn is conceived of as a Lady by a soldier-poet
bivouacked in a field:

> The naked pale limbs of the dawn lie sheathed
>   in dove-white folds of lawn
> But from one scarlet breast I see the cloudy
>   cover slowly drawn.

That something more than an eighteenth-century personification is envisioned here rapidly becomes apparent:

> Ah, bend above me, dear, and take my life breath
>   with your lips and break
> My body up as wheaten bread, and use my very
>   blood to slake
>
> Your parching sudden thirst of lust. Be cruel,
>   love, be fierce and thrust
> Your white teeth in my flesh and taste how
>   honey-sweet is amorous dust.
>
> Ah! slay me with your lips. . . .[18]

The mystical-sensual self-abasement, ending in a vision of
ecstatic annihilation, is, as we have just seen in Fletcher's
"Shadow on the Prairie," the common denominator between
an aesthetic response to nature and an erotic-spiritual response to the Lady. That the expression, or evocation, of
such an emotion is paramount in this poem is suggested by
the fact that in the two last stanzas just quoted, the personification collapses into virtual meaninglessness: there is no
literal referent for the Dawn's "lust" and destructive passion. In short, it is the poetic response, not description of the
object, that is important.

In F. S. Flint, we similarly find the tendency to regard
the Lady in some connection with a mystical empathetic experience with nature:

> O my love
> I am at your window singing; I am a bird.
> Look on me not in body; think of me
> only as the music you have heard. . . .
>
> it is my song, and I
> am Earth and Earth is I.
>
> ("April—an Old Tune")[19]

If the Lady here is no more than an excuse to explain an
elevated emotion, she appears elsewhere as no more than an

abstract "cause" of an effect in the mind. Her concrete identity is irrelevant and, indeed, she may be conceived as a force among forces represented in an image among images. Thus in "Chrysanthemums":

> O golden-red and tall chrysanthemums,
> you are the graceful soul of the china vase. . . .
> . . . .
> you are the symbol of my patient heart. . . .
> my love who comes
> will wave wide ripples of disquiet there. . . .
>
> you have no presage of the power that comes
> to fill with anguish the essential calm.[20]

In "Melody," she again becomes a "presence":

> I was making a melody of my love,
> knowing what it was to be
> a nightingale. . . .

The song inspires the Lady to "cling . . . more closely,"

> And then she raised her golden head and laughed
> not knowing how to take the day and hour . . .
> nor why it gave relief.[21]

Reminiscent of "April—an Old Tune," this poem takes as its center of interest neither love as such nor the lady as such, but the "melody of . . . love"; in short, the poet is interested in his song and its effect. The lady is necessary to the experience, but not primary, and the poet's real fulfillment is in being a poet, not a lover. The isolation implied in this poem is symptomatic, and we find that even when the poet has acquired domestic bliss ("Otherworld"), his wife is merely the goodly wife, a shadowy presence who exists but to understand the moods of her otherworldly lord and to inspire "tenderness." "She knows the meaning of my silence," says the poet, "And she will not jar the full cup of my morning treasures." This statement speaks for itself.

For Fletcher, aesthetic mysticism was an explicit philosophy as well as an implicit mode of responding to experience. It is not surprising to find him reflecting, late in his career, that it

> was the fault of imagism never to let its devotees draw clear conclusions about life and to force the poet to state too much and to deduce rather too little—to lead its disciples too often into a barren aestheticism which was, and is, empty of content. . . . Poetry merely descriptive of nature as such, however vivid, no longer seems to me enough; there has to be added to it the human judgment, the human evaluation.[22]

The difference between a "barren aestheticism" and the kind of aestheticism that Fletcher himself practiced is exactly a matter of raising the "sensation" to a metaphysical level and conceiving of it, ultimately, in moralistic terms.

As Fletcher said of the themes of "Midsummer Dreams" and "Poppies of the Red Year" in particular, those of his poetry in general involve loneliness, wandering, conflict, mysticism, and quiescence. These elements, reflected in both his personal life and the universe he created, come together in his quest to discover and perpetuate the ideal experience and, later in his career, to recapture its "magic." In this quest, the poet was eventually envisioned as a "black rock," who with "grim, silent struggle," covered its "strength with gay flowers," one of the "outcast sons of men / Who see, but will not yield to their despair." [23] The gay flowers Fletcher mentioned were, clearly, the rose of beauty, the aster of love, and the poppy of death. The pose is Byronic, perhaps, as well as Nietzschean, but it nonetheless provides us with a simplified example of the whole stoic rationale in modern poetry.

Fletcher eventually moved from a vision of personal to one of social salvation, a phenomenon that, again, occurs in the work of his more talented contemporaries and is, not surprisingly, particularly noticeable in Crane. Just as the latter projected a primitivistic myth in which life in a technological society would be revitalized, so Fletcher asserted the values of regionalism to counter those that led to world war, to "the boundless orgy of greed and display of the twenties," and finally to the Depression:

> I no longer felt pessimistic concerning my country's cultural future, no longer doubted that it would achieve its own great cultural forms and expressions . . . if the temper of the common people still could sustain a faith in this country, then it was presumably immortal, and there was an undying hope for democracy. . . .
> American culture, then, must be primarily regional, not metropolitan. The Southwest and the South were the more likely to achieve it, being regions where the over-successful propaganda of "prosperity" had not drugged the people too far into acquiescence.[24]

I do not contend that this kind of primitivism is less concrete than Crane's. In fact, it is probably altogether too concrete, for Fletcher's poems about his native state of Arkansas are not really "epics" but simply narrative poems on historical subjects. They are the work of a man who has succeeded, at least for the moment, in going home again:

> After a long hard journey, and mighty cities seen:
> The pure sweet scent of a southern long-leafed pine,
> Dangling with chains and balls of glass and toys,
> Into my nostrils breathed, soft, rich, and clean.[25]

A passage like this one is as much a matter of sentiment as aesthetics. But weariness, both actual and metaphysical, the desire for literal tranquillity and mystical repose, are scarcely alien to one another—just as it is not surprising that the kind of "suicide" that marks the aesthetic experience may be followed by actual suicide, as in the cases of both Crane and Fletcher.

2

Aesthetic mysticism rests, as we have seen in Leconte de Lisle and Fletcher, upon renunciation in that it presupposes the repudiation of conventional sentiment and passion in favor of a total response to nature. Accordingly, it may involve a tragic vision in which the conditions for achieving the ideal experience are emotional austerity and suffering. It is in the Hellenism of H.D., however, that we find a full expansion of stoical values. Unlike Fletcher's, H.D.'s stoicism does not involve a Dionysian mode of perception; the final experience is for her not a sensuous empathy with nature so much as an aesthetic vision of its austere forms. (One might go so far as to say that her view is reminiscent of the formalism described in Hulme's essay on modern art.) The point, however, is that the austere form, the aesthetic object, remains an ultimate that requires a particular kind of sensibility to which it may reveal itself.

The stoical beauty apparent in H.D.'s world as early as the initial poem in *Sea Garden*, her first volume, is not of the kind to be perceived by the conventional eye. Thus the poet asks of the sea rose, which, "stunted, with small leaf," is "flung on the sand," whether the spice rose can "drip such acrid fragrance hardened in a leaf." In other poems we learn that the sea lily, "slashed and torn," is still lifted up by the wind; that the sea iris, with its roots tangled in the sand and its petals broken, is nonetheless a "fortunate one," "wind / in our nostrils"; and that the sea violet, although its "grasp is frail / on the edge of the sand-hill," is still "frost, a star edges with its fire." The significance of these flower poems is made all the more explicit in "Sheltered Garden," in which the poet rejects the luxuriant, fragrant garden, the "beauty without strength" that "chokes out life" and seeks "a new beauty / in some terrible / wind-tortured place." [26]

Other manifestations of this attitude appear in the struggles of seafarers, as, for example, in "The Shrine." Located on a headland with treacherous currents, a shrine lures sailors to near-destruction; yet men survive and are redeemed:

> Though oak-beams split,
> though boats and sea-men flounder
> . . . .

> your eyes have pardoned our faults,
> your hands have touched us . . .
> and the waves can never thrust us back.[27]

To the landsmen the shrine is useless, and, accordingly, in the poem called "Sea Gods," there are men who "say there is no hope" to "conjure" the tritons, who, "twisted by the sea," will not respond to human appeal. Yet the seafarers have a higher knowledge, and, in bringing a gift of violets, believe that the gods will come, "answer our taut hearts . . . / break the lie of men's thoughts, / and cherish and shelter us." One scarcely need add that the knowledge of the seafarer is the wholly or partly mystical, nonconventional, "nonhumanistic" knowledge of the aestheticist and that the violets are the images of beauty through which salvation is attained. Again, it is not a distant step from this experience to the experience of the drowned mariner in Crane's "Voyages" who is resurrected by the sea goddess on the Belle Isle of the imagination.

In classifying H.D.'s innumerable Greek personae, both divine and human, Thomas Swann perceptively observes that chastity, renunciation, and independence are idealized and that erotic love is generally condemned: Artemis is the image of the heroine and Aphrodite of the villainess. Accordingly, idealized men are those who meet such women on their own terms, and those who fail to do so, who act out of lust, are villainous.[28] That such a predisposition is natural to, or helps define, an aestheticist view, is clear enough. On the other hand, H.D. was not insensible to the implications of an ethos in which conventional human passion was denigrated. For example, in the three poems concerned with Phaedra (who, as we recall, was inflamed by Venus with desire for Hippolytus, son of her husband, Theseus, and his first wife, the Amazon, Hippolyta), the woman of passion comments on the woman devoted only to hunting and war. Denied by Hippolytus, Phaedra causes his banishment and death by falsely denouncing him, and she finally hangs herself in despair. The conflict that emerges in the poems ("Phaedra,"

"She Contrasts Herself with Hippolyta," "She Rebukes Hippolyta") is, again, but a variation of that in the original legend as interpreted by Frazer: the conflict between Aphrodite—the life of passion—and Artemis—the life of dedication. "Was she so chaste?" asks Phaedra, and the answer implied is that her passion for the fields was no purer than that of a real woman for a lover:

> the broken ridge of the hills
> was the line of a lover's shoulder,
> his arm-turn, the path to the hills,
> the sudden leap and swift thunder
> of mountain boulders, his laugh
>
> She was mad. . . .[29]

The madness of Hippolyta is, in a sense, the madness of the dehumanized poetic sensibility that requires the antidote of human feeling, just as the madness of Phaedra is that of the earthy woman, who, committed to passion, requires the antidote of detachment and independence. The successful courtesan, like Lais, grows old and is left with nothing; but the fate of the prophetess, who, like Cassandra, must finally make a desperate appeal to Hymen for love, is no more satisfactory.

Although H.D.'s two major works, the wartime trilogy ("The Walls Do Not Fall," "Tribute to the Angels," and "The Flowering of the Rod") and *Helen in Egypt*, can scarcely be called imagistic poems, their theses are philosophic elaborations of the attitudes toward beauty and experience that appeared in H.D.'s earlier work. In presenting a poetic vision in all ways comparable to those found in the major neo-epics, both these poems deal with the attempt to ascertain the nature of "eternal realities"—psychological, historical, and cosmic—and to define the kind of perception and knowledge necessary to apprehend them. While the trilogy is concerned primarily with the identity and destiny of the poet as poet, *Helen in Egypt*, ostensibly concerned with the identity and destiny of Helen of Troy, is actually an inquiry into the nature of mystical being, knowledge, and cosmic fate in general.

As an elaboration of the lyrics (particularly "The Shrine"), the trilogy presents the single theme that, in spite of the destructiveness, both physical and moral, that has characterized society, and despite the degradation of the poet in such a world, poetry survives. Strengthened rather than defeated by suffering, the poet maintains his integrity in the quest for illumination and salvation that is his destiny. This essentially Nietzschean proposition is expressed in *The Walls Do Not Fall*,[30] through a series of parallel metaphors; the poet (or poetic mind) is compared to a shrine whose walls remain even though its roof has been destroyed, an oyster that, "living within" and begetting "self-out-of-self," is protected against the "sea-thrust," a worm that rides out storms on the back of a leaf and profits by every calamity. As in the *Quartets*—indeed, as in all the neo-epics—the means to salvation, or better, the sign of salvation, is the magic word that represents ideal, nonconventional perception and poetic logos: "Let us search the old highways / for the true-rune, the right spell, / recover old values." The Word is the poet's Caduceus, "the rod of power," that heals the sick and effects rebirth of the dead, or, manifesting itself in "concrete objects" that are "symbols of eternity," it becomes "grape, knife, cup, wheat," all images associated with fertility rites.

Thus, in his "dream," the poet plays a role analogous to that of the devotee of an ancient religion centering around a Hanged God; specifically the god acknowledged is the Egyptian Ammon (spelled *Amen* by H.D. to take advantage of a pun and an ambiguity), a ram-headed deity associated with the Greek Zeus and occasionally identified, as in H.D., with both Ra, the sun god, and his offspring, the corn god Osiris. In the dream, he appears "in a spacious, bare meeting-house," in "eighteenth-century / simplicity and grace." The locale is significant, of course, for it stands for the poetic world of H.D. herself, a world of "not sentiment but enchantment." Ammon is as different from the usual forms of Christ as, let us suppose, the new poetry from the "art-craft

junk-shop / paint and plaster" ornamentation of the old. I
have taken some liberties with the imagery here, but the
general pattern seems clear: the new religion and poetry
takes as its emblem

> the bare, clean
> early colonial interior,
>
> without stained-glass, picture,
> image or colour,
>
> for now it appears obvious
> that *Amen* is our Christos.   (XVIII)

Characteristically, the poet-devotee seeks from the god the
death that precedes rebirth, a rebirth that means communion
with eternity and the stars, which, invoked "by prayer, spell, /
litany, incantation / will reveal their individual fragrance
. . . / become . . . / personified messengers, / healers,
helpers / of the One, Amen, All-father."

   It is not surprising that the experience with which H.D. is
dealing should provide an interesting parallel to the speaker's
passage through the dark night of the soul in his quest for
the Word at the still point of the turning world in the
Quartets. Compare, for instance, the despairing self-appraisal
of the half-redeemed poet,

> Wistfulness, exaltation,
> a pure core of burning cerebration,
>
> jottings on a margin,
> indecipherable palimpsest scribbled over
>
> with too many contradictory emotions,
> search for finite definition
>
> of the infinite. . . .   (XXXI)

with Eliot's famous

> So here I am, in the middle way . . .
> Trying to learn to use words, and every
>   attempt

> Is a wholly new start, and a different kind
>   of failure . . .
>   a raid on the inarticulate
> With shabby equipment always deteriorating
> In the general mess of imprecision of feeling,
> Undisciplined squads of emotion.

But whereas Eliot seeks a Christian resolution, H.D. seeks one more generally aestheticistic: "Let us re-dedicate our gifts / to spiritual realism," she says, a statement which means, we later discover, "the search for historical parallels," and "research into psychic affinities." Even though such a search has been "done to death," its justification is that each poet has a "personal approach / to the eternal realities" that "differs from every other." In short, Ammon is the god of every poet, each of whom works out his own salvation as best he can. "For us," said Eliot, as we have seen, "there is only the trying. The rest is not our business." And similarly for H.D. what the poet has is the act of affirmation; powerless, his lungs filled with dust and powder, wandering in a dark wood on the edge of a grimpen, he continues his quest, and because he does, the walls do not fall and the possibility remains that he will "reach haven, heaven."

   Tribute to the Angels[31] does not advance what is really the unadvanceable argument of *The Walls Do Not Fall;* it simply changes the context of the quest from a pagan to a predominantly Christian myth. This is not to say that H.D., like Eliot, is presenting a Christian experience in substance; she is, I think, merely using its form insofar as it provides an expanded analogue to the fertility myth and the poet's search for logos. The invocation of and tribute to all seven of the holy angels is in essence an acceptance of life—and death or war, the latter taken as an inevitable part of the scheme of things. Uriel, the angel of war, becomes the "judgment and will of God, / God's very breath," for in the ruins of a blasted city lies the flowering rood, where "we pause to give / thanks that we rise again from death and live" (VII). This tribute, and the vision it entails, is part of an alchemy of the word that changes the bitter "mar" ("sea, brine, breaker, seducer") into the bright "mere, mater . . . Mary, / Star of the Sea, / Mother." Furthermore, in seeking to revive the "old values," spoken of in the first part of the trilogy, the poet must restore to their original meaning the debased forms of the name of the goddess; Venus and Astarte, both associated with the sea (as, incidentally, is the Egyptian Isis), are merely other images of Mary. The corruption of the name of the former (for example, in "venerous") is symptomatic of a world that has forgotten "the light at dusk" (Hesperus) and the "prayer at dawn" (Phosphorus):

> return, O holiest one,
> Venus whose name is kin
> to venerate,
> venerator.

(Compare Eliot's "Our Lady of the Promontory.") Similarly, along with Mary-Venus, Annael, the angel of peace, is invoked to be hailed along with Uriel, since "one must inexorably / take fire from the other / as spring from winter." This invocation is but an elaboration of that to Uriel; Annael also presides over the flowering rood, now viewed as a blossoming "half-burnt-out apple tree," an image that carries all the associations of the fall and partial resurrection of man. Out of this vision comes the major invocation, that to Mary as queen of the angels. She appears to the poet in a dream, as did Ammon, and just as this Egyptian deity was envisioned in a bare, eighteenth-century room, so Mary is seen in bare simplicity, not "flanked by Corinthian capitals, / or in a Coptic nave." She is, in effect, a characteristic projection of the imagist sensibility, not "hieratic" carrying the Child or a book of ancient wisdom, but like "Psyche, the butterfly, / out of the cocoon." Thus, far from being overwhelming, "She carried a book, either to imply / she was one of us, / with us, / or to suggest she was satisfied / with our purpose, / a tribute to the Angels" (XLI). Because of this sign, which implies at least the hope of salvation, the poet can make her final tribute to Zadkiel, the angel of the righteousness of

God, in which she can say "we are satisfied, we are happy, /
we begin again." In a sense, *Tribute to the Angels* represents
the search for "historic parallels" and "psychic affinities"
mentioned in *The Walls Do Not Fall.* For H.D., all the
gods and goddesses celebrated were reducible to the one god
and goddess of poetic creativity, deities whose abode was the
imagination itself.

The *Flowering of the Rod* [32] presents the third and final
vision of salvation. But despite the continued use of Christian mythology, the salvation imagined becomes all the
more apparently that of the aestheticist in an aestheticist
universe. "Having given all, let us leave all," says the poet;
"let us leave pity and mount higher / to love—resurrection."
What is actually being asked for here is detachment from
the world and from worldly emotion—the personal salvation
of the stoic: "does the first wild goose stop to explain / to
the others? no—he is off; / to follow or not, / that is their
affair." And such an appeal is made because the poet has
despaired of all success in fulfilling a prophetic role in society. She sees herself as a bird following her compulsion
for flight (quest), a flight from which she may fall "exhausted, numb, blind," but not without a "certain ecstasy,"
and, once again, therein lies her hope. Although a lonely
"frozen priestess," who sings doom "in broken hexameters,"
she contains within herself the vision that is "heal-all, everlasting." On the other hand, even though she is aware that
she is ignored by the majority of men, she, like Christ, may
redeem the few whom the world has cast out, "the twisted
or tortured individuals," who, so obviously like herself, are
"out of step" with "progress."

The mythic "affinity" illustrating this theme is a recon-
structed tale of Mary Magdalene's attempt to procure the
myrrh that Gaspar, third of the magi, presented to the Virgin
Mary. Magdalene announces to an uncomprehending Gaspar, "I am Mary . . . / through my will and my power, /
Mary shall be myrrh." And again: "*I am Mary, the incense-
flower of the incense-tree, / myself worshipping, weeping,
shall be changed to myrrh*" (XIX). She departs, but after

an illumination Gaspar sends the jar after her with a messenger. The point here is that Gaspar does in fact recognize Magdalene as Mary, and in this recognition is revelation, for at the same time he sees "the whole scope and plan / of our and his civilization / on this, his and our earth, before Adam" (XXXI). Gaspar is clearly the poet figure and his awareness that Magdalene is Mary carries with it faith in the eternal principle that the burnt rod always flowers (faith in "Christos," in other words); and the vision of a paradise before Eden is the prophetic apprehension of the past, mentioned previously, that is the poetic heritage, the seed from which the new grain will be brought forth. Contrasting with Gaspar's recognition of Magdalene as Mary is the failure to do so of Simon, host of the feast at which Magdalene appears; to him she seems only profane, a siren with a song bringing shipwreck and death. Christ's recognition of her serves only to arouse Simon's doubts of Christ's powers: "This man if he were a prophet, would have known / who and what manner of woman this is." Simon, of course, is of society, the conventional man who would see only "venery" in Venus. He does not know, as does Gaspar, that the "demons" possessing Magdalene are all "part of the picture" and that their true names are Isis, Astarte, Cyprus, and Demeter.

It is regrettable but understandable that Thomas Swann provides only a superficial review of *Helen in Egypt*, H.D.'s second and final long poem. Horace Gregory avoids the vast obscurity of this work by uttering impressionistic platitudes.[33] Yet although the poem is a baffling series of "endless, intricate questions" asked by a heroine in quest of identity, justification, and realization in various mystical realms of being and knowledge, a certain logic is perceptible and it is a logic that returns us to the basic themes we've been discussing. "explosive" scenes or to make the action of the Trojan War appear "before our eyes." [34] Neither is the poem a "medita- Despite its mythic content, the poem is not dramatic in either conception or execution and nothing is to be gained by condemning, as Swann does, H.D.'s failure to develop

tion" in the usual sense since something considerably more than rational appraisal is involved. For Helen, who exists and does not exist, *being* depends upon mystical knowledge; the primary source of emotion is uncertainty and the goal lies at the end of a labyrinth, at the bottom of a "spiral staircase," or within a convoluted seashell.

The various legends of Helen in Egypt are derived from the belief that Helen was transported to Egypt by Zeus and that Paris actually abducted a phantom. H.D. expresses an indebtedness to Stesichorus and Euripides, but it is clear that she is concerned not with the possibilities of plot and action or myth as such, but with the psychological and mystical implications inherent in the experience—such implications being of value not so much to resurrect a classical Helen as to provide a general vision of life. Swann's argument that H.D. has not been as successful as MacLeish in *Trojan Horse* or Jeffers in *At the Fall of an Age* is, I feel, irrelevant.[35]

For Helen, "inhabiting" the temple of "Amen-Zeus," an encounter with Achilles on a desolate beach represents a hieroglyph that holds the meaning of her life. And, indeed, just as she has been attempting to translate the symbols on the temple walls, to comprehend the Egyptian Mysteries, so she seeks to "translate" the details of the mystical meeting that is the human embodiment of the hieroglyphics. We find, for example, that at one point, "*Helen achieves the difficult task of translating a symbol in time, into timeless-time or hieroglyph or ancient Egyptian time.*" Specifically, "*she invokes . . . the symbol or the 'letter' that represents or recalls the protective mother-goddess.* [A bird has appeared.] *This is no death-symbol but a life-symbol, it is Isis or her Greek counterpart, Thetis, the mother of Achilles*" (p. 7).[36] The ability to translate a symbol in time into timeless-time (or vice versa) is precisely Helen's problem, for such translation really means the ability to make identities of opposites no less than of likes and to perceive an ultimate cosmic pattern. Thus Helen posits a whole series of identities unified by a concept of Proteus and the principle of metamorphosis he represents. Greek figures are "translated" into Egyptian, myth into mystery, action into idea. Just as Helen herself, for example, is "accused" of being related to Isis, so she sees Achilles partly as Osiris, partly as Typhon— preserver and destroyer. On this dimension of vision her meeting with Achilles resolves itself into a spiritual struggle conceived of in Egyptian terms: *"As Isis seeks to reclaim Osiris with the help of their child, the sun-god Horus, so Helen, with the aid of 'the unnumbered hosts . . . [dead Greek warriors] . . . would gain spiritual recognition and ascendency over 'Typhon, the Destroyer'* (p. 29).

Despite all her translations, postulations, reconstructions, and intuitions, Helen's "intricate questionings" never come to rest. Her inquiries are circular rather than linear and for every dimension of vision she reaches another appears to lie beyond, often to negate the one that preceded it. What is consistent, however, is the demand to reconcile dualism, a demand that ends in a tragic fatalism characteristic of H.D.'s poetry. Achilles emerges as the image of the Spartan warrior-death cult, an "icy fortress," the austere, single-minded masculine ego. Accordingly, he is associated with the sea (literally, through his mother, Thetis) and all it represents in H.D.'s earlier poems. His ultimate guise is that of Dis, the "Dark Absolute." Helen's supposed marriage with Achilles on Leuké (the White Island) represents her attainment of "immaculate purity," the "Absolute of Negation," death. Thus "she compares herself to Persephone." But the attraction of the "Achilles concept" for Helen, and as we have seen for H.D. herself, is counteracted by the demands of Paris, who envisions her not as the Spartan Helen but as the Rhodes Helen of the Trees (Helen Dendritis). If Achilles represents "winter-love," Paris represents "spring-love," Eros, Adonis, the counterpart of whom, again, is Helen as Persephone returned to earth, or Aphrodite. These dualisms are each dualistic in themselves, a phenomenon that actually holds out hope for an ultimate correspondence and reconciliation.

Regarded as a character, rather than as a symbol, Achilles,

no less than Helen, requires salvation or completion. Although "king of the Myrmidons," the iron-ring or death cult subservient to the "Command" (a military-spiritual oracle), Achilles finds himself seeking prophecy in the gestures of Helen as she walks the ramparts of Troy, a "game of chance," responsible for his deviation from the Command and his consequent death. The proposed significance of this action is that the "icy fortress" of Achilles was melted by Love; thus, "some said a bowman from the Walls / let fly the dart, some said it was Apollo, / but I, Helena, knew it was Love's arrow" (p. 9). And this is precisely a manifestation of the pattern that Helen has been seeking to apprehend:

> Is Fate inexorable?
> does Zeus decree that, forever,
> Love should be born of War?   (p. 33)

Correspondingly, Paris, the slayer of Achilles ("Wolf-slayer"), is identified with Eros, but through his Judgment and its consequences for Troy, he is also identified with Eris, the female personification of Strife with whose "apple of discord" the legend began. The tragic thesis that Love and War, life and death, harmony and discord, are twin aspects of a single process, a pattern, underlies the entire range of Helen's thought: *"Is the 'veil of Cytherea' or of Love, Death? Is the disguise of Death or the 'veil' of Death, Love?"* (p. 47)— such is the central question of the poem. The essential Translation, then, is explanation of the "subtle genealogy" that relates the various, opposing characters. Since Love is born of War, Paris is the son of Achilles, "the fire-brand . . . born of the Star" (p. 192). He is thus identified with Euphorion, the child of Helen and Achilles of the alleged marriage on Leuké; and as the lover of his mother and the slayer of his father, he is associated with Oedipus (p. 162);

> so the dart of Love
> is the dart of Death,
> and the secret is no secret;
> the simple path

refutes at last
the threat of the Labyrinth. . . .   (p. 314)

The ultimate identity is *La Mort l'Amour*, and the ultimate starscript or zodiak "the circle of god-like beasts": "would they turn and rend each other, / or form a frieze, / the Zodiac hieroglyph, / on a temple wall?" (p. 281).

Love and death are the archetypal dualities to be reconciled in Helen's psychological and cosmic experience, and in their reconciliation, Helen can comprehend that she has been part of a pattern and thereby be relieved of whatever guilt she may have felt for her role in the ruin of Troy and the carnage among the Greeks. Further dualities are those of time and eternity, intellect and intuition, action and stasis, will and fate, body and soul. Greek intellect, represented by Theseus, is opposed to Egyptian Mystery; Helen's intuitive apprehension of the meaning of the hieroglyphs must be repeated on the intellectual plane, with Theseus becoming, in a sense, an Ariadne to guide Helen through the labyrinth into which her quest has led her: *"The magic of Crete was inherited from Egypt. Parnassus, or Greek creative thought, must not be entangled in the Labyrinth or dissolved or washed away by "the ancient Nile"* (p. 176). The logic here, if I am not being far-fetched, is objectivistic: Helen, we are told, *"must be reborn, that is, her soul must return wholly to her body"* (p. 169). "I found perfection in the Mysteries," she says, "but I was home-sick for familiar trees" (p. 160). For Helen to return to her body is to recall the experience with Paris and Troy, an experience with "spring-love" and youth which in turn recalls her childhood and the episode in which she was kidnapped by Theseus himself. Again, Theseus preaches the reconciliation of opposites and he defines an ideal love that lies "beyond Trojan and Greek," an Eros that awaits somewhere between or beyond the hieroglyphs of Egypt (involving Achilles) and the "blackened Walls" of Troy (involving Paris). If Theseus is "half-way to that Lover" it is because he has provided Helen with Myth (the "one reality") that is the experiential basis of Mystery, a "reconciliation with Greek time"

after which Helen "is called back to Egypt" to seek a final
revelation of the cosmic meaning of her life. Furthermore,
Theseus is himself a lover of Helen and is implicitly an
Orpheus trying to save a Eurydice; he must bring her "back
from Death" by "singing" of his own analogous quest and
by arguing the merits of "spring-love." (We recall incidentally that he was involved in an attempt to kidnap Persephone.)

Another of the dualities involves the "Dark Absolute"
and the "Light Absolute" and centers about the Castor and
Pollux legend. Of the children Helen, Clytaemnestra, Castor,
and Pollux, "*Zeus-Amen decreed that two . . . should be
born of light, the other two of darkness. The child of light
will strive to redeem the child of darkness, 'Castor received
immortality through Pollux, you sought . . . Clytaemnestra
in Egypt?'*" (p. 194). The symbol of this "subtle genealogy"
is the nenuphar (the "thousand-petalled lily") also associated with "the script" of the stars, Fate, the twin principle
or the primal dualities of Life and Death, Love and War
(pp. 22, 108). Helen pursues her role by attempting to see in
her sister's story an analogue to her own, and to find justification in the assertion of the "female-principle" (love) over the
male (war). The sacrifice of Iphigenia is viewed as the crime
against women of the warrior cult, to which Achilles himself
belongs, and Clytemnestra's subsequent murder of Agamemnon as nemesis. Helen is warned that Clytemnestra's was a
different story, that

> if a woman fights,
> she must fight by stealth,
>
> with invisible gear;
> no sword, no dagger, no spear
> in a woman's hands
>
> can make wrong, right. . . .   (p. 101)

But this is merely saying that Clytemnestra is demonic while
Helen is not—the one "dark" while the other is "light."
"*That 'flash in the heaven at noon that blinds the sun'*

claims Helen [the meeting with Achilles], *while Clytaemnestra is 'called to another Star'* " (p. 105). Clytemnestra is
called the "Mistress of Magic" and is identified with Astarte
and the Orient (Egypt); Helen is called the "Mistress of
Fate" and is identified, in this contrast, implicitly, with
Aphrodite and Greece. But the revelation is that *"when
they reach a certain degree, / they are one, alike utterly"*
(p. 105). The story of Helen and Achilles ("Achilles awoke
from the dark") is therefore the apocalyptic version of that
of Clytemnestra and Agamemnon ("her Lord was cast / into
the lowest depths / of Cimmerian night"). But the point
is that both stories are part of the will of Heaven, the decree
of Zeus-Amen-Proteus.

This brief analysis can scarcely do justice to the involuted
structure of Helen's experience, or to the numerous images,
symbols, and quasi-symbols in which she is trying to find
meaning. Objects such as her scarf or veil, perceived by
Achilles as she walked on the walls, her broken sandal strap,
as she paused before her descent down a spiral staircase
(into Death, Hades, Myth, and Eternity), as perceived by
Paris in his final sight of her, Achilles' flint used to start a
fire in the brazier during the apocalyptic meeting ("was
there ever such a brazier?"), Theseus' own brazier used to
warm a Helen frozen by her wanderings on Ida in search of
Paris, the caravel that carried Achilles from Troy to Egypt
after his death, are all physical hieroglyphics, the final translation of which is never actually attained. In other complexities, the Helen-Dendritis image is elaborated to include
Thetis as a carven figure upon the prow of Achilles' ship, an
eidolon worshiped by him, and in one of its meanings signifies the principle of womanhood in its opposition to Spartan manhood ("what is 'the living grain of the tree' and
'the rose-vein of the wood' to 'one brandished spear that
enflames a thousand others' "). If the meaning of these
images is never fixed, if their meanings often shift with their
context, they at least point toward the basic dualities of the
poem, which themselves are in a state of flux. The flint
Achilles uses to start a fire is in one sense the "brandished

spear that enflames a thousand others" and in another sense
an index of his "awakening" into Helen's love and the
thawing of the "icy fortress" of his masculine warrior-ego.
Helen's broken sandal strap is equated with Achilles' heel
("why did she limp and turn / at the stair-head and half
turn back?" [p. 127]). The containment of one's opposite
in oneself, the mergence of one into one's opposite, the
assertion of multiple contrasts and identities, momentarily
emphasized, then dropped only to be restated in a different
situation, are all the conditions of Helen's experience in a
protean universe, the ultimate fixity of which is constantly
sought but never finally attained except in the notion of a
dynamic dualism.

At one point, we learn that Helen's effort to discover her
past is related to that of poets trying to comprehend the
meaning of Troy:

> Was it Apollo's snare
> so that poets forever,
> should be caught in the maze of the Walls
>
> of a Troy that never fell?
> . . . .
> I am called back to the Walls
> to find the answer,
>
> to wander as in a maze
> (Theseus' Labyrinth),
> to explore each turn of the street. . . .   (p. 241)

Helen, both "poet" and subject of the poem, a victim of
"Apollo's snare" and, so to speak, its bait, a translator seeking
to translate herself, is, finally, a projection of the aestheticist
imagination: narcissistic and objectivistic at once, introspec-
tive and dramatic, alternately committed to a conception of
free will and of fate. *Helen in Egypt* is a series of "endless,
intricate questionings" about endless, intricate questionings
—itself a hieroglyphic, an "Apollo's snare" and a maze, in-
timating but never yielding revelation. Like Pound's *Cantos*

it is clearly intended to represent, in a sense, the mystification and endless philosophic elaboration of an image and a
"moment" in an art epiphany that blossoms like "a thousand-
petalled lily" without ever coming to bloom.

3

Aestheticism in the poetry of both Fletcher and H.D.
reaches the level of vision—whatever the eventual ravages of
sentimentality in the former. Aestheticism in the poetry of
Amy Lowell never really crystallizes into a mystical or stoic
ethos; it merely takes the loose form of a romanticized view
of the "mystery" of "beauty" and "reality" and of the struggles of the poet. Her purely Imagist predilections were expressed in translations, with Florence Ayscough, from the
Chinese, and in a number of pictorial poems, but her chief
interest was in the dramatic monologue and the art ballad,
and her assertion that Coleridge, Keats, and Poe were her
masters is not entirely without foundation, whatever her
abilities as a poet. Her reservations about Browning, who,
she said, had "robustness" but no such "vivid, bold imagination as Coleridge" and "lacked the fantastic note," provides
us with a curious insight into the sensibility of a woman
whose call for realism was the key element in her propaganda
for the New Poetry.[37] We recall, however, that Coleridge
himself was also concerned with the relations between the
real and the imaginary, and his comments about what he
felt was necessary to procure the willing suspension of dis-
belief are relevant: in regard to supernatural or romantic
characters, his intention was to "transfer from our inward
nature a human interest and a semblance of truth" and,
conversely, to awaken "the mind's attention from the leth-
argy of custom" and to direct it "to the loveliness and
wonders of the world." We can recognize the genesis of
aestheticism in this last statement; undeveloped into a rigorous ethos, it resolves itself into the broadly romantic notion
of the "reality of wonder" and the "wonder of reality," a
notion behind much of Coleridge's poetry and, indeed, of

Amy Lowell's. Accordingly, such a conception, concerned at once with externalities and "mysteries," loosely accommodates attitudes, predilections, and themes that could appear, tightly organized, in a more highly developed aestheticist ethos.

For example, the title poem of *Sword Blades and Poppy Seed*, Amy Lowell's second volume but first mature work, presents a "legend" in which an aspiring poet learns from a Magic Man, Ephraim Bard, the nature of the craft that he would master. As a "Dealer in Words," the latter has a shop filled with swords and drugs, one for poetry that would "carve a breach / through old abuses the world condones," the other for romance, or "light whiff of a dream for a summer night." He is willing to serve the aspirant but requires payment: "Life, / Your nervous force, your strife!" After a violent reply by the young poet, who fears that the bargain will be Faustian, the proprietor vows that he is no fiend:

> "I have no wish to barter souls. . . .
> Surely the age of fear is gone.
> We live within a daylight world
> Lit by the sun." . . .[38]

More hysterics ensue, but the young poet finally leaves with his parcels just as dawn breaks.

Trite though it may be in conception as well as in execution, the poem is noteworthy on two counts. First, the allegory notwithstanding, no supernatural element intervenes and we have an example of the "reality of wonder." The experience is, at bottom, psychological—one that is comprehensible in a daylight world—even though in tone the piece attempts to create an exotic atmosphere. One might also deduce that the juxtaposition of sword blades and poppy seeds is one of stark reality and the imaginative world. Equally interesting is that the poet must give up part of his personality to acquire special perception—a principle we have seen at work in both Fletcher and H.D. Whether or not the proprietor of the shop is a devil, the poet does surrender his soul, for he is an eater, no less than a producer, of opium. Indeed, the moonstruck poet may well be led on by the image of a goddess in a fountain and his drowned body be discovered the following morning ("Clear, with Light Variable Winds"). No less can the poet militant be destroyed by the conditions of life:

> How should I sing when buffeting salt waves
>> And stung with bitter surges, in whose might
>> I toss, a cockleshell. . . .
> My eyes with hope o'erstrained, are growing blind,
>> But painted on the sky great visions burn,
>> My voice, oblation from a shattered urn.
>>>>>> ("Storm-Racked")

Yet this is precisely the fate chosen by the poet. To pick up the sword of poetry and expose oneself to the storms of the world is to assume the knowledge that one is really giving "one's soul to gain / Life's quintessence":

>> Rapture's self is three parts sorrow.
>> Although we must die to-morrow,
>> Losing every thought but this;
>> Torn, triumphant, drowned in bliss.
>>>>>> ("Happiness")

There is an obviously Nietzschean cast to these lines, and it would seem that for Amy Lowell—although not in a way approaching the mysticism of Fletcher—a thin line distinguishes "life's quintessence," art death, and actual death:

>> I crave to be lost like a wind-blown flame.
>> Pushed into nothingness by a breath,
>>> And quench in a wreath
>>> Of engulfing death
>> This fight for a god, or this devil's game.
>>>>>> ("The Last Quarter of the Moon")

Those art ballads concerned more or less directly with the artistic experience, such as "The Book of Hours of Sister Clotilde" or "The Shadow," present in terms of legend the implications of poetic narcosis. In the former example, a nun, painting a "Book of Hours," is bitten by a snake in whose skin she believes she has found the exact array of colors with which she wishes to paint the clothing of Mary. Fascinated by the discovery, she is heedless of the bite and would have perished were it not for the action of the gardener, who tells the other sisters that she has been bitten but not that he had saved her. They take her survival to be a miracle and the painting of Mary she has made during the night to be a product of divine inspiration. One can see in this legend another example of the "reality of wonder"—the miracle is wholly explicable—but also the "wonder of reality," for Clotilde is in fact inspired and her book has become "a choir / Of rainbow fire." Equally important, however, is that the snakeskin was a form of poppy seed that easily could have destroyed the artist had it not been for the banal but sober realist.

The Keatsian qualities of this theme are even more clearly manifest in "The Shadow," the legend of a watchmaker who sees the shadow of a beautiful woman on his wall, a shadow that, despite all his obsessed efforts, remains incommunicable:

> And everything he made he placed
> Before his lady. The Shadow kept
> Its perfect passiveness. Paul wept. . . .
> No word, no motion
> Eased the ache of his devotion.

The image here is, of course, suggestive of La Belle Dame sans Merci, who, precisely because of her nonhuman nature, must be without "tenderness." And the poet must suffer because as a human being he must humanize her. Thus, in a final effort, the watchmaker prepares a feast with wine "red as blood," which should "bring the lustihood / Of human life to his lady's veins." When he fails, he poisons himself in the hope of joining her in her world, but just before he dies, he discovers that her image has vanished. He can no more enter her world by death (since she is a product of his mind) than she can enter his by life (since her very nature is to be a shadow). For Amy Lowell, as for Keats, the poet was committed to a never-ending quest for eternity that, if it did end, would do so only in the grave.

Although many of the dramatic poems really can be read only for their stories and characterizations, a large number readily yield themselves to allegorical or semiallegorical interpretation. "The Great Adventure of Max Breuck," for instance, is the story of a man who, given a narcotic by his friends as a practical joke, dreams about a romance that, having lasted two years is about to be consummated, and then awakens to discover that he has been asleep only a short time. The dream has been so vivid and his sense of loss so profound that he kills himself. The sword blade and poppy seed theme is again evident here: Breuck is a Keatsian hero who, having once been drugged, finds the real world unbearable.

Less obvious are narratives like "The Cremona Violin," in which a sensitive young wife is driven to adultery by a husband devoted solely to his music. Perhaps reflected here is the obsession with loneliness that characterizes many of the dramatic poems, but the difference is that this kind of loneliness is directly involved with the artistic life. One might go so far as to suggest that, in a sense, the violinist and his wife represent two sides of the poet, the aesthetic and the human, with the latter paying the penalty for the achievements of the former. The poem concludes with the wife's breaking her husband's violin and deserting him, but this action is probably as much a matter of theater as of prophecy. We have already seen that the fate of the poet is dehumanization or death, and Amy Lowell was perhaps summing up her career, as well as anticipating her death, when she wrote in "Still Life": "Cousin Moon, our kinship is curiously demonstrated, / For I, too, am a bright, cold corpse / Perpetually circling above a living world." Amy Lowell may have been an enthusiastic woman and proclaimed optimism in poetry, but a sense of despair is noticeable in much of her work.

The historical impulse in the American aestheticist sensibility was anticipated, again loosely and romantically, by Amy Lowell, in the prose poem *Can Grande's Castle*, a series of vignettes of the high point and actual or potential destruction by war of a number of civilizations. Commenting on the theory of history behind the work, S. Foster Damon has said,

> To her, art was not only the expression of a civilization: it was life's highest achievement and its only permanence —it was almost civilization itself. The economic system is the root, the popular pleasures are the transient flowers, and the arts are the seed-bearing fruit. . . .

The vignettes, which include Nelson's victory over the French fleet at the Nile and his subsequent affair with Emma Hamilton in Naples, the opening of Japan by Perry, the vitality of England in Napoleonic times as reflected in its coach system of transportation, along with the portrayal of crucial moments in the history of Rome, Byzantium, and Venice, are all, as Damon says, pictures of life and the "acquisitive and destructive forces" behind it. True to her poetic, Amy Lowell seems to withhold moral judgment, and in so doing perhaps commits herself to a deterministic view of experience. The technique, itself, of presenting tableaux, is characteristically imagistic and is a diluted counterpart to Pound's ideogrammic method. But the poem is really more noteworthy in conception than in execution. In many ways the impulse that led to the writing of *Can Grande's Castle* —the desire to reveal the "truth" about history in an epiphanetic language—was similar to that which led to the writing of *The Bridge, The Cantos, Paterson,* and *In the American Grain*. Had Amy Lowell had the ability to sustain a poetic idiom, to rise above a style too frequently banal, the work would have been of more than documentary interest.

Whatever the specific forms of their conceptions of reality, the poets we have been discussing all presuppose some kind of transcendent mode of perception and response available chiefly to the artist; they are similarly all concerned with the fate of the artist who seeks to acquire and reveal the special knowledge of things in their pure beauty. Thus they can be said to establish an "aestheticist logic." We might now look at the "objectivists," in whom this logic reaches a metaphysical extreme.

3. WILLIAM CARLOS WILLIAMS: OBJECTIVIST MATHEMATICS

"A course in mathematics," wrote William Carlos Williams in an essay on Marianne Moore,

> would not be wasted on a poet, or a reader of poetry, if he remember no more from it than the geometric principle of the intersection of loci: from all angles lines converging and crossing establish points. He might carry it further and say in his imagination that apprehension perforates at places, through to understanding—as white is at the intersection of blue and green and yellow and red. It is this white light that is the background of all good work.[1]

Williams later extends the analogy in remarking that "poetry has taken many disguises which by cross reading or intense penetration it is possible to go through to the core. Through intersection of loci their multiplicity may become revelatory." The "intersection" meant for Williams the bare reality of an object seen without bias or association. "To Miss Moore an apple remains an apple whether it be in Eden or the fruit bowl where it curls. . . . One is not made to feel that as an apple it has anything particularly to do with poetry or that as such it needs special treatment; one goes on. Because of this, the direct object does seem unaffected." Thus, in describing his mother's sensibility in the prologue to *Kora in Hell*, Williams gives us a picture of the true objectivist poet:

> . . . seeing the thing itself without forethought or afterthought but with great intensity of perception, my mother loses her bearings or associates with some disreputable person or translates a dark mood. She is a creature of great imagination. . . . She is a despoiled, molted cast-

away but by this power she still breaks life between her fingers.[2]

If the objectivist poet sees the "thing itself" with "great intensity of perception" and devoid of all preconception,[3] the poem he writes must be the verbal reflection of the object perceived and hence itself a kind of object. "The poem being an object," says Williams in his autobiography, "it must be the purpose of the poet to make of his words a new form: to invent, that is, an object consonant with his day. This was what we wished to imply by Objectivism, an antidote, in a sense, to the bare image haphazardly presented in loose verse." [4] This obscure statement is considerably clarified by Williams' remarks in the introduction to *The Wedge*:

> When a man makes a poem, makes it, mind you, he takes words as he finds them interrelated about him and composes them—without distortion which would mar their exact significances—into an intense expression of his perceptions and ardors that they may constitute a *revelation* in the speech that he uses. It isn't what he says that counts as a work of art, it's what he makes, with such *intensity of perception* that it lives with an intrinsic movement of its own to verify its authenticity. [Italics mine.] [5]

I have emphasized the words "revelation" and "intensity of perception" because of their recurrence in Williams' thought. Here, as in Pound, and to some extent in all aestheticist poets, the concern for exact meaning is actually a part of the belief that poetic language has the power of a logos that immediately reveals the poet's encounter with bare reality and bare beauty. Conversely, the notion that the poem "verifies its authenticity" with "an intrinsic movement of its own" appears to mean precisely that: its authenticity to the object, perception, or experience is proved when it becomes a thing-in-itself with its own life. The ability to "invent" is the ability to make a poem into an object, a feat that depends upon "intensity of perception"—perception of the original

object or situation and discovery of the exact language
appropriate to it.[6]

The geometrical analogy that Williams used in respect
to Marianne Moore's poetry was not, perhaps, selected at
random. For the objectivist experience itself involves a kind
of aesthetic geometry, as the poem called "Della Primavera
Trasportata Al Morale" makes clear:

> The forms
> of the emotions are crystalline,
> geometric-faceted. So we recognize
> only in the white heat of
> understanding, when a flame
> runs through the gap made
> by learning, the shapes of things—
> the ovoid sun, the pointed trees. . . .[7]

"Curious shapes / awake / to plague me," writes Williams
in "Full Moon," and that, I think, is as succinct a statement
of his inspiration as one will find. Hence, in "To a Solitary
Disciple," we find advice upon the proper observation of a
moonlit steeple—observation that is a "white penetration"
to reality. The poet asks his student to see how the converg-
ing lines of the steeple

> meet at the pinnacle—
> perceive how
> its little ornament
> tries to stop them—
>
> See how it fails!
> See how the converging lines
> of the hexagonal spire
> escape upward. . . .   (CEP)

The geometrical relation of the moon to the lines of the
steeple, suddenly revealed to be akin to that of a flower to
its sepals, becomes an objectivist epiphany: "It is true: / . . .
the oppressive weight / of the squat edifice! / . . . the jas-
mine lightness / of the moon." It is in terms of vision such as

this that we find Williams talking about "the favorable /
distortion of eyeglasses / that see everything and remain /
related to mathematics" ("The Eyeglasses"), and celebrating the mathematician, Aigeltinger, who has

> stuck in my conk
> illuminating, for nearly half a century I
> could never beat you at your specialty   (CLP)[8]

As we learn in *Paterson*, the aim of the poet is to achieve
"a mathematics for particulars," to discover the universal
in the local, the abstract in the concrete. Herein lies the
process of invention and revelation.

What is equally interesting about the passage quoted
from "Della Primavera Trasportata Al Morale" is the assertion that "the emotions are crystalline, / geometric-faceted,"
for it implies that the poetic imagination, no less than the
object apprehended, has an independent reality of its own;
because the imagination is of such a character, it can apprehend "the shapes of things," the "geometrical" reality of the
world around it. This notion is, I think, behind Williams'
statement in "Revelation" that the aim of writing is to
reveal "that which is inside the man." "The gap made by
learning" becomes in this essay the corruption of the imagination by social convention and the other influences of
adult life that categorize and limit the individual and, in
effect, destroy perception. The mind, we learn in such poems
as "Two Deliberate Exercises," must be liberated from
itself; only then can "that which is inside the man" be
realized and revealed:

> Well, we live among
> the birds and bees in vain unless
> there result—now or then—
> a presentation . . .
>   to invoke
> for us a whole realm, compact of
> inverted nature, straining
> within the imprisoned mind to

> free us. Well, to free us.
>   At which, seeing in the pasture
> horses among the brambles,
> hearing the wind sigh,
> we broach the chaos . . .
>   where stand waiting
> for us or nowhere the tree-
> lined avenues of our desires.   (CLP)

The "inverted nature" refers, perhaps, to the "crystalline emotions" that are a counterpart to crystalline reality. This ideal and latent condition of the mind was described in "Writer's Prologue to a Play in Verse" (the play of human life realized through poetry) as a "gist" and both the term and the idea reappear in *Paterson*—significantly, in a passage on radium.

The poem "The Black Winds," fifth in the "Spring and All" sequence, is a typical expression of Williams' abiding concern with purging responses of all sentiment and objects of all association, so that the "liberated" imagination beholds a bare reality. The argument is that men have always committed the pathetic fallacy ("Black winds from the north / enter black hearts"); the poet asserts that "There is nothing in the twist / of the wind but—dashes of cold rain" and, through sensual contact, he achieves an epiphany:

> Black wind, I have poured my heart out
> to you until I am sick of it—
>
> Now I run my hand over you feeling
> the play of your body—the quiver
> of its strength. . . .

The old associations begin to return:

> The grief of the bowmen of Shu
> moves nearer—There is
> an approach with difficulty from
> the dead—the winter casing of grief

And the poet concludes, "How easy to slip / into the old mode, how hard to / cling firmly to the advance" (CEP).

This experience is an indication of what Williams meant when he asserted in "Against the Weather," "I am seeking but a sensual 'reality' ":

> If I succeed in keeping myself objective enough, sensual enough, I can produce the factors, the concretions of materials by which others shall understand and so be led to use—that they may better see, touch, taste, enjoy— their own world. . . .
>
> [Art is] most theoretical when it is most down on the ground, most sensual, most real. Picking out a flower or a bird in detail that becomes an abstract term of enlightenment.[9]

Again, sensuality did not mean hedonism or even innocent spontaneity (as, for example, in the manner of Cummings); what it did mean was psychological austerity—freedom from traditional attitudes and feelings—and a corresponding aesthetic independence.

One of the chief expressions of contact with sensual reality and of discovery of the universal in the particular was Williams' attempt to find beauty in mean or common objects or in places where it might not be suspected. And when he argued in the prologue to *Kora in Hell* that "a stained-glass window that had fallen out and lay more or less together on the ground was of far greater interest than the thing conventionally composed *in situ*," [10] he was providing the epigraph to a poetic career. Here is a characteristic passage taken from "Struggle of Wings":

> It is Poesy, born of a man and two women
> Exit No. 4, the string from the windowshade
> has a noose at the bottom, a noose? or
> a ring—bound with a white cord, knotted
> around the circumference in a design—
>   And all there is won

The poet has had a successful vision—he has made, in a
sense, a "white penetration." Similarly:

> And it is Innes on the meadows and fruit is
> yellow ripening in windows every minute
> growing brighter in the bulblight by the
> cabbages and spuds—
> > And all there is won

There follows a stanza that restates the theme of "The Black
Winds":

> What are black 4 a.m.'s after all but black
> 4 a.m.'s like anything else: a tree
> a fork, a leaf, a pane of glass—?
> > And all there is won

What is happening here, as in the entire poem, is made
explicit in a stanza that explains the technique and the vision
of the objectivist poet:

> Out of such drab trash as this
> by a metamorphosis
> bright as wallpaper or crayon
> or where the sun casts ray on ray on
> flowers in a dish, you shall weave
> for Poesy a gaudy sleeve
> a scarf, a cap and find him gloves
> whiter than the backs of doves   (CEP)

One recalls the eighteenth-century notion of "suggestive-
ness" as explained by Hazlitt in "On Imitation": "Imitation
renders an object, displeasing in itself, a source of pleasure
. . . by suggesting new ideas, by detecting new properties,
and endless shades of difference, just as a close and continued contemplation of the object itself would do."

And in "The Principles of Genial Criticism," Coleridge
presents this example of beauty:

> An old coach-wheel lies in the coach maker's yard, dis-
> figured with tar and dirt . . . . if I turn my attention

from these, and regard the figure abstractly, 'still,' I might say to my companion, 'there is beauty in that wheel, and you yourself would not only admit, but would feel it, had you never seen a wheel before.

This poetic, developed to its extreme, lies behind lines like "The beauty of / the terrible faces / of our nonentities / stirs me" ("Apology"); "My stuff / is the feel of good legs / and a broad pelvis / under the gold hair ornaments / of skyscrapers" ("Drink"); "You exquisite chunk of mud / Kathleen—just like / any other chunk of mud!" ("K.McB."); "silver mist lies upon the back yards / among the outhouses" ("Winter Quiet"). It is typical of Williams to admire "the houses / of the very poor: / roof out of line with sides" ("Pastoral"), or to be astonished "beyond words" by an old man with "majestic tread" who "goes about / gathering dog lime" and "walks in the gutter" ("Pastoral II"). Through "intensity of perception," homely objects—a pair of slippers, a dishmop, shoelaces, a red paper box, freightcars, even the numeral "five" on a fire engine—reveal their "antipoetical" poetical beauty in an objectivist experience approaching epiphany. Here, for example, is what Williams sees in a dishmop:

> I bought a dishmop—
> having no daughter—
> for they had twisted
> fine ribbons of shining copper
> about white twine
> and made a tousled head
> of it, fastened it
> upon a turned ash stick
> slender at the neck. . . .
>
> . . . .
> to be a light for me
> and naked
> as a girl should seem
> to her father.   ("Youth and Beauty," CEP)

A pair of shoes standing out against a design of flowers in
a carpet reminds the poet of nightingales ("The Nightingales") and his wife's "new pink slippers" elicit "I talk to
them / in my secret mind / out of pure happiness" ("The
Thinker").

This response, a way of poetry and a way of life, lasted
throughout Williams' career; in so late a poem as "The
Desert Music," which describes a trip to Juárez, Mexico,
Williams asks,

> What in the form of an old whore in
> a cheap Mexican joint in Juárez, her bare
> can waggling crazily can be
> so refreshing to me, raise to my ear
> so sweet a tune, built of such slime?

Music built of slime, the music heard only by the ear of the
"sensual realist," the poet in contact with his object, is also
associated with the figure of a tramp, asleep on the bridge
between Juarez and El Paso, who appears as

> a child in the womb prepared to imitate life. . . .
>   The music
> guards it, a mucus, a film that surrounds it . . .
> a music! a protecting music   .

In perceiving this music, the speaker asserts his identity as
a poet; he senses a "dance" around him in which some kind
of logos is manifest ("The verb detaches itself seeking to
become articulate"), and he expresses awe at his vision:

> And I could not help thinking
> of the wonders of the brain that
> hears that music and of our
> skill sometimes to record it.[11]

This experience epitomizes the whole mystique of objectivist
revelation. Earlier in the poem Williams asserted that "The
law gives us nothing / but a corpse, wrapped in a dirty
mantle"; that is, the law of normal perception and of appar-

ent Nature. It is in "following the insensate music" that the
poet achieves "an agony of self-realization / bound into a
whole / by that which surrounds us." And with this notion
of self-revaluation achieved through "intensity of perception," we return to the idea of poem-as-object: "Only the
made poem, the verb calls it / into being."

The first principle of objectivism—that "associational or
sentimental value is false"—and the second—that the objectivist poet must have "earthy tastes" ("God, if I could
fathom / the guts of shadows!")—have profoundly influenced Williams' portrayal of human subjects no less than
they have his treatment of objects in nature. The poems in
this manner are offered without comment and usually without implication:

> A big young bareheaded woman
> in an apron. . . .
>
> Her shoe in her hand. Looking
> intently into it
>
> She pulls out the paper insole
> to find the nail
>
> That has been hurting her   (CEP)

The poem is entitled "Proletarian Portrait," but Williams
is hardly talking about the woman's need for new shoes,
nor her pathos, nor her innocence, nor even her earthiness,
as such. He is merely capturing an earthy pose that, like
other earthy images, has revealed its form to the poet.

Again, in "Canthara" (Spanish fly), an old Negro imi-
tates the naked dancing girls he saw in his youth:

> his gestures, against the
> tiled wall of the dingy bath-room,
> swished with ecstasy to
> the familiar music of
>   his old emotion.   (CEP)

The bland title holds the clue to the poet's interpretation
of the scene—not that the old man is bawdy or innocent,

but simply that his behavior is incongruous enough to imply, facetiously, that he is under the influence of an aphrodisiac. Once more, it is the pose that makes the poem.[12]

When the response is not wholly aesthetic, it is generally ironic—the irony, with exceptions, not being blatant. Here is an example of how Williams can take a situation charged with conventional association and neutralize it:

> O tongue
> licking
> the sore on
> her nether lip
>
> O toppled belly
>
> . . . .
> I can't die
>
> —moaned the old
> jaundiced woman . . .
>
> I can't die
> I can't die
>   ("To an Old Jaundiced Woman," CEP)

Dying old women are pathetic, but we are looking at this old woman through the eyes of a doctor who is more taken by the ironic incongruity of her cry than by the pathos of her circumstances and really betrays no emotional involvement. Actually, the daring in this poem is minuscule when compared to that in "The Ogre," in which the poet appears to display an outright perversion:

> Sweet child,
> little girl with well-shaped legs
> you cannot touch the thoughts
> I put over and under and around you.
> This is fortunate for they would
> burn you to an ash otherwise.
> Your petals would be quite curled up.   (CEP)

One may argue that the title absolves the poet of all responsibility and that the poem is really a dramatic monologue. I am inclined to doubt it. If there is irony, it is probably in the title itself, the suggestion being that it is conventional to look upon the utterance that follows as being that of an "ogre," when in reality it is but another aspect of the poet's sense of beauty, sexually motivated or not, and therefore not only legitimate but laudable.

Incidentally, I might draw the obvious conclusion at this point that sexuality or sexual allusion in Williams' poetry is generally more an aesthetic than an erotic matter. Again, the aim is to achieve a bizarre vision and perhaps there is no more bizarre a sexual analogy, presented for aesthetic purposes, in American poetry, than the one that appears in the unassuming poem called "Winter Quiet":

> Limb to limb, mouth to mouth
> with the bleached grass
> silver mist lies upon the back yards
> among the outhouses.
>
> . . . .
> Tense with suppressed excitement
> the fences watch where the ground
> has humped an aching shoulder for
> the ecstasy.   (CEP)

Consistent with its paradoxical nature, the objectivist vision was one in which emotion was felt only against a background of psychological austerity, and one in which the poet, who would share his experience with the world, remained essentially an isolated figure defying a universe. "Who shall hear of us / in the time to come?" writes Williams in one of the brief poems called "Love Song," "Let him say there was / a burst of fragrance / from black branches." And in "A Prelude," he asserts, "I know only the bare rocks of today. / In these lies my brown sea-weed." [13] Thus we find him admiring Leonardo da Vinci's Last Supper, not because of its subject, but because

> of the severity and simplicity
> of the background. . . .
>
> . . . .
> ignoring the subject, I fell upon

the perpendiculars of the paneled
woodwork standing there, submissive,
in exaggerated perspective.

There you have it. It's that background
from which my dreams have sprung. . . .
                                    ("Russia," CLP)

The "stark dignity" ("Spring and All") of geometrical vision
is again apparent. And in "The Farmer" we are given an
image of the poet as starkly dignified in a desolate world:

On all sides
the world rolls coldly away:
black orchards
darkened by the March clouds—
leaving room for thought.   (CEP)

Thus "looms the artist figure of / the farmer—composing /
—antagonist." This vision of the "antagonistic" poet, the
man who at once knows reality and "invents" an order out
of desolation, reappears in the poetry of Wallace Stevens,
as does the entire metaphysic in which realism and idealism
are forcibly joined. And just as Stevens was to view the poet
essentially as a Narcissus, so we find Williams writing,

if I in my north room
dance naked, grotesquely
before my mirror . . .
and singing softly to myself:
"I am lonely, lonely.
I was born to be lonely,
I am best so!"
If I admire my arms, my face,
my shoulders, flanks, buttocks
against the yellow drawn shades,—

Who shall say I am not
the happy genius of my household?
                                    ("Danse Russe," CEP)

Here, the poet has turned himself into an object and there is no more egoism in his self-admiration than there was sexual desire in the "ogre's" admiration of the body of a little girl. The last lines are particularly appropriate, suggesting as they do that the poet has found a moment of self-sufficiency: the viewer and the viewed, the revealer and the revealed, the poet and the audience are one; and loneliness becomes freedom.

But "Danse Russe" presents the objectivist-narcissistic experience only at its ideal. Again, as in Stevens, a demonic aspect exists in which the lonely poet has a vision of reality-as-chaos and is unable to create order through the poem; when the farmer cannot compose, loneliness becomes not freedom but terror:

> The mass
> of yellow tulips in the bowl is shrunken.
> Every familiar object is changed and dwarfed.
> I am shaken, broken against a might
> that splits comfort, blows apart
> my careful partitions, crushes my house
> and leaves me—with shrinking heart
> and startled, empty eyes—peering out
> into a cold world.   ("Portrait of the Author," CEP)

It is in poems like this that we can appreciate the similarity of objectivist to existential thought, for the thesis that existence precedes essence, that a reality exists that is prior to all conceptions by which the mind seeks to understand it, is precisely Williams' premise. The speaker, unable to create the ordering idea ("Oh, I cannot say it. There is no word"), faces the contingency of a once-familiar world with sensations akin to those of the Sartrian hero, Roquentin, who beholds a garden that has suddenly become monstrous to him. "The yards in a fury / of lilac blossoms," writes Williams, "are driving me mad with terror." Such is the price of objectivist, no less than of existential, perception.

2

Although poems like "Portrait of the Author" have a nightmarish quality, they do not really prepare the reader for the vast epistemological and moral crisis of Williams' epic poem, *Paterson*, in which the problem of "invention" is extended to include industrial civilization as well as the natural world.[14] The premise of this work is that modern life is characterized by "divorce"—of knowledge from reality, of "idea" from "thing," of language from truth, and, literally and symbolically, of man from woman. Impotent, the poet seeks to master a language, discover a logos, by which meaning in the details of life will be apprehended, order imposed upon flux, and beauty, "locked in the mind," released. Stated in terms of the allegory Williams has set forth, Paterson the poet is Paterson the city, but instead of "living well in his body," he is lost in a sleep from which he cannot waken; his mind, identified with the Falls, is a cataract of things, facts, persons, and events, whose roar is too strong for his voice. The "roar / of eternal sleep . . . challenging / our waking" persists throughout the entire poem, despite the poet's occasional vision of "music," and even as late as the end of the third book, his struggle has proved fruitless:

No meaning. And yet, unless I find a place
apart from it, I am its slave,
its sleeper, bewildered—dazzled. . . .
. . . .
I must
find my meaning and lay it, white,
beside the sliding water: myself—
comb out the language—or succumb. . . .[15]

The concept of "marriage" is dramatized by the figure of the Goddess, a Muse-Nature-Fertility image associated with the woods and park that adjoin the river (Paterson); it is with her that the poet seeks a union, one that represents the reconciliation of imagination and object and the achievement of Knowledge, Beauty, and Poetic Creativity.

Presented in characteristically objectivist terms, the problem of knowledge, identical with the problem of beauty, is posed at the beginning of the preface to Book One:

> To make a start,
> out of particulars
> and make them general, rolling
> up the sum, by defective means—   (p. 11)

We have already seen that the aim of finding the general in the particular has been one of the chief principles in Williams' nature poetry; in commenting on Paterson, Williams says that, "I wanted, if I was to write in a larger way than of the birds and flowers, to write about the people close to me: to know in detail, minutely what I was talking about —to the whites of their eyes, to their very smells." Accordingly, he explains what is virtually the motto of the poem: "But, who, if he chose, could not touch the bottom of thought? The poet does not, however, permit himself to go beyond the thought to be discovered in the context of that with which he is dealing: no ideas but in things." [16] "Touching the bottom of thought" means, of course, following the semimystical mode of pure perception. Ideas without things are the mere abstractions of rationalism (to be associated with the University); things without ideas are mere chaos. The ideal, again, is to find an objectivist mathematic, a higher logic, in which dualism is reconciled and the "mass of detail" interrelated "on a new ground." "By multiplication, a reduction to one" is to be the magic equation in the poem:

> Who are these people (how complex
> the mathematic). . . .
> They walk incommunicado, the
> equation is beyond solution, yet
> its sense is clear—that they may live
> his thought is listed in the Telephone
> Directory—   (p. 18)

The communication made possible by the telephone direc-
tory is, by implication, an ironic counterpart to that which
would be made possible by the Poem; as the opening of
Book One makes clear, multiplicity ("detail") remains multiplicity, the people being but

> a thousand automatons. Who because they
> neither know their sources nor the sills of their
> disappointments walk outside their bodies aimlessly
>   for the most part,
> locked and forgot in their desires—unroused.   (p. 14)

On his part, Paterson cannot objectify his "ideas" or transcend his own dreams; beauty remains "locked in the mind"
and unattached to things. And at one point in his despair,
the poet envisions the nullification of the whole unsolved
formula:

> Look for the nul
> defeats it all
>
> the N of all
> equations . . .
>
> the death of all
> that's past
>
> all being   •   (p. 95)

Conceived of in terms of natural imagery, and thereby
associated with the Goddess and Beauty, Knowledge, the
unfulfilled vision of the many-in-the-one and the one-in-the-
many, becomes a "multiple seed, / packed tight with detail,"
and rotting in a mind, which, possessed by chaos and condi-
tioned by "learning," cannot bring it to fruition and disperse
it. Similarly, the Goddess herself is multiple and awaits
fulfillment from Paterson:

> A man like a city and a woman like a flower
> —who are in love. Two women. Three women.
> Innumerable women, each like a flower.
>   But
> only one man—like a city.   (p. 15)

Here too failure is manifest:

> The flower spreads its colored petals
> > wide in the sun
> But the tongue of the bee
> > misses them
> They sink back into the loam. . . .   (p. 20)

The image reappears as two "halfgrown girls hailing hallowed Easter," while playing with a willow branch, and eventually as a harem of African wives "astraddle a log" in a "descending scale" of freshness and beauty. This ambiguous image is interpreted by Vivienne Koch as indicating "a primitive and vigorous sexuality in a vital and coordinated society" and one can accept this view as far as it goes.[17] In terms of the context, the African chief who is their husband has succeeded in doing on a sexual level what the poet has failed to do on the literary:

> The brain is weak. It fails mastery,
> never a fact.
> >   To bring himself in,
> hold together wives in one wife and
> at the same time scatter it,
> the one in all of them   .   (pp. 223–224)

Elsewhere, we find an account of African fertility rites that seems to confirm the idea that the wives on the log have been truly "married," in contrast to the condition of "divorce" that marks life in Paterson; when a warrior is killed, the women

> cut young branches from a sacred tree and wave the bough over the genital organs of the warrior to extract the spirit of fertility into the leaves. Knowledge of the rites must be kept from men and from unmarried girls. Only married women, who have felt the fertility of men in their bodies, can know the secret of life.   (p. 171)

The obverse condition is signified by the young sisters in the park who hold a willow twig that represents, along with the girls themselves,

> a bud forever green,
> tight-curled, upon the pavement, perfect
> in juice and substance but divorced, divorced
> from its fellows, fallen low—   (p. 28)

The "young branches cut from a sacred tree" and the "willow twig" represent the Golden Bough potent and the Bough powerless ("You also, I am sure, have read / Frazer's *Golden Bough*," Williams says at one point). Similarly, the Goddess in Paterson is like a bush or branch that "trembles frantically / in the indifferent gale: male—stands / rooted there." Yet at one point the poet has a vision of mastery of language; thus he sees the Golden Bough becoming potent:

> one branch
> of the tree at the fall's edge, one
> mottled branch, withheld,
> among the gyrate branches
> of the waist-thick sycamore,
> sway less, among the rest, separate, slowly. . . .
>   (p. 31)

And the image merges into that of the eldest of the African wives, envisioned as the primal source of beauty and fertility realized,

> her old thighs
> gripping the log reverently, that,
> all of a piece, holds up the others—
> alert: begin to know the mottled branch
> that sings. . . .   (p. 32)

only to be contrasted once more with the Bough impotent

> certainly NOT the university,
> a green bud fallen upon the pavement its
> sweet breath suppressed: Divorce. . . .   (p. 32)

The "sweet breath" here mentioned is part of another series of images that reflects the theme of poetic impotence. If the sweet breath of the bud is suppressed, the poet's own breath is accordingly "stale as a whale's." In the moment of vision mentiond above, he says,

> Only of late, late! begun to know, to
> know clearly . . . whence
> I draw my breath or how to employ it
> clearly—if not well. . . .   (p. 31)

But this vision is temporary at best, and the "history" of beauty as it occurs within his mind is best expressed by the hunt for a jungle cat whose "stinking breath would fell us." For the poet the "flower within a flower," the multiple seed, appears only to rot; thus, although in some ideal external reality beauty is integral and constant, in the poet's "weak" mind, it is able to be grasped only momentarily at best:

> Why should I move from this place. . . .
>   knowing
> how futile would be the search
> for you in the multiplicity
> of your debacle. The world spreads
> for me like a flower opening—and
> will close for me as might a rose—
>
> wither and fall to the ground
> and rot and be drawn up
> into a flower again. But you
> never wither—but blossom
> all about me . . .
>   in your
> composition and decomposition
> I find my   .   .
>   despair!   (p. 93)

Hence, the history of the poem and of the poet: "But Spring shall come and flowers will bloom / and man must chatter of his doom" (p. 95).

The doom mentioned here is perhaps what Williams had in mind when he wrote that the "brunt of the four books of Paterson is a search for the redeeming language by which a

man's premature death might have been prevented." Or, to
recall a previous citation, "I must . . . / comb out the
language—or succumb." Correspondingly, we find that in
the poet's mind beauty has become a tiger "made to spring,
/ at the rifle-shot of learning: to kill / and grind those bones"
(p. 33). As becomes apparent sometime later, the bones are,
of course, those of Paterson forced to try to trap beauty by
learning:

> that the poet,
> in disgrace, should borrow from erudition (to
> unslave the mind) . . .
> seeks to induce his bones to rise into a scene,
> his dry bones, above the scene, (they will not). . . .
>   (p. 99)

The plea of the Goddess, "Marry us! Marry us! / Or! be
dragged down, dragged / under and lost" (p. 102), is never
really answered and consequently the fate of Paterson is that
of Sam Patch, who jumps into the falls:

> A speech! What could he say that he must leap so des-
> perately to complete it. . . . Speech had failed him. He
> was confused. The word had been drained of its meaning.
> . . . He struck the water on his side and disappeared.
>   (p. 27)

The poet's failure to acquire the Golden Bough reaches
a climax in the nightmare of the library episode, which begins as a vision of paradise and turns into a vision of hell.
Paterson goes to the library seeking a "cool of books," which
have inspired in his mind "a scent . . . of locust blossoms."
But, as we are to discover, the scent, like the "multiple
seed" that sours, will become a reek within the brain, and
conversely the cool breeze becomes a cyclone that in its
violence is equal to the falls. The cyclone itself will be followed by a holocaust (a "cataract reversed") and a deluge,
other instances of the violence and destructiveness of nature
that ideally precede rebirth—but not in the internal world
that Paterson inhabits. Thus the library is precisely a model

for the mind of the poet. The "dreams" of "dead men" are "unobjectified," locked in books, just as Paterson's are imprisoned within him:

> confined by these walls, risen
> [they] seek an outlet. The spirit languishes,
> unable, unable not from lack of innate ability. . . .
>
> but from that which immures them pressed here. . . .
>
> they sought safety (in books)
> but ended battering against glass
> at the high windows
>
> The Library is desolation, it has a smell of its own
> of stagnation and death   .   (p. 123)

On the other hand, what is locked within print is like a chaotic torrent in which the poet can sometimes read his own fate:

> Old newspaper files,
> to find—a child burned in a field,
> no language. . . .
> Two others,
> boy and girl, clasped in each others' arms
> (clasped also by the water) So be it. Drowned
> wordless in the canal. . . .
> The mind
> reels, starts back amazed from the reading . (p. 120)

The point, then, is that the library is merely an extension of life in the city itself, and things, facts, ideas, and dreams bear no different a relationship to one another. The poet lends "blood / to the past . . . risking life" (as do the books themselves), but he can "never separate that stain / of sense from the inert mass. Never. / Never that radiance / quartered apart, / unapproached by symbols" (p. 132).

Conceived of as a cyclone, behind which is hidden the image of Beauty, the contents of books are also conceived of

as a holocaust from which the poet attempts to separate the
stain of sense,

> (breathing the books in)
> the acrid fumes,
>   for what they could decipher   .
> warping the sense to detect the norm, to break
> through the skull of custom. . . .   (p. 139)

But again, allegorically, Paterson is the books, and just as
he cannot awaken from his dream neither can the books
come to life:

> under the malignity of the hush
> they cannot penetrate and cannot waken, to be again
> active but remain—books
>   that is, men in hell,
> their reign over the living ended. . . .   (p. 140)

Still, they contain within them the vast energy associated
with reality and in a climactic, virtually hysterical moment,
Paterson imagines he has discovered some kind of "meaning":

> A bottle, mauled
> by the flames, belly-bent with laughter. . . .
>
> An old bottle, mauled by the fire
> gets a new glaze, the glass warped
> to a new distinction, reclaiming the
> undefined. A hot stone, reached
> by the tide, crackled over by fine
> lines, the glaze unspoiled   . . . .
> ·
>   The bottle!
> the bottle! the bottle! the bottle! . . . (pp. 142–143)

This objectivist epiphany is ultimately associated with the
revelation of the Goddess:

> Beautiful thing
>
> —intertwined with the fire. An identity
> surmounting the world, its core— . . .   (p. 145)

"An old bottle, mauled by the fire" is vulgarity made radiant, and consequently the poet announces that the "vulgarity of beauty surpasses all . . . perfections." But because Paterson is not the Objectivist but a man haunted by learning, he shrinks "along with the rest, squirting at the fire." The entire fire episode is summarized in this comment:

> We read: not the flames
> but the ruin left
> by the conflagration
>
> Not the enormous burning
> but the dead (the books
> remaining). Let us read   .
>
> and digest: the surface
> glistens, only the surface. . . .   (pp. 148–149)

And beneath the surface is Néant, a "white-hot man become / a book, the emptiness of / a cavern resounding" (p. 149).

When, earlier, the flood was considered along with the wind and the fire as a "counter to all staleness," Williams perhaps had the image of the falls in mind,

> no lullaby but a piston,
> cohabitous, scouring the stones   .
>
> the rock
> floating on the water (as at Mt Katmai
> the pumice-covered sea was white as milk) (p. 163)

But this is not the vision of the flood pertinent to Paterson in the library; rather it is the flood represented as a "muddy flux" in which, literally and symbolically, flowers, dogs, and men are drowned—the flood of learning and convention that inheres in books:

> Texts mount and complicate them-
> selves, lead to further texts and those
> to synopses, digests and emendations. . . .
> Until the words break loose or—sadly
> hold, unshaken. . . .   (p. 156)

Thus, "when the water has receded most things have lost their forms"; what is left is not fertile mud but "a pustular scum," "an acrid, a revolting stench" that "fouls the mind." Once again, it is Paterson's mind that is a flood, as well as the books themselves, and when he says "there is no re-currence / The past is dead" (p. 169), the suggestion is both that the past is unrecoverable from books and that Paterson himself has no memory but is like the "amnesic crowd (the scattered)" in the park that he has visited. What distinguishes him is his awareness of his condition and his refusal to yield despite the knowledge of the perpetual impossibility of his ever obtaining Knowledge:

> But somehow a man must lift himself
> again—
>   again is the magic word   .
>   turning the in out   :
> Speed against the inundation   (p. 162)

Corollary to the problem of knowledge and poetic cre-ativity is the problem of love and personal involvement, a failure of Paterson that is explored most fully in the park episode (Book Two). Appearing throughout this section are excerpts of a letter from C (Cressida), "a woman dying of loneliness," with whom "Doctor P." has broken off, and her indictment is the indictment of the Goddess against Pater-son for his inability to transcend the barriers of his own mind and enter into life:

> You've never had to live, Dr. P—not in any of the by-ways and dark underground passages where life so often has to be tested. The very circumstances of your birth and social background provided you with an escape from life in the raw; and you confuse that protection from life with an *inability* to live. . . .
> But living . . . isn't something one just sits back and decides about. It happens to one. . . . Or else it doesn't happen. . . . when it doesn't then one brings to life (as you do) purely literary sympathies and understandings,

the insights and humanity of words on paper *only*. . . .
(p. 111)

As he walks through the park, the allegorical embodiment of
the Goddess, Paterson's thoughts are excited by grasshoppers,
couriers "to the ceremonial of love," but this image proves
to be but a variation of the multiple-seed, the momentary
inspiration that is never fulfilled. The kind of love that
Paterson witnesses in the park—the kind of love emblematic
of his own condition—is less than ideal:

> But the white girl, her head
> upon an arm, a butt between her fingers
> lies under the bush   .   .
>
> Semi-naked, facing her, a sunshade
> over his eyes,
> he talks with her. . . .
>
> . . . .
> Minds beaten thin
> by waste—among
>
> the working classes SOME sort
> of breakdown
> has occurred. . . .   (pp. 66–67)

Elsewhere, Paterson looks down at an image of himself:

> She stirs, distraught,
> against him—wounded (drunk), moves
> against him (a lump) desiring,
> against him, bored   .
>
> flagrantly bored and sleeping. . . .   (p. 75)

Characteristically, he has, at the end of the sequence, a momentary vision of awakening, stated both whimsically and
lyrically:

> His mind would reawaken:
>
> He   Me with my pants, coat and vest still on!
>
> She   And me still in my galoshes!
>
> . . . .

Her belly . her belly is like a white cloud . a
white cloud at evening . before the shuddering night!

(pp. 104, 105)

Thus ends the episode, ominously.

The poet's crime against the Goddess is reflected in the
crime of the people—the "great beast"—against the park
itself:

flowers uprooted, columbine, yellow and red,
strewn upon the path; dogwoods in full flower,
the trees dismembered; its women
shallow, its men steadfastly refusing—at
the best   .
    The language . words
without style!

(p. 100)

And, ironically, the dominant voice in the park is that of a
revivalist haranguing on behalf of Christ and against sin.

Contrasted with the revivalist's account of how he rid
himself of all his wealth are excerpts from documents describing the fiscal policy of the early Republic and the plans
of Alexander Hamilton for Paterson. And contrasted with
these excerpts, in turn, are those from a Poundian argument
against the Federal Reserve System and money in general.
The question of money reappears in the fourth book and at
least one critic, Randall Jarrell, has read "with sinking heart"
what seems to be a clear imitation of Pound's economics.[18]
Yet the whole presentation has its ambiguities and one may
well inquire whether Williams has in fact envisioned an
economic solution to the metaphysical problem of poetic
knowledge. To begin with, although Williams often defended Pound, he never subscribed to his ideas and was at
least mildly resentful of Pound's lecturing him on what to
read. Perhaps significantly, a letter of "advice" from Pound is
quoted in the flood sequence, preceded by a page in which
the lines are out of kilter and followed by a table of substratum layers that reflects the futile attempt to find potable
water. In the one instance, the disalignment suggests the
breaking up (or flooding) of the poet's mind and, ominously

enough, Pound's letter is headed "S. Liz" (that is, from the mental hospital to which he was committed). Similarly, the table of substratum layers is clearly a metaphor for Paterson's unsuccessful quest and an analogue of the barren condition of his mind. The point, then, is that Pound may represent simply another face of Paterson, and his economic vision simply another multiple seed that has soured or another false route followed by the questing poet. Thus, after an excerpt marking the initial attack on money, we find

> The bird, the eagle, made himself
> small—to creep into the hinged egg
> until therein he disappeared, all
> but one leg upon which a claw opened
> and closed wretchedly gripping
> the air, and would not—for all
> the effort of the struggle, remain
> inside   .   (p. 91)

This may or may not be intended as a description of Pound (on the next page we find, "I had a friend . . . / let it pass"), but, were it so intended, one would not be surprised.

It is true that the conclusion of Part II, Book Four identifies "invention," "radium," "the gist," with social credit; on the other hand, Williams told Horace Gregory,

> I have maintained from the first that Eliot and Pound by virtue of their hypersensitivity (which is their greatness) were too quick to find a culture . . . ready made for their assertions. They ran from something else, something cruder but, at the same time, newer, more dangerous but heavy with rewards for the sensibility that could reap them. They couldn't. Or didn't. But they both ended by avoiding not only the possibilities offered but, at the same time, the deeper implications intellectually which our nascent culture accented.[19]

This statement was made in the context of what Williams called the "clarification of form," "new alignments, in our own language and culture" achieved by "invention, by rediscovery, by reassertion, by the intelligence and the emotions in any and every age." In other words, invention transcends "ready-made" systems. The last six pages of Part II can therefore easily be taken as a parody, not an imitation, of Pound's ideas and style:

> just because they ain't no water fit to drink in that
> spot (or you ain't found none) don't mean there ain't
> no fresh water to be had NOWHERE . .   (p. 215)

and:

> IN
>   venshun.
> O.KAY
>   In venshun
>
> and seeinz az how you hv / started. Will you consider
> a remedy of a lot:
>   i.e. LOCAL control of local purchasing
>   power .
>   ?   ?
>   (p. 218)

Similarly, the opening lines of Part Three are:

> Haven't you forgot your virgin purpose,
> the language?
>
> What language? "The past is for those who
> lived in the past," is all she told me.
>
> Shh! the old man's asleep. . . .   (p. 219)

This passage may imply that for all its possible value, the idea of social credit is not the primary instrument to be used by the poet, whose true province is "form" and language; the old man—Paterson, Pound, Williams (as he sees himself)—remains asleep. And indeed we find in "To My Friend Ezra Pound," "Your English / is not specific enough / As a writer of poems / You show yourself to be inept not to say / usurious." [20] On the other hand, as I have indicated, the economic theme as such remains ambiguous and I offer my interpretation as a possibility, not a certainty.

Whatever the case, repeated throughout all four books, both in the main text and through newspaper articles, historical tracts, letters, and poems, is the myth of the impotent poet and the unfulfilled, wronged, yet lethal goddess with its implications of incomplete knowledge, inadequate love, and unmastered language. The pursuit of the giant "striped bass" dragged ashore (p. 19), the attempt to kill a mink (p. 64), the shooting of a member of a German singing club and the consequent degeneration of the group into a mob (p. 60), the mutilation of an Indian by Dutch soldiers (p. 125), the burial of another Indian, a chief of "gigantic stature" (p. 158), each is in its own way suggestive of Paterson's condition, as well as being an actual occurrence in the history of the city—occurrences from which no "meaning" can be derived. One of Paterson's most striking personae is the dwarf that lives (lived) near the falls, "a monster in human form"; "his face from the upper part of his forehead to the end of his chin, measures *twenty-seven* inches . . . his body is twenty-seven inches in length, his limbs are small and much deformed . . . he cannot support the enormous weight of his head." Such is the head of Paterson, bloated by the "din of fracturing thought / as it falls tinnily to nothing upon the streets." At the end of the poem, after the vision of an ideal pre-Industrial Paterson and of "many women like flowers," the poet, hopefully it would seem, "awakens" and emerges from the sea (an image primarily associated with the chaos of life, death, and reality); yet the last lines of the poem include a typical excerpt from a newspaper describing the hanging of a man "in full view of thousands who had gathered . . . to witness the spectacle" and one realizes that Paterson's emergence from the sea is merely the repetition of the cycle described in the Preface: "Yet there is / no return: rolling up out of chaos, / a nine months' wonder." Thus the nightmare ends only because the poem must end:

> This is the blast
> the eternal close
> the spiral
> the final somersault
>   the end.   (p. 238)

But perhaps it is in the very acceptance of his condition that Paterson attains an almost existential kind of heroism, and the single imperative that emerges from his experience is "Be reconciled, poet, with your world, it is the only truth," *La Vertue est toute dans l'effort*. This essentially tragic vision reappears in a number of the meditative lyrics that Williams wrote in the fifties. We find in "The Pink Locust," for example,

> I'm persistent as the pink locust,
>   once admitted
>   to the garden,
> you will not easily get rid of it.
>   Tear it from the ground,
>   if one hair-thin rootlet
> remain
>   it will come again.[21]

The speaker concludes that he persists with poetry "for what there may be in it" even though he is not in the "galaxy of poets / a rose." In "The Yellow Flower," the poet asserts that he has eyes made to see, and if

> they see ruin for myself
>   and all that I hold
>   dear, they see
> also
>   through the eyes
>   and through the lips
> and tongue the power
>   to free myself
>   and speak of it. . . .[22]

In "To a Dog Injured in the Street," he tells René Char,

> you are a poet who believes
> in the power of beauty
> to right all wrongs.
> I believe it also.
> With invention and courage
> we shall surpass
> the pitiful dumb beasts. . . .[23]

Thus, like the Asphodel, That Greeny Flower, the poet, "having known ruin and the failure of love," continues to "celebrate the light" and love, and, in doing so, achieves his "partial victory."

Furthermore, with the appearance of Book Five in 1958, the story of Paterson took a seemingly new course with the thesis that poetic salvation lay not in the conquest of meaning but in the liberation of beauty from it, and the entrance of the poet into the realm of art, music, and dance. In "The Clouds," as in *Paterson III*, Toulouse-Lautrec, to whom the book is dedicated, appears as one of those gifted with the authentic vision of beauty:

> Toulouse-Lautrec, the
>
> deformed who lived in a brothel and painted
> the beauty of whores. These were
> the truth-tellers of whom we are the sole heirs
> beneath the clouds that bring
>
> shadow and darkness full of thought deepened
> by rain against the clatter
> of an empty sky. . . .   (CLP)

Only in the objectivist vision of Toulouse-Lautrec (and other artists such as Brueghel, Dürer, Klee, and Picasso) is the Goddess really appreciated in her image as a prostitute, and the identity of Mary and Magdalene, whore and virgin, comprehended (p. 245). Paterson, we recall, has told the Goddess,

> You smell like a whore. I ask you to bathe in my
> opinions, the astonishing virtue of your
> lost body. . . .

Williams has, in short, come full circle here, for his poetry
began in an attempt to reveal the aesthetic (nonrational)
identity of the earthy and the exalted object. Similarly, we
learn in *Paterson* V that everything depends upon form and
nothing upon content:

> the world
> of the imagination most endures:
>
> Pollock's blobs of paint squeezed out
> with design!
> pure from the tube. Nothing else
> is real   .   .   (pp. 248–249)

The Dionysian spontaneity of jazz (represented in the poem
by a quasi-mystical musical experience recounted by Mezz
Mezzrow), the tragic emotions of the dance ("We know
nothing and can know nothing . / but / the dance, to dance
to a measure / contrapuntally, / Satyrically, the tragic foot"
[p. 278]) is Paterson's final mode of escape from the flux into
which thought and learning have hurled him. Williams gives
us the direct transcription of an interview in which he asserted the need for poetry to rise above "practical sense" into
an ultimate "rhythm" that justifies a content that may be
no more than "a fashionable grocery list." That such a
rhythm could be associated with the object as well as the
poem is made clear, one recalls, in "The Desert Music."

Yet despite the affirmative tone in this characteristically
aestheticist solution to the metaphysical and moral problems of the poetic experience, the conclusion of Book Five
is really no more conclusive than that of Book Four. Paterson does not emerge as the hero triumphant but only as the
hero pursued (a unicorn). But, given the conditions of life
on the Passaic, the mere fact that he has survived, has
reached the age where he can "instruct the young," was
heroism enough. And the letter from Allen Ginsberg, reprinted in Book Five, suggests that the young were in fact
ready to listen.

4. WALLACE STEVENS:
META-MEN AND PARA-THINGS

"Sentimentality," Wallace Stevens wrote in the *Adagia*, "is a failure of feeling." The remark is symptomatic, and if we consider what Stevens thought authentic feeling to be, we will soon find ourselves involved in the metaphysics of imagination and reality, the inevitable subject of Stevens' poetry.[1] For Stevens, as for Williams, authentic feeling was the result of a direct perception of, or contact with, "reality," and even though that reality was often variously defined, it remained the first principle of Stevens' world. "Sentimentality" and other "romantic" responses by which man established a "blissful liaison with his environment" were distortions of the imagination that in its authentic form did not act independently of external reality. Thus, for Stevens, as for Williams, and as, indeed, for the whole aestheticist tradition, the initial poetic act is to "observe." Mere reverie, we learn in two of the "anecdotes," can lead to insanity: "In the moonlight / I met Berserk," a figure who sets his traps "in the midst of dreams." Similarly, the poet X, dreaming of tropical herbs, "In sleep may never meet another thought / Or thing"; he must awaken:

> Now day-break comes . . .
>
> X promenades the dewy stones,
> Observes the canna with a clinging eye,
> Observes and then continues to observe.
> ("Anecdote of Canna")[2]

In at least one of its phases, the imagination is merely responsive to its environment:

> As the immense dew of Florida
> Brings forth hymn and hymn
> From the beholder,

Beholding all these green sides
And gold sides of green sides,

And blessed mornings,
Meet for the eye of the young alligator,
And lightning colors
So, in me, come flinging
Forms, flames, and the flakes of flames.

(*"Nomad Exquisite"*)

And in poems like "Waving Adieu, Adieu, Adieu," we learn that pure observation is the basis of self-fulfillment:

Just to be there and just to behold.

To be one's singular self. . . .

. . . .
Ever-jubilant,
What is there here but weather, what spirit
Have I except it comes from the sun?

The question is not an idle one, for we are told elsewhere that the "soul" is in fact "composed / Of the external world" and that man is his environment; "There are men of the East . . . / Who are the East" (*"Anecdote of Men by the Thousands"*). Thus, although "it is not every day the world arranges itself in a poem" (*Adagia*) and "One's tootings at the weddings of the soul [with reality] / Occur as they occur" in a chance world, life as it is offered to man is the final truth and the aesthetic enjoyment of it is the most meaningful experience:

Could you have said the blue jay suddenly
Would swoop to earth? It is a wheel, the rays
Around the sun. The wheel survives the myths.
The fire eye in the clouds survives the gods. . . .
It may be that the ignorant man, alone,
Has any chance to mate his life with life
That is the sensual, pearly spouse, the life
That is fluent in even the wintriest bronze.

(*"The Sense of the Sleight-of-hand Man"*)

Given this context, it is no surprise to find in *The Adagia* and elsewhere statements about poetry, reality, and feeling that call to mind the arguments of Williams. Here is a counterpart to Williams on "invention" and the need for the unusual response: "The exquisite environment of fact. The final poem will be the poem of fact in the language of fact. But it will be the poem of fact not realized before." [3] And on "revelation": "Poetry has to be something more than a conception of the mind. It has to be a revelation of nature. Conceptions are artificial. Perceptions are essential." [4]

The truth is, however, that even in the early poems, Stevens reveals complexities that make an easy definition of his attitudes impossible. In "Evening without Angels," prefaced by the quotation, *"the great interests of man: air and light, the joy of having a body, the voluptuousness of looking,"* there appears a characteristic vision of the Earth as man's natural home. Here we are told that "air is air," that light was made for men, not angels, and that "Bare night is best. Bare earth is best." An evening without angels is an evening without myths made by sad men, an evening in which one senses and responds to an identity with Nature:

> Men that repeat antiquest sounds of air
> In an accord of repetitions. Yet,
> If we repeat, it is because the wind
> Encircling us, speaks always with our speech.

Yet if the world was made for men, there is a counter-thesis in Stevens that it was men who made it themselves and that the reality of which the soul is composed is also composed in part of the soul. The *Adagia* contains almost as many apparently idealistic as realistic pronouncements:

> The mind is the most powerful thing in the world.
> Things seen are things as seen.
> There is nothing in life except what one thinks of it.
> Reality is a vacuum.[5]

But as we shall see momentarily, if Stevens' realism is modified by his impulse toward idealism, his idealism is held in check by his abiding sense of realism.

In the essay "Three Academic Pieces," Stevens asserted that the imaginative act (now conceived of as a positive rather than a responsive process) involved the creation of resemblances—an act that bound the internal to the external world and expressed itself in a poetry that was part of the "structure of reality." [6] Like men in general, the poet created resemblances in terms of his own sensibility, a narcissistic act from which he derived "pleasure." As stated in another essay, "The Effects of Analogy," "poetry becomes and is a transcendent analogue composed of the particulars of reality, created by the poet's sense of the world . . . his attitude, as he intervenes and interposes the appearances of that sense." [7] In the poem called "Of the Surface of Things," written a quarter of a century earlier than these essays, we find Stevens' notion of this aspect of the poetic experience manifested in three brief stanzas. The first states the objectivist premise:

> In my room, the world is beyond my understanding;
> But when I walk I see that it consists of three or four
>   hills and a cloud.

Having left his "room" (recall that "Anecdote of Canna" and "Anecdote of the Prince of Peacocks" describe the dangers of mental life out of touch with external reality), the poet creates a resemblance in his own image, or, perhaps one should say, after his own desire:

> From my balcony, I survey the yellow air,
> Reading where I have written,
> "The spring is like a belle undressing."

And concludes, in the third stanza, with the total manipulation of reality:

> The gold tree is blue.
> The singer has pulled his cloak over his head.
> The moon is in the folds of the cloak.

"Six Significant Landscapes" goes even farther in demonstrating the identity of human and natural worlds through imaginative manipulation:

> An old man sits
> In the shadow of a pine tree
> In China. . . .
> His beard moves in the wind.
> The pine tree moves in the wind.
> Thus water flows
> Over weeds.

The intended effect here is, I think, both impressionistic—one is supposed to be looking at a "landscape" in which man and nature are fused—and expressionistic, insofar as the figure in the picture is, we can assume, supposedly undergoing an imaginative experience and is a projection of the poet himself. If, in this stanza, man is absorbed by nature, in the next, nature is absorbed into the human world:

> The night is of the color
> Of a woman's arm:
> Night, the female,
> Obscure,
> Fragrant and supple,
> Conceals herself.

But in "Three Academic Pieces" Stevens was to write that although the imagination could manipulate nature, it could not create a new one—that, in effect, it was ultimately circumscribed by the material upon which it acted. That manipulation is possible is a source of pride; the mind is gigantic:

> I measure myself
> Against a tall tree.
> I find that I am much taller,
> For I reach right up to the sun,
> With my eye. . . .

That manipulation is only manipulation, that the mind cannot escape reality, that the perceiver can be no more than

what he perceives, is a source of mock-heroic self-irony. If
the imagination encompasses a tree, it *is* a tree:

> Nevertheless, I dislike
> The way ants crawl
> In and out of my shadow.

On the other hand, if the mind does not transcend the realities of nature, neither does nature escape the resemblances,
the commonly human elements, to which the mind is habit-
uated. The moon itself takes on a human shape ("The soles
of its feet / Grew red. / Its hair filled") when apprehended
by the dreaming poet. In the fifth landscape a star is considered a supreme aesthetic artisan with more precise instru-
ments than the "knives of lamp-posts," "chisels of the long
streets," and so forth. All these resemblances, it is suggested
in the final stanza, are those of an imaginative geometer,
who, unlike the "rationalists," does not limit himself to
squares and right angles but tries "rhomboids, / Cones,
waving lines, ellipses," and wears a flamboyant "sombrero." [8]
Poems like "Six Significant Landscapes" and "Of the Surface of Things" are, in essence, demonstrations of both sides
of Stevens' vision—first, of the idea that novel perception is
necessary, and second, of the idea, stated in "To the One of
Fictive Music," that "so retentive of themselves are men /
That music is intensest which proclaims / The near, the
clear, and vaunts the clearest bloom."

  It is further testimony to the complexities of Stevens'
mind that the realistic-idealistic paradox is repeated on what
is, in a sense, another dimension of attitudes. The appearance of an active imagination, as in the poems just discussed,
is alone sufficient to suggest a reality that is not a "fluent
life" naturally married to human life, but, in fact, to repeat
one of the adages, a "vacuum," or, to make explicit the implicit, a "Néant" in which nature is not continuous with the
human world but is contingent. Here, the benign "bare
earth" of "Evening without Angels" becomes merely "Absolute Fact," *ding-an-sich*. Yet significantly even this trans-

human reality draws the poet to it no less than it repels him
through terror:

> Shine alone, shine nakedly, shine like bronze,
> that reflects neither my face nor any inner part
> of my being, shine like fire, that mirrors nothing.

Thus Stevens addresses a star in "Nuances of a Theme by
Williams." The vision is elaborated in "Stars at Tallapoosa":

> The lines are straight and swift between the stars.
> The night is not the cradle that they cry,
> The criers, undulating the deep-oceaned phrase.
> The lines are much too dark and much too sharp.
>
> The mind herein attains simplicity.
> There is no moon, on single, silvered leaf,
> The body is no body to be seen
> But is an eye that studies its black lid.

Once again, we have returned to the idea of pure perception,
but it is perception of a distant world. The apprehension of
this guise of reality requires that the mind yield up its narcissistic imaginative powers, as we learn in "The Snow
Man":

> One must have a mind of winter
> To regard the frost and the boughs
> Of the pine-trees crusted with snow . . .
>
>   and not to think
> Of any misery in the sound of the wind. . . .

One who achieves the "mind of winter," being "nothing
himself, beholds / Nothing that is not there and the nothing
that is." That is, he perceives the Nothing that is the true
being of reality.

The attempt of the poet to sustain a snowman's vision
and, paradoxically, because he is human, to build a world
upon it, is the subject of one of the major pieces in *Har-
monium*, "The Comedian as the Letter C." Trying to reduce

himself to the letter C (that is, to the "ABC of being"),
Crispin, the hero, succeeds only in confirming that he is in
fact "comedian" and human.[9] Yet Stevens' investigation of
what in his world is a central aesthetic and metaphysical
problem, for all the ironies it uncovers, does not end in
despair or even in exasperation, and one must finally ask
whether the "doleful heroics" are as "mock" as much of the
tone of the work would lead us to believe.

Having been exposed to a vision of Absolute Fact (the sea,
"veritable ding an sich") in which his "mythology of self"
(imagination) has been "Blotched out beyond unblotching,"
and having been reduced to "some starker, barer self / In a
starker, barer world," Crispin seeks to become a "connoisseur
of chaos," the poet of "an elemental fate" and "beautiful
barenesses as yet unseen." His old role as a dilettante of
nature, a "Socrates of snails" and a "musician of pears,"
afforded an altogether too "blissful liaison" with the external
world; such a role was characteristic of "lunar" thought or
a dreamy and "misty" romanticism. (Although the lunar
mind is identified with the Arctic, and its opposite, the solar
mind, is identified with the tropics, the latter is really but a
variation of the mind of the snowman; Crispin is a "nihilist,"
a "searcher for the fecund minimum.") Hence, "all dreams
are vexing. Let them be expunged." The new poetry as a
reflection of a new sensibility will actually be dehumanized,
for the aim of the poet is "to drive away / The shadow of
his fellows from the skies, / And, from their stale intelligence
released, / . . . make a new intelligence prevail." Freedom
means escape from moonlight that haunts the human mind
and gives rise to the dream of the romantic; conversely, when
the self of the poet is possessed by the "self" of reality, the
mind is set free and the poetry it "records" is "veracious page
on page, exact."

It is not difficult to see the direction of this objectivist
argument. The escape from moonlight is the escape from
the personal and lyrical into the impersonal and descriptive,
from the limited to the extensive. Crispin wants to become
a "clerk of experience" and the natural end of this desire is

the "annotation" or "accounting" of an empire. "The idea of
a colony" is not simply the establishment of a new school
of poets, but the expansion of the self that comes from
surrender of the self to reality. Crispin's vision of empire—
based on Stevens' abiding notion that the soil (environment) determines the intelligence (poetry)—directs that the
Georgian be "pine-spokesman," the Floridan play a banjo,
the Peruvian make the "Sierra scan," and the Brazilian write
"pampean dits." Crispin's imagined extension of himself (as
"progenitor") is, as we shall see later, a prototype of Stevens'
conception of the poet as a giant who, in identifying himself with reality, dominates it.

But the idea of a colony, of a "comprehensive island hemi-
sphere," in the tropics, is doomed, and precisely because the
element of the personal, the human, cannot be transcended.
Gradually, Crispin not only gives up his idea of a continent
and concentrates on "things within his actual eye," but he
finds himself virtually in the position he was in before his
voyage: a poet of plums:

> It seemed haphazard denouement.
> He first, as realist, admitted that
> Whoever hunts a matinal continent
> May, after all, stop short before a plum
> And be content and still be realist.[10]

The difference is that he is now, partly perhaps in rationalization, trying to see the plum as a *ding-an-sich*, a bare reality
that survives its descriptions and remains "good, fat, guzzly
fruit." Nonetheless, he is aware that something essential has
been lost and he contemplates the possible responses he
might make: that of the "tragedian" lamenting his fate with
"fugal requiems" or that of the philosopher seeing in his own
fate "an instance of all fate." The latter involves the admission that all men are subject to personal limitations that
make ideal identification with absolute reality impossible:

> Can one man think one thing and think it long?
> Can one man be one thing and be it long?

> The very man despising honest quilts
> Lies quilted to his poll in his despite.[11]

Ironically, one can go so far as to say that the very idea of a
colony is but another example of a personal dream and that
the very quest for identification with sea and jungle is but
an illusion of the mind.

The self-defeating nature of the poetic experience as Crispin conceives it is a truth the realist comes to perceive and,
if he is to remain faithful to truth, must accept, since "For
realist, what is is what should be." The conclusion of the
poem, which describes Crispin's lapse into domestic life with
a blond wife and "daughters with curls," far from evading
the problem of realism, is the only logical resolution of it.
Given the inevitability of failure, the only position of the
realist is "indulgent fatalism" and the acceptance of a com-
fortable "quotidian," even though it detracts from the (already doomed) pursuit of the "knaves of thought."

Felicity is the reward for finding one's poetry in one's
daughters and the external world in one's family:

> The world, a turnip once so readily plucked . . .
> Came reproduced in purple, family font,
> The same insoluble lump. The fatalist
> Stepped in and dropped the chuckling down his craw,
> Without grace or grumble.[12]

But for Stevens, this conclusion, implying as it did the logical
self-effacement of the poet, was really no answer; the passion
for reconciling the human and the nonhuman absolute, the
personal and the universal, the dream and the fact, the idea
and the reality was to provide him with a "motive for metaphor" throughout a lifetime.

The sequel to the realism of "The Comedian as the Letter
C" is the idealism of "The Idea of Order at Key West" in
which the poet, instead of identifying himself with "absolute
fact," identifies absolute fact with himself through the power
of the imagination:

> when she sang, the sea,
> Whatever self it had, became the self
> That was her song, for she was the maker. Then we,
> As we beheld her striding there alone,
> Knew that there never was a world for her
> Except the one she sang and, singing, made.

Far from being "blotched out," "mythology of self" (for Stevens the only legitimate mythology) has proven itself "the strongest force in the world." But what is particularly important is that the speaker can share the singer's triumph:

> Ramon Fernandez, tell me, if you know,
> Why, when the singing ended . . .
> The lights in the fishing boats at anchor there,
> As the night descended, tilting in the air,
> Mastered the night and portioned out the sea,
> Fixing emblazoned zones and fiery poles,
> Arranging, deepening, enchanting night.

Thus, in "The Noble Rider and the Sound of Words," Stevens wrote that the function of the poet is to make his imagination that of his readers:

> . . . he fulfills himself only as he sees his imagination become the light in the minds of others. His role . . . is to help people to live their lives. . . . He has had immensely to do with giving life whatever savor it possesses . . . whatever the imagination and senses have made of the world. . . .
>   . . . what makes the poet the potent figure that he is . . . is that he creates the world to which we turn incessantly and without knowing it and that he gives to life the supreme fictions without which we are unable to conceive of it.[13]

The singer has not only mastered reality but she has, in a sense, made the personal universal—she has created a supreme fiction that has satisfied her listeners', as well as her own, "rage for order." And perhaps one can say that this new "mythology of self" is suitable for a "colony," whereas Crispin's loss of self left him capable of doing no more than raising a family. In "The Irrational Element in Poetry," Stevens wrote that "Resistance to the pressure of ominous and destructive circumstance consists of its conversion, so far as possible, into a different, an explicable, an amenable circumstance." [14] Although he is talking specifically about the pressure of events that characterize modern life, the remark holds true for the kind of reality represented by the sea. We discover at the end of the poem that the singer has triumphed because she has been able to translate the sound of the ocean into something meaningful to the human ear, into "Words of the fragrant portals, dimly-starred, / And of ourselves and of our origins."

It is a testament to Stevens' realism, however, that the experience at Key West represents but a moment in the poet's resistance to the pressure of the "ominous and destructive." There are occasions when the mind is overwhelmed:

> Out of the window,
> I saw how the planets gathered
> Like the leaves themselves
> Turning in the wind.
> I saw how the night came,
> Came striding like the color of the heavy
>   hemlocks
> I felt afraid.   ("Domination of Black")

"Valley Candle" may be read symbolically:

> My candle burned alone in an immense valley.
> Beams of the huge night converged upon it,
> Until the wind blew.

In "A Weak Mind in the Mountains," we find:

> The black wind of the sea
> And the green wind
> Whirled upon me.
> The blood of the mind fell
> To the floor. I slept.

> Yet there was a man within me
> Could have risen to the clouds,
> Could have touched these winds,
> Bent and broken them down,
> Could have stood up sharply in the sky.

Less dramatic but no less illustrative of Stevens' vision of the limitations imposed by reality on the mind are the "maladies of the quotidian" ("Disillusionment of Ten O'Clock," "The Man Whose Pharynx Was Bad," "Loneliness in Jersey City," and so on) in which, under the pressure of dull weather or banal surroundings, the poet suffers a paralyzing ennui.

2

Behind the obscurities and ambiguities of Stevens' middle and late poetry lies a vision of perception, of poetry, and of belief that is a culmination, often hypersubtle in its logic, of the paradoxes of realism and idealism visible in his earlier work. Transconceptual knowledge of Absolute Fact remains the starting point, as the appeal in "Credences of Summer" exemplifies:

> Postpone the anatomy of summer, as
> The physical pine, the metaphysical pine.
> Let's see the very thing and nothing else.
> Let's see it with the hottest fire of sight.
> Burn everything not part of it to ash.
>
> Trace the gold sun about the whitened sky
> Without evasion by a single metaphor.　.　.　.　.
> Look at it in its essential barrenness
> And say this, this is the centre that I seek.[15]

The explicit meaning of this imperative can be found in a passage from "Notes toward a Supreme Fiction":

> To discover an order as of
> A season, to discover summer and know it,

> To discover winter and know it well, to find,
> Not to impose, not to have reasoned at all,
> Out of nothing to have come on major weather,
>
> It is possible, possible, possible. . . .
> . . . .
>   To find the real,
> To be stripped of every fiction except one,
>
> The fiction of an absolute. . . .[16]

And in "An Ordinary Evening in New Haven," Stevens' intricate disquisition on reality, the "poem of pure reality" is described as being

>   untouched
> By trope or deviation, straight to the word,
> Straight to the transfixing object, to the object
>
> At the exactest point at which it is itself,
> Transfixing by being purely what it is,
> A view of New Haven, say, through the certain eye. . . .[17]

The "certain eye" is, however, inevitably "inexquisite," for "We do not know what is real and what is not"; visions of reality are always modified by "prolongations of the human." Thus, an earlier section:

> Inescapable romance, inescapable choice
> Of dreams, disillusion as the last illusion,
> Reality as a thing seen by the mind,
>
> Not that which is but that which is apprehended,
> A mirror, a lake of reflections in a room. . . .
> . . . .
> Everything as unreal as real can be. . . .[18]

Conversely, we are told in "Notes toward a Supreme Fiction" that

> Two things of opposite natures seem to depend
> On one another, as a man depends
> On a woman, day on night, the imagined
>
> On the real.[19]

Consequently, "The Bouquet" speaks of a world of "medium nature," "The place of meta-men and para-things," in which reality and human imagination find an ideal coexistence. "Para-things" are things whose existence is partly absolute and partly a matter of poetic insight:

> The rose, the delphinium, the red, the blue,
> Are questions of the looks they get. The bouquet,
> Regarded by the meta-men, is quirked
>
> And queered by lavishings of their will to see.
> . . . .
>   an appanage
> Of indolent summer not quite physical
>
> And yet of summer. . . .
>
> The infinite of the actual perceived . . .
> The real made more acute by an unreal.[20]

In one sense, meta-men are men whose imaginations are not divorced from a sense of the "absolutely real," men for whom "no blue in the sky" is a hindrance to their becoming "clear, transparent magistrates." The para-thing represents what Stevens called, in "A Collect of Philosophy," an "integration," the desire for which was part of a "will to order" shared by poet and philosopher. Perception of "the infinite of the actual," just mentioned, is an "inherently poetic" act (or idea):

> Certainly a sense of the infinity of the world is a sense of something cosmic. It is cosmic poetry because it makes us realize . . . that we are creatures, not of a part . . . but of a whole for which, for the most part, we have as yet no language. This sudden change of a lesser life for a greater one is like a change of winter for spring or any other transmutation of poetry.[21]

It is precisely through the "transmutation of poetry" that things become para-things and men become meta-men; on the other hand, "the infinite of the actual perceived" does not obscure the actual itself, insofar as it can be "transfixed, transpierced and well perceived": "The meta-men behold the idea as part / Of the image, behold it with exactness through beads / And dewy bearings of their light-locked beards."

This vision of an ideal "medium nature" receives one of its clearest elaborations in "An Ordinary Evening in New Haven," that "endlessly elaborating poem" about "things seen and unseen, created from nothingness." I quote the passage at length because it contains details that may be fruitfully pursued:

> Suppose these houses are composed of ourselves,
> So that they become an impalpable town, full of
> Impalpable bells, transparencies of sound,
>
> Sounding in transparent dwellings of the self. . . .
> . . . .
> Coming together *in a sense* in which we are poised,
> Without regard to time or where we are,
>
> In the perpetual reference, object
> Of the perpetual meditation, point
> Of the enduring, visionary love,
>
> Obscure, in colors whether of the sun
> Or mind, uncertain in the clearest bells,
> The spirit's speeches, the indefinite,
>
> Confused illuminations and sonorities,
> So much ourselves, we cannot tell apart
> The idea and the bearer-being of the idea.
>
>   [italics mine][22]

In its resolution of time and timelessness, this experience with a fourth dimension is perhaps reminiscent of Eliot's in the *Four Quartets*. Whatever the case, in "St. Armorer's Church from the Outside," Stevens speaks of a "mystic eye" through which not the "sign of life but life, / Itself" is revealed. And such mystic vision begins and ends with a "sense," the poet's "sense of the world," discussed in "The Effects of Analogy," cited earlier in this chapter. Poetry transforms reality, but "the poetic nature of any idea," we learn in "A Collect of Philosophy," "depends on the mind through which it passes. This is as true of the poetic aspect of nature as it is of the poetic aspect of ideas. The sun rises and sets every day and yet it brings to few men and to those men only infrequently a *sense* of the universe of space" (italics mine).[23] The point, then, is that "sense" or feeling is the crucial element in poetic vision, not mere perception by itself. Thus, in "Poem Written at Morning":

> The truth must be
> That you do not see, you experience, you feel,
> That the buxom eye brings merely its element
> To the total thing, a shapeless giant forced
> Upward.

And "The Ultimate Poem Is Abstract" confirms this notion:

> It would be enough
> If we were ever, just once, at the middle, fixed
> In This Beautiful World Of Ours and not as now,
>
> Helplessly at the edge, enough to be
> Complete, because at the middle, if only in sense,
> And in that enormous sense, merely enjoy.

The extreme of idealism to which the idea of sense can lead appears in "Bouquet of Roses in Sunlight," in which flowers appear "Too actual, things that in being real / Make any imaginings of them lesser things." Yet this very appearance of Absolute Reality is but "a consequence of the way / We feel and, therefore, is not real, except / In our sense of it." On the other hand, when ideal sense is absent (and such is the condition that prevails), the eye looks down a "crude foyer," not in perception of an absolute, but, since the conception of the absolute is itself an idea of order, in

> An innocence of an absolute,
> False happiness, since we know that we use
> Only the eye as faculty, that the mind
> Is the eye, and that this landscape of the mind

> Is a landscape only of the eye; and that
> We are ignorant men incapable
> Of the least, minor, vital metaphor, content,
> At last, there, when it turns out to be here.
>
> ("Crude Foyer")

This despairing vision is a part of the aesthetics of sickness:

> To lose sensibility, to see what one sees . . .
> To hear only what one hears, one meaning alone,
> As if the paradise of meaning ceased
> To be paradise, it is this to be destitute.
> This is the sky divested of its fountains.
> Here in the west indifferent crickets chant
> Through our indifferent crises.[24]

The theory of "sensibility," with its corollary on "inherently poetic ideas," is similarly responsible for the paradoxes involved in Stevens' famous "Supreme Fiction." This notion, which, so to speak, contains wheels within wheels, can best be defined as the *idea* of reality and the *idea* of man, both being "inherently poetic" and therefore capable of the transformations of the Nameless Universe (imaginatively conceived of as Absolute Reality) which make it possible for men to satisfy their "will to order" and to live their lives with "pleasure" and "savor." (One might add that the mere *idea* of *a* supreme fiction [apart from *the* Supreme Fiction] is itself an "inherently poetic idea.") The requirements for a supreme fiction, we learn in the "Notes," are that "It Must Be Abstract; It Must Change; It Must Give Pleasure"— each of these values corresponding to a human need.[25] The first problem then is to find a "name for something that never could be named": establish an abstraction for the thing-in-itself:

> Begin, ephebe, by perceiving the idea
> Of this invention, this invented world,
> The inconceivable idea of the sun.
>
> . . . .
> Never suppose an inventing mind as source

> Of this idea nor for that mind compose
> A voluminous master folded in his fire.

> How clean the sun when seen in its idea,
> Washed in the remotest cleanliness of a heaven
> That has expelled us and our images. . . .[26]

The "inventing mind" is probably that of God; it may just as logically be that of man himself, since we discover that even though Adam and Eve created a paradise that bore the image of themselves, "a second earth" of a "very varnished green," the truth is that

> The clouds preceded us

> There was a muddy centre before we breathed.
> There was a myth before the myth began,
> Venerable and articulate and complete.[27]

But to return to our argument, that is to say, the myth of creation, the difference between the thing-in-itself and the idea-of-the-thing (the abstraction or "first idea") is the difference between

> The weather and the giant of the weather,
> Say the weather, the mere weather, the mere air:
> An abstraction blooded, as a man by thought.[28]

And the "giant of the weather" has its counterpart in the "pensive giant" that is the abstraction of man considering manhood:

> The major abstraction is the idea of man
> And major man is its exponent, abler
> In the abstract than in his singular,

> More fecund as principle than particle.[29]

That is, the *idea* of major man expounding the idea of man is itself a major abstraction or poetic idea. The *idea* of "heroism" is more fruitful than any individual act of heroism.

And when Stevens writes, as he does in "The Noble Rider and the Sound of Words," that the "idea of nobility exists in art today only in degenerate forms . . . if, in fact, it exists at all," he is seeking to reestablish literally what in his view is one of the chief abstractions of poetry and therefore of life (and vice versa). It might be added, incidentally, that Stevens' frequent remarks on the relation of poetry to life are intended to apply to his own genre of poetry—in short, that his poetry, like that of most of his contemporaries, is intended to accomplish in fact what it proposes as theory. To say that "The poet is the subject of the poem" need not involve us in a metaphysic; to suggest that the poet is the subject of the poem because the subject of the poet is "inherently poetic" is something else again. Thus Stevens' assertion in "The Figure of the Youth as a Virile Poet" that the poem comes to "possess the reader . . . naturalizes him in its own imagination and liberates him there," and that the experience of the poet is "no less a degree than the experience of the mystic," [30] is merely a statement proposing literally what might be proposed in his poetry as part of a vision.

When we come to the second requirement, "It Must Change," we again face a notion of deceptive simplicity. For example, we learn that the cycle of the year, so conceived, does not represent change but mere repetition—the suggestion being that the idea of death and rebirth or of immortality is not an inherently poetic idea and does not correspond to anything authentic in the human psyche or in absolute reality. "Repetition" or "immortality" is an idea of permanence, as is expressed in a statue that changes "true flesh to inhuman bronze" and consequently is "rubbish in the end." To appreciate the drift of this argument, we might recall the lines in "An Ordinary Evening in New Haven" in which the ideal experience was described as being a "sense in which we are poised, / Without regard to time or where we are." The experience occurs in an eternal present having no connection with what comes before or after including other such ideal experiences. In "Montrachet-le-Jardin," for instance, this ideal imperative appears:

> Breathe, breathe upon the centre of
> The breath life's latest, thousand senses.
> But let this one sense be the single main.

Only to be followed by:

> And yet what good were yesterday's devotions?
> I affirm and then at midnight the great cat
> Leaps quickly from the fireside and is gone.[31]

To return to the original image of spring and to the problem
of how it should be conceived:

> Why . . . when in golden fury

> Spring vanishes the scraps of winter, why
> Should there be a question of returning or
> Of death in memory's dream? Is spring a sleep?

> This warmth is for lovers at last accomplishing
> Their love, this beginning, not resuming, this
> Booming and booming of the new-come bee.[32]

The point, then, is that the true idea of change is the idea of
contingency, a state-in-itself for which there is no causation
and no sequence; each experience with the ideal is thus a
"new beginning." To appreciate contingency is to appreciate
the reality of "changing essences," the "freshness of a world."
And since that world is, in essence, the world with which
men are identified, its "presentations" of freshness "Are rub-
bings in a glass in which we peer": "It is our own, / It is
ourselves, the freshness of ourselves." Thus the argument
comes full circle: Since the external world is contingent,
men's natures are contingent; and when those natures sense
the contingency of the world they fulfill themselves according to their own character or are "liberated." Therefore, to
be a fiction suitable to human needs, the Supreme Fiction
must "change" or be eternally fresh, and the only fiction
that can be eternally fresh is the idea of reality or the idea
of man as being eternally fresh. These are complications perhaps beyond those intended by Stevens, but they are nonetheless complications to which his logic inevitably leads.

In any event, man possesses a "will to change" (along with a "will to order") that it is the function of poetry to satisfy, and "one's motive in writing is renewal." (Furthermore, just as the Fiction must be eternally fresh, so we find that "As a man becomes familiar with his own poetry, it becomes obsolete.") In the first part of the "Notes" Stevens asserts that

> It is the celestial ennui of apartments
> That sends us back to the first idea. . . .
>
> . . . .
> May there be an ennui of the first idea?
> What else, prodigious scholar, should there be?

The argument continues,

> The poem refreshes life so that we share,
> For a moment, the first idea. . . . It satisfies
> Belief in an immaculate beginning. . . .[33]

To share in the first idea is to begin by apprehending essence and freshness, but the suggestion is that if the first idea were held for more than "a moment," it would become dull and no longer a source of "pleasure." "The ravishments of truth" (which delude one into believing that one has captured an essence permanently) are "fatal to / The truth itself" (that essence is eternally changing and fresh). In actuality, the first idea becomes "The hermit in a poet's metaphors, / Who comes and goes and comes and goes all day." Thus man's craving for change, a reflection of the changeability of truth (and first ideas) is a desire that prevents him from succumbing to the "ravishments" of truth:

> The philosopher
> Appoints man's place in music, say, today.
> But the priest desires. The philosopher desires.

And such desire

> knows that what it has is what is not
> And throws it away like a thing of another time,
> As morning throws off stale moonlight and shabby
>   sleep.[34]

Finally, in "The Irrational Element in Poetry," Stevens declares that the irrational, associated with the "unknown" and therefore with freshness, is the very essence of poetic energy and part of the "individuality" (or eccentricity) of the poet—in short, of his own element of freshness. Accordingly, the poem is determined by the nature of the poet's sensibility and is automatic in that "it is what I wanted it to be without knowing before it was written what I wanted it to be, even though I knew before it was written what I wanted to do." [35] To the extent that a poem is beyond the poet's power to change it (i.e., "automatic"), it is "irrational." Hence, the Supreme Fiction, in the final part ("It Must Give Pleasure"), becomes

> the soft-footed-phantom, the irrational

> Distortion, however fragrant, however dear.
> That's it: the more than rational distortion,
> The fiction that results from feeling.[36]

And "What is it my feeling seeks?" asks Stevens in an earlier poem called "Country Words":

> It wants the diamond pivot bright.
> It wants Belshazzar reading right
> The luminous pages on his knee,
> Of being, more than birth or death.
> It wants words virile with his breath.

To read right the luminous pages of being is to read the idea of man (as hero) or, again, the first idea of one's self; but since the self is "irrational" (a "fated eccentricity"), the feeling (desire) for apprehension of being must be the desire to apprehend a feeling defined, not an "image," for an image would convey a permanent rather than a "changing" abstraction. "Examination of the Hero in a Time of War" declares:

> There is no image of the hero.
> There is a feeling as definition.
> How could there be an image, an outline,
> A design, a marble soiled by pigeons?

The hero is a feeling, a man seen
As if the eye was an emotion,
As if in seeing we saw our feeling
In the object seen and saved that mystic
Against the sight, the penetrating,
Pure eye. Instead of allegory,
We have and are the man, capable
Of his brave quickenings, the human
Accelerations that seem inhuman.[37]

"We have and are the man"—a crucial assertion given meaning by such statements as "Life consists / Of propositions about life" and "The whole race is a poet that writes down / The eccentric propositions of its fate" ("Men Made Out of Words"). "That's it," concludes "A Primitive like an Orb,"

The lover writes, the believer hears,
The poet mumbles and the painter sees,
Each one, his fated eccentricity,
As a part, but part, but tenacious particle,
Of the skeleton of the ether, the total
Of letters, prophecies, perceptions, clods
Of color, the giant of nothingness, each one
And the giant ever changing, living in change.

The giant of nothingness is referred to elsewhere, most explicitly in "Asides on the Oboe," as "the glass man," glass in that he is "the transparence of the place in which / He is." Since the place is the mind and the mind is characterized by its will to change, only a substance whose nature could change with the changes of its environment—change in the light directed upon them, as glass, crystal or diamond—would be logical for the abstraction of the hero. Yet if the man of glass "in a million diamonds sums us up," he is also "without external reference"—just as the mind itself is at once transparent and without external reference. "Sea Surface Full of Clouds" is an early poem describing the responses of the mind to changing light on a seascape—that is, as a transparence of the place in which it is. On the other hand, as we have seen, the mind is "eccentric"—a sensibility that is a thing-in-itself characterized by a will to order and a will to change, paradoxical characteristics that reflect a para-doxical reality. The glass hero in a crystal world (the poet's "fluent mundo") is thus the first idea of mankind in the natural world—a "human acceleration that seems inhuman," and, one might add, an acceleration of nature that seems unnatural.

Finally, the "auroral creature musing in the mind" is de-scribed as "the naked man" who paradoxically becomes the "plus gaudiest vir," a man constantly rejuvenated by the "cataracts" of "facts" ("Montrachet-le-Jardin"). The naked-ness of the naked man is a reflection of the identity of the mind with the natural world of reality; to say that such nakedness should make him "gaudy" is to associate him with the imagination. When the "Well Dressed Man with a Beard" is well dressed because he is naked, the transforming imagination and the sense of fact, the will to order and the will to change, necessity and contingency, abstraction and feeling, speech and speechlessness—the "super man" and the "root-man"—are all united, poetry becomes belief, belief be-comes truth, and truth is established in its permanent image as changing fiction.

3

Michel Benamou has argued that the poetry of Stevens incorporates conflicting elements from Impressionism and Cubism, naturalness and artificiality, and he asks where in these extreme ranges is the identity of the poet's sensibility.[38] He answers that it is in Stevens' concern with change, Im-pressionism showing the passive principle of change and Cubism the active, which transforms and extends the object by multiplying resemblances. The distinctions that Mr. Benamou makes are interesting ones, even though the ques-tion, I think, is really idle and the answer unsatisfying. Or perhaps I should say that he asks a question that virtually answers itself. If anything, Stevens reveals an obsession with

unity, and it is precisely that obsession that has brought to
fruition the intricate logicality of his mind, a mind that finds
its final expression not in dualism but in paradox. Stevens
does indeed incorporate conflicting elements of Impressionism and Cubism, naturalness and artificiality, since both are
essential parts of his vision. And no one can deny that he is
concerned with change, passive or active, so long as one
appreciates that the rage for change is part of a concept of
order, just as the rage for order is part of a concept of
change. Even in "So-and-So Reclining on Her Couch," the
poem Mr. Benamou uses as an illustration of Cubism,
Stevens is actually presenting a characteristic paradox. A
sculptured model is seen as a projection:

> To get at the thing
> Without gestures is to get at it as
> Idea. She floats in the contention, the flux
>
> Between the thing as idea and
> The idea as thing. She is half who made her. . . .
> . . . .
> The arrangement contains the desire of
> The artist.

This notion sounds familiar enough; the poem concludes,
however;

> But one confides in what has no
> Concealed creator. One walks easily
>
> The unpainted shore, accepts the world
> As anything but sculpture. Good-bye,
> Mrs. Pappadopoulos, and thanks.

It is not that all sculpture is necessarily "rubbish," as was the
statue of the general in "Notes." The problem is that the
model has remained So-and-So in the statue when she is
really Mrs. Pappadopoulos, and that the statue has failed to
have any human appeal; it doesn't give "pleasure" (in Stevens'
sense of the word) and the artist might as well dismiss the
lady with the perfunctory thanks that he gives her. The

poem, then, is not simply an exercise in Cubism; quite the contrary, it is an expression of one of the unifying principles of Stevens' world, a world predicated on the belief that So-and-So *must be* Mrs. Pappadopoulos and that the artist who succeeds in making her so will be the artist who most reveals himself, just as the imagination is most realized when it realizes reality.

5. MARIANNE MOORE:
UNPARTICULARITIES

One need not read deeply into the poetry of Marianne Moore with its descriptive-meditative investigation of flora and fauna, its detached tone, and its unusual logic, to appreciate why it would elicit praise from both William Carlos Williams and Wallace Stevens. Neither would one be surprised to find Miss Moore saying during an interview that she was sufficiently exhilarated by her laboratory course at Bryn Mawr to consider studying medicine. "Precision, economy of statement, logic employed to ends that are disinterested, drawing and identifying, liberate—at least have some bearing on—the imagination," she added in a comment that reveals the objectivist tendency of her thought.[1] The techniques that begin in the laboratory really end in the trans-rational world, for as we find in "He 'Digesteth Harde Yron,'" "the power of the visible is the invisible." Thus what Miss Moore has said about "people's surroundings" (in the poem so entitled) might, in part, be taken equally as a gloss on her own work:

> In these non-committal, personal-impersonal
>   expressions of appearance,
> the eye knows what to skip;
> the physiognomy of conduct must not reveal
>   the skeleton;
> 'a setting must not have the air of being one,'
> yet with X-ray-like inquisitive intensity upon it,
>   the surfaces go back;
> the interfering fringes of expression
>   are but a stain on what stands out,
> there is neither up nor down to it;
> we see the exterior and the fundamental structure. . . .

Ultimately, "X-ray-like inquisitive intensity" involves a theory of perception, of language, and of life in general—in short, a characteristically aestheticist vision.[2]

Indeed, as Kenneth Burke has noted, Miss Moore, no less than Williams, can be called an objectivist, and although Burke defines the word in terms of his own conceptions, his remarks at least provide a point of departure:

> In objectivism, though an object may be chosen for treatment because of its symbolic or subjective reference, once it has been chosen, it is to be studied in its own right.
>
> . . . a poet writing in an "objectivist" idiom might select his subject because of some secret reference or personal significance it has had for him; yet having selected it, he would find that its corresponding object had qualities to be featured and appraised for themselves. And he might pay so much attention to such appraisal that the treatment of the object would in effect "transcend" the motive behind its original singling-out.[3]

In terms of the present context, the treatment would reveal the object in its essentiality. Bernard Engel tries to make a further distinction when he argues that Marianne Moore's

> . . . grounds for faith in Objectivism . . . are not those of Williams. His belief may be described as scientific, a faith that values are inherent in objects because all are parts of the phenomenal world in which both reason and imagination begin. But Miss Moore believes in the existence of a spiritual world. To her, objects are important because they are or contain something more than the qualities of mere phenomena. . . . Belief in the existence of a spiritual understructure to the world of appearances gives her confidence in the rightness of her devotion to presentation of the object.[4]

The distinction is perhaps a dubious one. If Williams' objects do not contain a "spiritual understructure," they are scarcely presented as normally perceptible phenomena.

We might consider, to begin with, then, the brief poem called "By Disposition of Angels," which provides us with one of the sharpest clues about the nature of Miss Moore's universe. Looking at a star, the speaker finds himself incapable of giving an explanation:

> Messengers much like ourselves? Explain it.
> Steadfastness the darkness makes explicit?
> Something heard most clearly when not near it?
>   Above particularities,
> These unparticularities praise cannot violate.

Unable to be "particularized" by an adequate poetic speech, the star is both unapproachable and undemanding:

> Star that does not ask me if I see it?
> Fir that would not wish me to uproot it?
> Speech that does not ask me if I hear it?
>   Mysteries expound mysteries.   (p. 141)

When Miss Moore says that "praise cannot violate" the star, she is actually criticizing conventional perception and trite response. "If tribute cannot be implicit," she writes in "Armour's Undermining Modesty," another poem concerned with "unparticularities," "give me diatribes and the fragrance of iodine." Here, the appearance of a vividly colored moth on the speaker's wrist gives rise to reflections apparently about early man's clumsy attempts to praise and by analogy the whole tradition of trite laudatory poetry with its "faulty etymology." These efforts were more matters of self-expression than of "precise" apprehension:

> Once, self-determination
> made an axe of a stone
> and hacked things out with hairy paws. The conse-
>   quence—our mis-set
> alphabet   (p. 149)

And "Smooth Gnarled Crape Myrtle" provides the example of a carved box depicting a scene that includes "a brass-green bird" and a redbird, along with the motto, " 'joined in

friendship, crowned by love.' " "Art is unfortunate," says the
speaker, who is disturbed by the sentimentality. The redbird
of which she conceives—the "unparticularity"—is actually
without a mate, and

> comes where people are, knowing they
> have not made a point of
> being where he is—this bird
> which says not sings, 'with-
> out loneliness I should be more
> lonely, so I keep it'—half in
> Japanese.   (p. 106)

"What is more precise than precision?" asks the speaker
in "Armour's Undermining Modesty"; "Illusion," is the answer, and that is why only "mysteries expound mysteries."
Needless to say, the point is not that such mysteries are beyond all men; quite the contrary, the mind itself is, funda-
mentally, both a means for apprehending mystery and a
source of mystery itself—an "enchanting thing" and an "en-
chanted thing." Like the unparticularity, it has an aesthetic
being,

> like the glaze on a
> katydid-wing
>   subdivided by sun
>   till the nettings are legion.
> like Gieseking playing Scarlatti. . . .

As a means of perception,

> It tears off the veil; tears
>   the temptation, the
> mist the heart wears,
>   from its eyes,—if the heart
>   has a face. . . .
>   ("The Mind is an Enchanting Thing," p. 133)

The "mist" is that of sentiment and, one may assume, all
conventional association and response. It is the ability to
perceive with this kind of imagination that marks the "hero";

for example, the "decorous, frock-coated Negro / By the grotto" who

> answers the fearless sightseeing hobo
>   who asks the man she's with, what's this,
>   what's that . . .
>   not seeing her; with a
>   sense of human dignity
> and reverence for mystery. . . .

. . . .

>   He's not out
>   seeing a sight but the rock
>   crystal thing to see—the startling El Greco
>   brimming with inner light. . . .
>
> ("The Hero," p. 16)

What is required for "heroism" is, in a sense, the most important subject in Miss Moore's poetry, for the "reverence for mystery" and the ability to see without sentiment demand a particular kind of sensibility made "rigorous" by a particular kind of morality. Or, to put it another way, Miss Moore's primary concern is with the relations between aesthetic integrity and moral integrity, an obvious enough problem that underlies a great deal of the obscurity in her work. To begin with, crucial to the ideal mind is "propriety" or "nonassertiveness," a quality of unself-consciousness and internal repose that signifies the absence of egoism and excess. For example, Bach and Brahms, both "heroes," were like the "unintentional pansy-face"; if they were splendorous, like the jet black of the pansy, it is only because they were "born that way." "Unobtrusiveness is dazzling," says Miss Moore in "Voracities and Verities," and she warns, "Poets, do not make a fuss." The poets who do make a fuss, as we learn in pieces like "Novices," are not those who express "spontaneous, unforced passion," as did the ancient Hebrews, but rather those who are so "sophisticated" as to be bored by it.[5] Sophistication, she says "In the Days of Prismatic Color," is "at the antipodes from the great initial truths." Other pseudopoets who have made a fuss may be

"Writers trapped by teatime fame and by / commuter's comforts" ("Not for these / the paper nautilus / constructs her thin glass shell"). The speaker in "Critics and Connoisseurs" is willing to concede that "There is a great amount of poetry in unconscious / fastidiousness," such as in "certain Ming products," but she still expresses a preference for the unself-conscious and the uncomplicated: a

> mere childish attempt to make an imperfectly bal-
>   lasted animal stand up,
> similar determination to make a pup
>   eat his meat from a plate.   (p. 43)

The "conscious fastidiousness" of the critic represents an intellectuality to be rejected entirely.

What Miss Moore calls an "integration," an ideal art work reflecting an ideal sensibility, may be characterized by a "A Carriage from Sweden," a "country cart / that inner happiness made art." Such "inner happiness" entailed the rigor of moral integrity:

> in this city of freckled
> integrity it is a vein
>
> of resined straightness from north-wind
>   hardened Sweden's once-opposed-to-
>   compromise archipelago
> of rocks. Washington and Gustavus
> Adolphus, forgive us our decay.   (pp. 131–132)

What is meant here by "our decay" is perhaps best made clear by the poem called "The Icosasphere," which begins by contrasting the integration achieved by birds building a nest (they "leave spherical feats of rare efficiency") with an example of human disintegration through avarice:

> avid for someone's fortune,
>   three were slain and ten committed perjury,
> six died, two killed themselves, and two paid fines for
>   risks they'd run.

Hardly an example of "inner happiness." The creation of the icosasphere, however, suggests that men are also capable of "efficiency":

> at last we have steel-cutting at its summit of
>   economy,
> since twenty triangles conjoined, can wrap one
>
> ball or double-rounded shell
>   with almost no waste, so geometrically
>   neat, it's an icosahedron. . . . (p. 142)

And the achievement of the icosasphere is negligible when compared to that of the "seventy-eight-foot solid granite" monoliths erected by the Egyptians.

With their "economy," these objects have what Miss Moore calls, in "An Octopus," a "neatness of finish" that is the result of the "love of doing hard things," another quality associated with spiritual poise. In this latter poem, the "octopus" refers to an ice flow of "unimagined delicacy" that "lies 'in grandeur and in mass' / beneath a sea of shifting snow-dunes." "Relentless accuracy is the nature of this octopus / with its capacity for fact." And if it represents an overwhelming force that transforms all before it, its action is still called "unegoistic." Regarded from one point of view, the ice flow, along with the flora and fauna that it influences, is an unparticularity; regarded from another, it is a symbol of the ideal artist—

> damned for its sacrosanct remoteness—
> like Henry James 'damned by the public for decorum';
> not decorum, but restraint;
> it is the love of doing hard things
> that rebuffed and wore them out—a public out of sym-
>   pathy with neatness.   (p. 84)

The love of doing hard things is the poet's love for creation based upon "precision," just as it must be the reader's love for the inevitable difficulty involved in apprehending his work, a "hard mountain 'planed by ice and polished by the wind.' "

But the love of doing hard things and the "integration" that it reveals again depend upon inner happiness, or as the Greeks tried to define it, "a spiritual substance or the soul itself"—a quality they themselves possessed, but "we are still devoid of." [6] And once again we find that "disintegration," excess, lack of authentic happiness, is characteristic of the modern, as the regulations in the arctic game preserve imply:

'guns, nets, seines, traps and explosives,
hired vehicles, gambling and intoxicants are prohibited;
disobedient persons being summarily removed
and not allowed to return without permission in writing.'

The kind of person against whom this warning is directed is hardly the one who can enter a mysterious realm in which both physical and spiritual austerity is demanded:

It is self-evident
that it is frightful to have everything afraid of one;
that one must do as one is told
and eat rice, prunes, dates, raisins, hardtack, and tomatoes
if one would 'conquer the main peak of Mount Tacoma.' . . .
(p. 83)

Without moral integrity and "happiness," the implements that men use in ascending a mountain (eagle traps, snow-shoes, alpenstocks) are mere "toys." "Victory won't come / to me unless I go to it," says Miss Moore in "Nevertheless," and she exclaims, "What is there / like fortitude!" But her definition of the word is no simple one.

2

Miss Moore's poetic zoology, marked by a predilection for exotic animals, is at once an exercise in "X-ray-like inquisitive intensity" of vision into unparticularities and an assertion of the moral values that characterize her attitude toward experience in general. If her portrayals can scarcely be called allegorical, they at least suggest the same contrasts

between ideal and nonideal that appear elsewhere. The
ostrich, for example, in "He 'Digesteth Harde Yron,'" is described as being "a symbol of justice," but the point of the
poem is that human greed has led to large-scale destruction
of the bird: "Six hundred ostrich-brains served / at one ban-
quet . . . dramatize a meaning always missed / by the ex-
ternalist." To an internalist the meaning is clear:

> Heroism is exhausting, yet
>   it contradicts a greed that did not wisely spare
> the harmless solitaire
>
> or great auk in its grandeur. . . .   (p. 104)

There is perhaps a double irony here insofar as man's injus-
tice is shown in his destruction of the symbol of justice, a
bird whose habits entitled him to the honor.

The pangolin (anteater), we find, is a nonaggressive animal, "made graceful by adversities," which, with its neat
exterior, presents a model of "exactness." In light of "An
Octopus," one appreciates full well the meaning of these
qualities. "Grace," one of the chief traits of unparticularity,
requires, the poem tell us, "a curious hand" to explain it, and
is one of the permanent ideals (or why would those who
decorated cathedrals with animal figures seek to confuse
grace with Christian virtues?). The piece concludes, on the
other hand, with a contrasting anatomy of man as an animal
of contradictions and vacillations, a model of inexactness
and lack of poise, fearsome and fearful rather than nonaggressive and graceful, saved chiefly by his sense of humor
and his eternal hope. And a similar image of him appears in
contrast to that of the elephant in "Melancthon." The
elephant speaker is proud not of his power in general, but
of his power of soul ("spiritual poise"), an inner solidity
that matches the external solidity of his body and hide.[7]
Thus he asserts that his "ears are sensitized to more than
the sound of the wind," unlike the

> wandlike body of which one hears so much, which was
>   made

to see and not to see; to hear and not to hear . . .
   [that]
spiritual
brother to the coral-
    plant. . . .   (p. 47)

And correspondingly we learn in another poem on elephants
that "magic's masterpiece is theirs"—namely serenity and
equanimity, qualities that exist only rarely in men.

   Finally, Miss Moore's admiration of the jerboa (desert
rat) for its qualities of adaptation and economy lead her to
a survey of ancient Egyptian curios and artifacts, which present

                        a fantasy
          and a verisimilitude that were
          right to those with, everywhere

          power over the poor.   (pp. 18–19)

"One would not be he / who has nothing but plenty," she
says of the jerboa in her condemnation of an art and a class
that possessed "Too Much." Hedgehogs, salamanders, mock-
ingbirds, plumet basilisks, frigate pelicans, cats, buffaloes,
and unicorns are a part of a menagerie whose perfections
invariably reflect on human greed, aggressiveness, and insta-
bility. Nonetheless, despite passages like the one which concludes "Virginia Britannia"—"while clouds expanding above
/ the town's assertiveness, dwarf it, dwarf arrogance"—Miss
Moore can scarcely be called misanthropic. The implication
of her poetry is not that men are incapable of salvation, but
that their potential for salvation remains unrealized. Men
have "everlasting vigor, / power to grow." Like the Irish, in
particular, in "Spenser's Ireland," what they need is "fern
seed for unlearn / ing obduracy and for reinstating / the enchantment." The fern seed that supposedly brings actual
invisibility[8] is, in a sense, associated with the "invisible"
world of the unparticularity that is the "power of the visible."
And in Marianne Moore's Ireland that fern seed can be
nothing but poetry itself.

6. E. E. CUMMINGS:
THE NOW MAN

"Here is a thing," wrote E. E. Cummings in a little piece called "Fair Warning"; "To one somebody, this 'thing' is a totally flourishing universal joyous particular happening deep amazing miraculous indivisible being." To other "somebodies," the tree, here described, is something mechanical or functional:

> Somebody number one is a poet. Actually he is alive. His address is: Now. All the other somebodies are unpoets. They all aren't alive. They all merely are not unexisting—in a kind of an unkind of unreality or When. Here is another thing: whatever happens, everybody cannot turn the Nowman's Now into When; whatever doesn't, nobody can turn the Whenman's When into Now.[1]

This theme recurs in the introduction to the *Collected Poems*:

> We can never be born enough. We are human beings; for whom birth is a supremely welcome mystery, the mystery of growing: the mystery which happens only and whenever we are faithful to ourselves. You and I wear the dangerous looseness of doom and find it becoming. Life, for eternal us, is now; and now is much too busy being a little more than everything to seem anything, catastrophic included.[2]

This Bergsonian conception of spontaneous existence, for both subject and object, the idea of physical and mental life as perpetual birth and growth, as constant *becoming*, is, of course, reminiscent of the ultimate values of Williams, Stevens, and Hart Crane. And, again, as in these poets, the problem of perception and response is crucial.

118

Although in so frankly a primitivistic ethos as Cummings',
ideal perception and response are not really a matter of
exotic vision, Cummings is inclined to make the same kind
of distinctions that one would find in objectivist theory.
There are the deluded rationalists (bourgeois society) and
the enlightened irrationalists (poets):

> A poet is somebody who feels, and who expresses his
> feeling through words. . . .
> A lot of people think or believe or know they feel—but
> that's thinking or believing or knowing; not feeling. And
> poetry is feeling—not knowing or believing or think-
> ing. . . .[3]

As with the objectivist, the poet's experience with language
is experience with logos and ultimate truth:

> Ineluctable preoccupation with The Verb gives a poet one
> priceless advantage: whereas nonmakers must content
> themselves with the merely undeniable fact that two
> times two is four, he rejoices in an irresistible truth (to
> be found on the title page of the present volume) [Is 5].[4]

Similarly, Cummings' ideas concerning the "self" and its
relation to the external world, nature, follow a logic not
remote from the objectivist's. To begin with, identity with
"Life" means "self-transcendence" and what would be called
by "mostpeople" nonidentity, since to be "most truly alive"
means to transcend the social self and to acquire the natural
one (selflessness) that comes with response to the universe.[5]
The Now Man is "on the one hand a complete fanatic, dedicated to values beyond life and death," and on the other he
is "a profoundly alive and supremely human being."[6] He
dives "out of tinying time / (into supreme Now)," seeking
"new / textures of actual cool stupendous is" (p. 267).[7] As
"Being," stupendous Is represents both physical nature and
supernature, just as "Now" is both a moment and eternity.
Existence is, in a sense, the final "para-thing" (Stevens) and
it is not surprising to find that in Cummings, as in Fletcher,
Aldington, Crane, Williams, and Stevens, death itself is

regarded as a form of being, or at least intimately associated
with the process of *becoming*. The "sweet spontaneous
earth" defies the "fingers of prurient philosophers," and responds only to a more elemental suitor:

> true
> to the incomparable
> couch of death thy
> rhythmic
> lover
>   thou answerest
> them only with
>   spring)   (p. 39)

To "live suddenly without thinking / under honest trees"
(p. 121), to live with "feeling," then, implies a sympathetic
union (in the sense of Hazlitt) of mind and object, a union
in which the "organic" object, in a state of continual growth,
defines consciousness. The reply of the wind to the speaker
in "the wind is a Lady" (p. 79) suggests the indistinguish-
ability of mind and object in the ideal experience. To the
question, "why do you touch the flowers as if they were
ideas?," the green Lady replies,

> "because, sir
> things which in my mind blossom will
> stumble beneath a clumsiest disguise, appear
> capable of fragility and indecision
>
> —do not suppose these
> without any reason and otherwise . . .
> different from the i am who wanders
>
> imminently across the renewed world"

That is, despite appearances, the mind does not treat the
object as an "idea" in abstraction; rather the object, "blossoming" in the mind, constitutes its very nature. In short,
what seems "capable of fragility and indecision" is what
actually makes up the force of life. Looked at from another
point of view, the poet himself, ideally a nonidentity and

therefore an Individual, must be "slender and fragile," borrowing "contact from that you and from / this you sensations, imitating a few fatally / exquisite . . . things" (p.
237). "When my sensational moments are no more / unjoyously bullied by vilest mind" (active reason rather than passive feeling), only then is the Now of eternal spring possible.
Exquisite things, "fragile splendors," "luminous" objects—
para-things and unparticularities—are fatal to the reason and
social self; they are similarly part of the "doom" that is the
rhythmic lover of "life," the eternity that characterizes Now.
To die in time and be reborn in timelessness is the poetic
aim of life.

It is in these terms that one can understand Cummings'
appreciation of Hart Crane, whom he saw as being able "to
invent growth's likeness"—that is, to carry out the true function of poetry: "Drunk and becauseless (talking about a
cyclone, telling how at last with the disappearance even of
impossibility himself found actually himself and suddenly
becoming the cyclone; not perishing and not surviving;
Being). . . ." [8] The equivalent experience in Cummings is
suggested in a poem in which a tree, addressing the wind,
says

> i
> wait the sweet
> annihilation of swift
> flesh. . . .
>
> . . . .
> O haste
>   annihilator
> drawing into you my enchanting
> leaves.   (p. 135)

The absorption of the tree into the wind, of the poet into
eternity, is the death that is in reality growth.

The preoccupation with being-as-being has, as we saw in
both Williams and Stevens, its negative side: explicitly, confrontation with the contingent may involve terror no less
than joy. I am thinking specifically of Williams' "Portrait

of an Author," discussed earlier, in which the apprehension
of an existence that resisted all human conceptions of it left
the poet "with shrinking heart / and startled empty eyes—
peering out / into a cold world." A dialogue between lover
and lady walking alone at night appears to reflect this problem in Cummings' poem, "touching you i say" (p. 218).
"Everything / turns into something else, and slips away,"
says the frightened girl; "These leaves are Thingish with
moondrool." The poet tries to comfort her by providing a
humanized conception, even though he is himself partially
overcome with the changing reality of the spring night:

> "along this particular road the moon if you'll
> notice follows us like a big yellow dog. You
>
> don't believe? look back. (Along the sand
> behind us, a big yellow dog that's. . . . now it's red
> a big red dog that may be owned by who
> knows)
>   only turn a little your. so. And
>
> there's the moon, there's something faithful and mad"

That if one turns one's head the moon will become a dog
might be comforting, but even so, in a thingish world, the
dog will prove as mad as faithful—as changing as constant.
    Yet whatever the interpretation of such poems as this, the
"invention of growth's likeness," the imitation of being and
becoming, remains the central poetic in Cummings' work.
The dissolution of syntax ("Who pays attention to the
syntax of things will never wholly kiss you"), involving the
dissolution of conventional conceptualization, has been, of
course, a distinguishing feature of Cummings' poetry. Insofar
as Cummings is usually attempting to achieve an effect of
"Nowness," to remove all sense of temporal or causal (as
opposed to "organic") progression, we can profitably recall
Pound's definition of the "Image" as an instantaneous presentation that gives that "sense of freedom from time and
space limits; that sense of sudden growth." "Sudden growth"
(if I may use Pound's expression out of context) seems to be

precisely the paradoxical quality that Cummings is seeking
to effect in poems describing natural phenomena—sunsets,
moonrises, and thunderstorms, for example. "Growth" is
development in time, and the conception of "instantaneous
growth" is a logical contradiction that is the metalogical
verity of any vitalistic outlook.

A thunderstorm appears to Cummings as three moments,
coming in so rapid a succession as to constitute a single moment:

n (o) w
            the
how
        dis(appeared cleverly)world
iS Slapped:with;liGhtninG
!
    at
which (shal)lpounceupcrackw(ill)jumps
of
   THuNdeRB
            loSSo!M . . .

The next moment is similarly introduced with "n,o;w:":

            theraIncomIng
    o all the roofs roar
                drownInsound. . . .

And finally,

            But l!ook—
                s

U
    n:starT birDs(lEAp)Openi ng
t hing ; s(
—sing
)all are aLl(cry alL See)o(ver All) Th(e grEEn
?eartH)N,ew   (p. 250)

The graphic imitation, which is relatively straightforward in
this poem, contributes to the effect of spontaneous growth,

just as the whole experience is essentially an "imagistic" one.

The attempt to capture motion (that is, paradoxically, to give the illusion of motion in a "moment") is equally apparent in this poem about a striptease dancer (p. 320):

```
sh estiffl
ystrut sal
lif san
dbut sth

epoutin(gWh.ono:w
s li psh ergo
wnd ow n,
                    r
Eve
aling 2 a
-sprout (eyelands). . . .
```

(She stiffly struts, all ifs and buts; the pouting Who [proper name?] now slips her gown down, revealing two asprout islands.) And, again, in the poem about a grasshopper (p. 286):

```
         r-p-o-p-h-e-s-s-a-g-r
      who
   a)s w(e loo)k
   upnowgath
          PPEGORHRASS
                              eringint(o-
   aThe):l
         eA
           !p:
   S. . . .
```

The word "now" appears in each of the three poems cited, and, indeed, it is the quality of "nowness," immediacy, that is common to all of them. But in each of the poems there also appears a reference to vision ("But l!ook," "See," "Eyelands," "Eyes," "a)s w(e loo)k / up"); to say nothing of the whole matter of the graphic technique itself. The truth is that the act of perception, as distinct from the object as such, is the central element in these pieces. If the last poem cited attempts to imitate a leaping grasshopper, it also tries to create a verbal equivalent that has an effect on the eye similar to that of the actuality; just as the grasshopper is out of focus in the process, and comes into focus only after he has come to rest, so the word that signifies him, suddenly regarded ("as we look up"), is jumbled throughout the poem, finally to "become rearrangingly, 'grasshopper.'" The striptease dancer is similarly a chaos of broken movements transformed into broken words, and if her breasts are "islands," they are also a place where the eye lands. She represents an "object" with the power to "absorb" the beholder, psychologically and aesthetically as well as sexually:

> seethe firm swirl hips whirling climb to
> GIVE
> (yoursmine mineyours yoursmine
> !
> i()t)

As a beholder, the poet in Cummings' world is, like the objectivist, the man who apprehends and recreates the true nature of the object, the true nature here being "growth," "vitality," "rhythm." Thus the poet can say,

> myself is sculptor of
> your body's idiom:
> the musician of your wrists;
> the poet who is afraid
> only to mistranslate
>
> a rhythm in your hair. . . .   (p. 209)

But in empathizing with his subject as objectivist, the poet also involves himself with it as mystic; in the lines just cited, the speaker is lover as well as poet. "Art is a mystery," says Cummings; "all mysteries have their source in a mystery-of-mysteries who is love: and if lovers may reach eternity directly through love herself, their mystery remains essentially that of the loving artist whose way must lie through his art, and of the loving worshipper whose aim is oneness with his god." [9] And in another poem, we find,

> "to be, being, that i am alive
> this absurd fraction in its lowest terms
> with everything cancelled
> but shadows
> —what does it all come down to? love? Love." . . .
>   (p. 212)

If poetry is a form of love, what characterizes love characterizes poetry, and as the "mystery-of-mysteries" love is the quintessential awareness of being "alive," or, again, the ultimate form of "self-transcendence." The poet as aestheticist responds to the Lady's beauty:

> nothing which we are to perceive in this world equals
> the power of your intense fragility. . . .

As lover, he is transfigured:

> whose texture
> compels me with the colour of its countries,
> rendering death and forever with each breathing
>   (p. 263)

The kind of death the Lady renders (the "dooms of love") is the death from time into eternity, both sexually and spiritually:

> And then all her beauty is a vise
>
> whose stilling lips murder suddenly me,
>
> but of my corpse the tool her smile makes something
> suddenly luminous and precise
>
> —and then we are I and She. . . .
>
> what is that the hurdy-gurdy's playing   (p. 116)

The hurdy-gurdy, if not a distraction after the act, is possibly

an appropriate accompaniment, like the hand organ, in another poem, "at the corner of Nothing and Something . . .
/ playing like hell."

In Cummings' realism, the passivity of the lover before
the beauty of the Lady (or if not the beauty, the charisma
of her person) is analogous to the receptivity of the Now
Man before the power of existence. Just as the object determines consciousness, so the Lady determines the lover's
being:

create

me gradually (or as these emerging now
hills invent the air)
breathe simply my each how
my trembling where my still invisible when.   (p. 267)

The poet's role in this mystical experience is solely to express his feeling without conception and without evaluation
("nor has a syllable of the heart's eager dim / enormous
language loss or gain from blame or praise.") for it is only
the thought "born of dream"—the feeling that survives
"wish and world" that matters.

The primitivistic conception of experience that underlies
Cummings' poetry, for all its foundation in realism, can,
in one sense, be seen as resolving itself in the direction of
idealism. Since we have been talking about natural objects
as existents and phenomena as process, we might recall
Sartre's exposition of the problem in *What Is Literature?*:
"Each of our perceptions is accompanied by the consciousness that human reality is a 'revealer,' that is, it is through
human reality that 'there is' being, or, to put it differently,
that man is the means by which things are manifested. It is
our presence in the world which multiplies relations." [10] This
formulation, which finds its prototype in Renaissance humanism and idealism, implies that human consciousness,
being the means by which reality is expressed, "encompasses"
reality. Or, to recall Stevens again, the idea of reality is a
human "fiction." Bergson's statement on the aim of art is
in complete harmony with Cummings' poetic: "Could reality

come into direct contact with sense and consciousness, could
we enter into immediate communion with things and with
ourselves, probably art would be useless, or rather we should
all be artists, for then our soul would vibrate in perfect accord
with nature." [11] The idealistic converse of this realistic proposition is that nature requires the artist to make itself known,
just as a Now Man is necessary to the spontaneity (the *idea*
of spontaneity) that governs Cummings' world. The poet
might often feel that he has failed to invent growth's likeness or to "fabricate the unknown," but he never fails to
appreciate the nature of "growth" and the extent of his
failure, and it is precisely upon such appreciation that Cummings' world depends. Those poems in which the speaker
laments his inability to translate his experience are, needless
to say, part of the rhetoric of translating the experience of
defining reality. Beyond the translation is the subjective
apprehension; beyond the subjective apprehension there is
nothing. I would be foolish to insist that Cummings is
actually an idealist; he is indeed a realist—just so long as
one appreciates the truism that in poetic realism the aesthetic
response of the poet is a crucial element.

7. HART CRANE:
THE "NUCLEAR SELF"
AND THE FATAL OBJECT

In his description of Hart Crane as a mystic, Waldo Frank argued that "the mystic is a man who *knows*, by immediate experience, the organic continuity between his self and the cosmos." He asserted that denial of the sense of "organic continuity between the self and a seemingly chaotic world" merely perpetuated "the inward-and-outward chaos" and he proposed what he took to be the authentic solution to the problem:

> . . . by self-knowledge and self-discipline, it is to achieve within one's self a stable nucleus to bear and finally transfigure the world's impinging chaos. For the nucleus within the self, as it is gradually revealed, is impersonal and cosmic; is indeed the dynamic key to order in the "outward" world.[1]

In Frank's opinion, Crane never achieved this ideal; "yet he was too virile to deny the experience of continuity; he let the world pour in; and since his nuclear self was not disciplined to detachment from his nerves and passions, he lived exacerbated in a constant swing between ecstasy and exhaustion." This mystical description of an essentially mystical poet is not without its value, for it touches the essential problem in Crane's poetry as in contemporary poetry in general—the relation of subject and object in a universe in which objects are recognized as being absolutes. To seek "continuity" with a world outside one's self is, in at least one sense, to be a realist; to seek to "transfigure" that world by means of an inner discipline, an "idea," is to act as an idealist. Frank's argument is reminiscent of Schopenhauer's and the ideal of stoicism by which he judges Crane is the ideal to which

Schopenhauer's hero, man at once realist and idealist—committed to external forces and psychologically free from them —adheres. What makes Frank's assertions interesting is not their accuracy in appraising Crane so much as their relevance to Crane's own vision of himself and the world. The quest for a "nuclear self" paradoxically continuous with and free from "chaos," a self both passive to reality and generating order, is the central issue in nearly the whole span of Crane's work.

Early in his career Crane told Gorham Munson:

> The modern artist has got to harden himself, and the walls of an ivory tower are too delicate and brittle a coat of mail for substitute. . . . I think that you would do better to . . . forget all about aesthetics, and apply yourself closely to a conscious observation of the details of existence . . . let us be keen and humorous scientists anyway.[2]

Crane's response to this problem was to stop writing poems about "fragile gardens," "whispering lamps," and shadowy ladies and to begin investigating the qualities of objects in the external world.[3] For example, in "My Grandmother's Love Letters," he tried to discover the "essence" of a packet of letters. The speaker appreciates their physical fragility and the delicacy of feeling that their associations create in the beholder, but he does not know whether he has the sensitivity and the insight to recreate for himself the same emotions that his grandmother felt naturally.

Within its own limitations "My Grandmother's Love Letters" presents what was to become the abiding concern for Crane: the ability of the beholder to respond correctly to an "attractive" object—to perceive ultimate reality with "ungalvanized" eyes. An intimation of the fully developed vision of *The Bridge* is evident in this early assertion:

> How can you tell where beauty's to be found?
> I have heard hands praised for what they made;
> I have heard hands praised for line on line;
> Yet a gash with sunlight jerking through

> A mesh of bolts down into it, made me think
> I had never seen a hand before,
> And the hand was thick and heavily warted.
>
> ("The Bridge of Estador")[4]

The reference is to an occurrence that had been described in "Episode of Hands," in which a factory owner's son (Crane) finds a "communion" with a worker whose injured finger he tends. The first line of the quotation implies that beauty is to be found in unlikely places—in a factory as well as a garden, and in a normally ugly hand—and the remainder of the argument contrasts the poet's kind of vision (the response to the lighting) with ordinary vision.

Crane's belief in the transcendence of special aesthetic qualities in objects—qualities visible only to a certain kind of eye—over all other qualities, good or bad, becomes all the more evident when we take into account the background of the episode. Crane's hopes for a relationship with the worker were dashed, yet the fact did not prevent him from maintaining the impression of beauty, a purely visual response, in "The Bridge of Estador," written a year after "Episode of Hands."

The ability of the poet to respond in such a fashion was his justification. Commenting on "Chaplinesque," Crane wrote that the "pantomime of Charlie," which he was trying to "put in words," "represents fairly well the futile gesture of the poet in the U.S.A. today."[5] Chaplin is an impotent clown and his "game" with society "enforces smirks," but, concludes the poem,

> we have seen
> The moon in lonely alleys make
> A grail of laughter of an empty ash can,
> And through all sound of gaiety and quest
> Have heard a kitten in the wilderness.
>
> ("Chaplinesque")[6]

The interesting image here is the first one, not the second: the ability to see an ash can turned into a grail of laughter by the moon justifies both the object and the viewer, just as does the ability to see a warted hand changed into something beautiful by sunlight through machinery. In another poem, Crane, lamenting the death of a "brother poet" who, he believed, was destroyed by the world, wrote:

> Still, having in mind gold hair,
> I cannot see that broken brow
> And miss the dry sound of bees
> Stretching across a lucid space.
>
> ("Praise for an Urn")

Again, it is the visual association that inspires the poet, despite his knowledge of depressing reality.

Finally, in "Sunday Morning Apples," we discover the poet not merely responding to visual beauty, but, significantly for his mature work, becoming intoxicated by it:

> I have seen the apples there that toss you secrets,—
> Beloved apples of seasonable madness
> That feed your inquiries with aerial wine.
> Put them again beside a pitcher with a knife,
> And poise them full and ready for explosion. . . .

2

With this background in mind, one can perhaps fully appreciate Crane's chief pronouncement on the requirements for modern poetry. "For unless poetry can absorb the machine," he wrote in 1929, "i.e., *acclimatize* it as naturally and casually as trees, cattle, galleons, castles and all other human associations of the past, then poetry has failed of its full contemporary function." Then he added in a particularly revealing comment that the process of acclimatization demands "an extraordinary capacity for surrender, at least temporarily, to the sensations of urban life. This presupposes, of course, that the poet possesses sufficient spontaneity and gusto to convert this experience into positive terms." The machine will "act creatively" in men's lives when "like the unconscious nervous responses of our bodies, its connotations emanate from within—forming as spontaneous a terminology of poetic reference as the bucolic world of pasture, plow and barn." [7] The ideal that Crane is proposing here might well go by Frank's term, "organic continuity" of subject and object. By "surrender," Crane meant yielding one's self up to the essential, hidden beauty of objects—or again, seeing with the mystical eye. His use of "gusto" differs from Hazlitt's chiefly by virtue of its mystical intent, and insofar as the "object" is initially "unsympathetic" rather than "sympathetic." Quoting Blake—"We are led to believe in a lie / When we see with not through the eye"—Crane suggests that if the poet can regard an urban or industrial object with correct vision, its intractability, both moral and aesthetic, will vanish and a new aesthetic experience will be available. Again, one can recognize the objectivist element in Crane's reasoning—the concern for an ideal vision, which, purged of conventional sentiment, reveals the object as it is to the surrendering subject. Thus we find Crane asserting:

> It is my hope to go *through* the combined materials of the poem, using our "real" world somewhat as a springboard, and to give the poem as a whole an orbit or predetermined direction of its own. I would like to establish it as free from my own personality. . . . Such a poem is at least a stab at truth, and to such an extent may be . . . called "absolute."

The "spontaneity" that accompanied surrender to the object came to mean a casting off of reason, a development of the kind of response presented in "Sunday Morning Apples." As I have argued in another work, Crane's mature period began with his apparent adaptation of ideas found in Nietzsche's *Birth of Tragedy*, the chief of those being that of the Dionysian mode of response as a metaphysical act. Nietzsche's description of the Dionysian artist, who regarded life not with the despairing rationality of his Apollonian counterpart, but with "awe," and was spurred on by a "narcotic draught" to surrender his individuality in order to merge with his fellows in "mysterious Primordial Unity," clearly provided Crane with the intellectual rationale for his own proclivities and with what amounted to a philosophic "solution" to the problem of the poet in a hostile world.[9] Dionysian perception begins in suffering and the surrender to pain for the insight that it brings. Along with such insight comes transcendence of pain and in effect of personality—or as Frank might put it, the chaotic self is transformed into the nuclear self. For Crane, such suffering may be derived, as in "Possessions," from a personal sense of sexual (or homosexual) guilt:

> Tossed on these horns, who bleeding dies,
> Lacks all but piteous admissions to be spilt
> Upon the page whose blind sum finally burns
> Record of rage and partial appetites.

Yet in the piteous admission that burns upon the page there lies the prophecy of redemption:

> The pure possession, the inclusive cloud
> Whose heart is fire shall come,—the white wind raze
> All but bright stones wherein our smiling plays.

Through the idea of purgation, what is suffered personally is but an analogy first to the poetic experience in general, as we find in "Legend"—

> It is to be learned—
> This cleaving and this burning,
> But only by the one who
> Spends out himself again.
> . . . .
> Then, drop by caustic drop, a perfect cry
> Shall string some constant harmony. . . .

—and finally to universal experience, as in "Lachrymae Christi," in which the poet, identified with Christ, Dionysus, and nature itself, celebrates the process of destruction and rebirth as the principle of life.

In this latter poem, we learn that spring nights, although associated with death ("swart / Thorns freshen on the year's

/ First blood") are nonetheless "Anoint with innocence" and "recall / To Music what perjuries / Had galvanized the eyes." The "perjuries" are those of nontragic vision in a fragmented, quotidian world, as "For the Marriage of Faustus and Helen," Crane's first quasi-epic poem makes clear. A witness of and participant in the life-death principle of nature, the poet, identifying himself with hanged gods, finds that his tongue has "cleared";

> Betrayed stones slowly speak. . . .
>
> Names peeling from Thine eyes
> And their undimming lattices of flame,
> Spell out in palm and pain
> Compulsion of the year, O Nazarene.

The meaning of this experience is clarified in a poem in the Key West collection in which we learn that man has "betrayed" nature by categorizing rather than empathizing with it:

> we are usurpers, and chagrined—
> And take the wing and scar it in the hand.
> Names we have, even, to clap on the wind. . . .

True empathy means the knowledge of death:

> But we must die, as you, to understand.
>
> I dreamed that all men dropped their names, and sang
> As only they can praise, who build their days
> With fin and hoof, with wing and sweetened fang
> Struck free and holy in one Name always.
>
> ("A Name for All")

This notion, that only through a psychological and spiritual death is logos apprehended and the poem realized, recurs in "Voyages":

> Shall they not stem and close in our own steps
> Bright staves of flowers and quills to-day as I
> Must first be lost in fatal tides to tell?
> In signature of the incarnate word. . . .   (IV)

For Crane, the Dionysian metaphysic provided the solution to the problem of "organic continuity" with chaos and internal attainment of order, and this ideal lies behind his first major poem, "For the Marriage of Faustus and Helen," as well as behind *The Bridge*. Central to the character of Faustus, and to the vision of Crane, is the notion of suspension between two worlds: that of chaotic fact in a fragmented quotidian, Faust's natural world; and that of an imagined absolute, represented by Helen, "the world that comes to each of us alone." Thus the opening lines:

> The mind has shown itself at times
> Too much the baked and labeled dough
> Divided by accepted multitudes.

This, in a sense, is the same negative sensibility that Eliot's Tiresias, his soul determined by the objects of a wasteland, reveals. Yet just as Tiresias is stirred by the coming of spring, so Faust is stirred to vision beyond his own fragmentary world by the appearance of birds:

> Across the stacked partitions of the day—
> Across the memoranda, baseball scores,
> The stenographic smiles and stock quotations
> Smutty wings flash out equivocations.
>
> The mind is brushed by sparrow wings. . . .

It is precisely the fragmented mind of the poet that can be brushed by sparrow wings, for in society only a Tiresias or a Faust is conscious of his fate. In quest of a name in a nameless world, the poet is impelled to seek an imaginative night world of the absolute, that to which the sparrows return in the evening, "Somewhere virginal, perhaps, less fragmentary, cool."

As the poem develops, we find Faust riding in a streetcar without paying the fare since, unlike the "barber, druggist, and tobacconist," he has no place to go in "the world dimensional." On the other hand, he is a man whose hands have known the press of "steel and soil," and if he is to have a vision, it can be only in terms of the world he knows. Thus it is on the streetcar itself, "lost yet poised in traffic," that a contingent moment breaks into time and he sees the image of Helen,

> flickering with those prefigurations—
> Prodigal, yet uncontested now,
> Half-riant before the jerky window frame.

Faust's claim to union with Helen is precisely that he is a poet, a figure who, though condemned to quotidian, carries within him a dream of love and can offer words that are as light as the touch of moonlight on snow. As Crane has portrayed her in this section, Helen resembles not Aphrodite but Artemis, a moon goddess who, virgin and aloof, yields her "ecstasies" only after her lover has suffered. Similarly, Faustus, "the body of the world," must "weep in inventive dust" (poetry) for the "hiatus that winks above" (the "great wink of eternity," Helen).

In envisioning the mythic union, Crane began to use a Nietzschean logic:[10]

> I meet you, therefore, in that eventual flame
> You found in final chains, no captive then—
> Beyond their million brittle, bloodshot eyes;
> White, through white cities [you] passed on to assume
> That world which comes to each of us alone.

Faustus sees in the mythological Helen an analogue to the imaginative life he himself must achieve. Like Helen, he is the captive of an alien society, surrounded by a "million, brittle, bloodshot eyes," and he must attain the same kind of transcendent equanimity ("nuclear selfhood") that she did. As the epigraph cryptically informs us, Faust must, by a secret "Talmud skill and profane Greek" (poetic imagination), "raise the building up of Helen's house" (poetry) against the "Ismaelites" and other barbarians of the modern world.

Yet what did knowledge of the mystical Hebrew and Greek (and, in *The Bridge,* Sanskrit) involve? Relevant here is the Nietzschean contrast between the Apollonian and the

Dionysian sensibility, the former representing the art world of dreamland and the latter of intoxication. The Apollonian creates through meditation, by reading and unmasking his dreams; the Dionysian creates through ecstatic response. In the passage just discussed, Faust is Apollonian and Helen appears as the object of a dream; the mode of perception is meditative. (Consider, for example, the rhetoric of argumentation that pervades the poem: "*suppose* some evening," "there is some way, I *think*," "I meet you, *therefore*," and so on.) But as has been suggested, the Apollonian mode was, for Crane, insufficient in itself in the quest for "continuity with chaos" and the rational resolution of the section ("I meet you, therefore, in that eventual flame") anticipates a Dionysian experience. The mystical language will be comprehended only on a suprarational level, just as the mystical self can replace the chaotic self only when the poet abandons normal vision.

Thus Crane said that in the second part of the poem he wanted to "invent an idiom for the proper transposition of jazz into words. Something clean, sparkling, elusive." [11] One might well suppose that this "idiom" is related to the secret "Hebrew," just as jazz might be taken as the modern form of Dionysian music, the "highest musical orgasm of tragedy," which imparts to the listener "the sure presentiment of supreme joy to which the path through destruction leads." Under the "brazen hypnotics" of a jazz band, the Apollo in Faust is destroyed; what to the sober mind would be a kind of hell becomes to the intoxicated one a saturnalia, and an "opéra bouffe" becomes a "blest excursion." Surrendering to chaos, the poet sees Helen not as an image of absolute beauty but as an alluring embodiment of the "sensations of urban life," a "siren of the springs of guilty song"; he is fatally attracted to her, for her cupids (the jazz band), with their "snarling hails of melody" and "deft catastrophes of drums," turn orgy into Dionysian doom. Thus drugged, Faustus can "fall downstairs with perfect grace and equanimity" and believe that he can see beneath all distortion the "incunabula of the divine," the pristine Helen.

Even though the Dionysian scene is artificial (the "gardened skies" of the ballroom) and occurs not in spring but in mock winter (with cultivated storms, hails of melody, and skating dancers), Faust is resigned:

> Let us take her on the incandescent wax
> Striated with nuances, nervosities
> That we are heir to: she is still so young,
> We cannot frown upon her as she smiles. . . .

"Nuances and nervosities," striated upon the wax dance floor by the feet of the slim skaters (or perhaps the image refers simply to a jazz phonograph record), may be but a shadow of the highest musical orgasm of tragedy, but they are the modern poet's sole vision of immortality.

The conception of Faustus that emerges in the final section appears to be a synthesis of Apollonian and Dionysian sensibilities, a synthesis that Nietzsche himself described:

> In his Dionysian drunkenness and mystical self-abnegation, lonesome and apart from the revelling choruses, he sinks down, and . . . now through Apollonian dreaminspiration, his own state, i.e., his oneness with the primal source of the universe, reveals itself to him *in a symbolical dream picture*.[12]

This synthesis is the "tragic" response, through which the final union with Helen is envisioned. The last part, wrote Crane, "begins with *catharsis*, the acceptance of tragedy through destruction. . . . It is Dionysian in its attitude, the creator and the eternal destroyer dance arm in arm, etc., all ending in a restatement of the imagination as in Part I." [13] In becoming the tragic poet, Faustus has a renewed dream of Helen, but she is no longer the mere "Gioconda" of his imagination, as in Part I, nor even the hallucinatory siren, as in Part II; rather she is the personification of tragedy itself, experienced both soberly and in Dionysian elation. By "unbinding his throat of fear and pity," the poet, who has been involved in the war as an aviator, purges himself of guilt, and with Dionysian laughter attempts to give voice to the new society. His union with Helen is an Apollonian dream that presents a picture of his Dionysian oneness with society and the universe.

In planning this section, Crane said he knew only that it would concern the World War and be Promethean in mood. As it turned out, it presents a Promethean argument against war guilt and accordingly against despair in the face of chaos. Technology, with its potentiality for putting man in tune with the infinite (for reconciling reality with ideality, when "properly" comprehended), is the stolen fire; its destructive application in the war is the moral issue. In Nietzsche's interpretation, Prometheus (from Aeschylus) has committed the crime of ennobling mankind at the expense of the gods and brings down upon himself a "flood of sufferings"; he is a hanged god and mask of Dionysus. Tragedy forecasts Prometheus' redemption, just as it does the reintegration of the mangled god.

Faust plays a Promethean role in his dual identity as aviator (the conquest of space represents a peak of technological achievement) and poet. As aviator, he represents man's prideful aspirations and takes upon himself the guilt of a warring society. The crime of war carries its own punishment (the hands the flier extends to "thresh the heights" are themselves bleeding), and from punishment comes atonement. Faustus the poet is the voice of Faustus the aviator who "persists to speak again" and "spread with bells" word of the enlightened technological utopia that justifies the war.

Crane attempted to give this vision of social and personal redemption a mythical-historical basis by seeking an analogy in the Trojan war itself, which, although it brought the Greeks to Troy, led the Trojans to Rome ("Anchises' navel, dripping of the sea"), in the characteristic tragic process of death and rebirth. A second rebirth after the fall of Rome and the Dark Ages is heralded by Erasmus ("Hands . . . dipped in gleaming tides"), and a third rebirth will follow the World War; it will come, however, not through the sea, but through space. Faustus will "delve upward" for the "voltage of blown blood and wine"; his "blamed bleeding hands" will "thresh the heights," not be dipped in gleaming tides, for the fulfillment of the new "prophecies of heaven."

Therefore, the war does not call forth Christian asceticism, but the tragic laughter of Dionysus. "This crown of laughter," says Zarathustra, "this rose-garlanded crown. . . . Laughing have I consecrated: ye higher men, learn, I pray you—to laugh!" Thus Faustus:

> Laugh out the meager penance of their days
> Who dare not share with us the breath released. . . .
>
> The imagination spans beyond despair,
> Outpacing bargain, vocable and prayer.

Entering as it does into the second and third sections of "Faustus and Helen," the idea of guilt is of particular importance and I should like to investigate briefly its relevance to the theme of selfhood and the acceptance of reality. To gain some perspective on this problem we might look first at a passage that appears in the writings of Gauguin, whose sensibility has something in common with Crane's. In a characteristically primitivistic statement in *Noa Noa* Gauguin writes that the natives of Tahiti, because of their nakedness, do not have the sexual preoccupations found in civilization and are therefore possessed of a "natural innocence, a perfect purity." In spite of this desexualization about him, he finds himself caught in a moment of lust while following a young male guide through the forest, and in disgust he asks, "Why was it that there suddenly rose in the soul of a member of an old civilization, a horrible thought?" The boy turns to regard him as they cross a stream and Gauguin suddenly finds himself triumphing over his senses:

> I felt an infinite joy, a joy of the spirit . . . as I plunged into the fresh water of the brook.
> "*Toë, toë* (it is cold)," said Jotefa.
> "Oh, no!" I replied.
> This exclamation seemed to me also a fitting conclusion to the struggle which I had just fought out within myself against the corruption of an entire civilization. . . . And

I said to myself that Nature . . . was willing after the ordeal to receive me as one of her children.[14]

And later he concludes that "wholly destroyed, finished, dead, is from now on the old civilization within me. I was reborn; or rather another man, purer and stronger, came to life within me." [15]

What I wish to emphasize here is Gauguin's notion that an "evil" civilized self has been replaced by a purified self that is the product of nature. Crane's conception of Faust's guilt is, up to a point, similar: the idea of a consummation with Helen, "beyond that eventual flame" and after catharsis, suggests a condition of stoical purity and serenity that accompanies the redeemed poetic self. But what distinguishes Crane's vision from Gauguin's primitivism is that whereas the latter's victory is personal and simple, that proposed for the former is social as well—and in being so presents a paradox. Faust is attempting to escape civilization and to reach a state of absolute purity, but he tries to bring with him the very world that he is trying to transcend. Sexual guilt, suggested in Part II (and explicit in "Possessions") becomes war guilt—the personal and the social are one—with the result that there can be no redemption for Faust without there being one for the world with which he has identified himself. In finding peace, Gauguin gives up his civilized self and announces that he has become a savage Maori (at least for the moment); Faustus, Apollonian and Dionysian at once, tries to find Maori peace in terms of his civilized world, or, to return to our starting point, he tries to maintain "organic continuity" with the chaos of external reality while achieving the equanimity that characterizes the "nuclear self."

3

Behind the contrapuntal development of *The Bridge* lies the assumption that if the object-in-itself, truly perceived, yields a "spiritual illumination" (Crane's expression), then, conversely, the state of mind of the poet determines the aesthetic and moral quality of the object. We recall that the poet is asked to surrender, but he is still expected to have the "gusto" to convert his observations into "positive terms." In effect, "gusto," the ability to "sympathize" with an object, if we apply Hazlitt's meaning, becomes the mystical love, "Dionysian intoxication." The Nietzschean rationale notwithstanding, Crane's uncertainty about the metaphysical legitimacy of this response was recurrent, and what eludes the reader as well as it eluded Crane himself is the exact nature of the poetic experience in his universe. Is the poet actually a pantheist who feels himself able to reach a mystical state by surrendering to a reality in which ugliness and pain are mere appearances; or is he actually a nihilist who self-consciously induces in himself a narcotic state in which no ugliness and pain are perceivable, a state which he knows, ultimately, is only an illusion? While Crane wanted to believe that he was practicing the former, he was sophisticated enough to fear that he was practicing the latter. Notice, for example, this passage from "The Wine Menagerie," written a year before he began working in earnest on *The Bridge:*

> New thresholds, new anatomies! Wine talons
> Build freedom up about me and distill
> This competence—to travel in a tear
> Sparkling alone, within another's will.
>
> Until my blood dreams a receptive smile
> Wherein new purities are snared. . . .

His vision "redeemed" by wine, the poet is able to feel compassion for the dancers in a cocktail lounge, a compassion that in his intoxication he dreams will be returned, wherein new thresholds, new anatomies, and new purities (new forms of "spiritual illumination") will be available. But his rational self presents a more sobering argument:

> —Anguished, the wit that cries out of me:
>
> "Alas,—these frozen billows of your skill!
> Invent new dominoes of love and bile . . .

> Ruddy, the tooth implicit of the world
> Has followed you. . . .

It is attitudes such as this that distinguish Crane from
the figure with whom he so often has been associated—
Walt Whitman; for the vision of compassion here is seen
to be only the trick of an intoxicated mind, a poet's illusion;
the reality is that the world is a "tiger" and the poet a help-
less Petrushka. This Apollonian comment on a Dionysian
assertion was merely part of a dialectic that ran throughout
most of Crane's poetry and reached a climax in *The Bridge*.

The conception of the poetic hero in Crane's major poem
differs from that in "Faustus and Helen" chiefly in that the
milieu of the quest is the American continent and American
history and in that Faust's Dionysian self is envisioned in
the more obviously primitivistic terms of an Indian persona,
Maquokeeta, who, being burnt at the stake and merging with
the earth goddess, Pocahontas, represents the transcendent
self that meets Helen in "that eventual flame." The hero of
The Bridge is portrayed as having a fragmented, civilized
self, apparent in the Proem, just as his prototype was portrayed as having a mind "divided by accepted multitudes."
Accordingly, the same Apollonian dream of unity marks the
terms of regeneration; the vision of Helen is transformed
into that of Brooklyn Bridge:

> And Thee, across the harbor, silver-paced
> As though the sun took step of thee, yet left
> Some motion ever unspent in thy stride,—
> Implicitly thy freedom staying thee!

Again, the ideal was to achieve a union of reality—the conditions of modern life as determined by technological progress—and myth, the pantheistic spirit which involved knowledge of the Infinite. Crane's underlying argument is that the
Bridge in the modern world must come to stand for the
same things as Pocahontas (Gea) did in the past and that
it was the role of the poet to join both worlds by perceiving,
experiencing, interpreting, and announcing the apocalyptic

nature of his object. The idealistic implication of this reasoning is sufficiently clear: the nature of reality depends upon the poet's attitude toward it, and the poet's attitude is determined not only by what he observes rationally, but by a self-induced Dionysian inspiration, justified, externally, only by the general principle of tragedy: that negation and evil are but a prelude to affirmation and good.

The mystical characteristics of Crane's vision are, in a sense, anticipated in Frank's *Our America*, in which we are told that "America is yet in the inchoate state where it has subjective meaning only. . . . As a Unit it exists only in the eye of the beholder." America is a dream of young manhood, Frank continues, "to which the real must conform":

> . . . we are in revolt . . . against that organized anarchy to-day expressed in Industrialism which would deny to America any life—hence any unity at all—beyond the ties of traffic and the arteries of trade. We believe we are the true realists; we who insist that in the essence of all reality lies the Ideal.[16]

This statement, typically paradoxical, both Whitmanesque and Bergsonian, accordingly envisions the poet (or mystic) as the creator of a "spiritual reality," the figure who lifts "America into self-knowledge that shall be luminous so that she may shine, vibrant so that she may be articulate." This subjective realism (or realistic idealism) is brought to a focus in an assertion that can be taken as a succinct and accurate gloss on *The Bridge*: "In this infancy of our adventure, America is a mystic Word. We go forth all to seek America. And in the seeking we create her. In the quality of our search shall be the nature of the America that we create." [17] Visionary America—the American Dream—exists in vision; essence exists only in the intuition of it; "secret reality" is mystical consciousness and mystical consciousness is poetic articulation; in the quest for meaning lies the creation of meaning. In brief, the Word that the poet apprehends is the Word he himself speaks. Because the very nature of quest is apocalyptic, *The Bridge*, as a whole, is intended to be apocalyptic; if the poet fails, his failure has tragic (noble) implications; if he succeeds, his success is of the universal dimension beyond tragedy.

As to the quest itself, and the vision it reflects, it is in its essence dialectical. For Crane, the moral history of the continent began with its conquest by the white man, whose iron "dealt cleavage," both of space (the actual surface of the land) and time (the connection with the past). Civilization meant the ruin of Eden, but the New World was redeemable and, in the apocalyptic moment represented by "The Dance," the poet, by identifying himself with the Indian, received the legacy of the past. This legacy, the "crucial sign" of the goddess, represented an insight into the absolute, whose manifestations had become obscure yet needed only to be reasserted to live again.

As early as the second stanza of the prologue Crane expressed despair over modern life and over the possibilities of realizing the ideal (an Apollonian response), and as early as the fourth stanza he expressed a Dionysian faith in the Bridge. These two attitudes are responsible for the contrapuntal form the poem was to take, that is to say, the fluctuations between rational pessimism and tragic optimism that mark the course of the work. Thus, as I have argued elsewhere, "The Harbor Dawn" presents a dream vision of Pocahontas that vanishes; in "The River," the awakened dreamer makes a rational appraisal of modern America and tries to find in it the elements that will help him recapture the goddess; in the ecstasy of "The Dance" lies the answer to all meditation. During the sections that follow, the poet indicates that, having returned from the mythic past to the modern world, he can now apprehend the goddess only by extrarational means. Contemplation of the realities of technological society—war in "Cape Hatteras," the deterioration of love and beauty in "Three Songs," Philistinism in "Quaker Hill," and metropolitan chaos in "The Tunnel"—brings only despair. Yet in nearly every instance we find the poet reasserting his faith, either "ecstatically," as in "Cape Hatteras"; with a note of determination not logically justified by the context, as in "Quaker Hill"; or with an unrestrained hymn, as in the finale.

The central question in *The Bridge*, then, is perhaps best expressed in the lines,

> So, must we from the hawk's far stemming view,
> Must we descend as worm's eye to construe
> Our love of all we touch. . . .   ("Quaker Hill")

The truth is that while the poet consistently refuses to descend from the hawk's view, the question is never really settled. Thus despite the coherence lent to the work by the Nietzschean argument, there is, in a sense, nothing but the literary principle of anticlimax to prevent another cycle of despair and ecstasy from being added to the poem and extended indefinitely. Such is the phenomenon inherent, it would seem, in any attempt to achieve "continuity with chaos," when that chaos is represented by modern industrial life.

That Crane found it impossible to sustain the Faustian "self" is apparent in "Voyages" and the Key West poems, as well as in *The Bridge* itself, which, along with Dionysian doom, presents a vision of death by water, a death marked by absolute serenity separated from, rather than part of, social experience. Much in the Key West collection recalls the desire of Gauguin to purge his civilized self in order to attain harmony with nature. Yet, ironically, even here Crane was not wholly at peace, for although he found his images of "power in repose"—a royal palm "launched beyond mortality, an air plant ("Angelic Dynamo!")—he was also aware of the "tarantula rattling the lily's foot" that represented not a death in which the poet returned to "natal power," but one in which he was meaninglessly obliterated in a tropical hell ("O Carib Isle!"). But most important is that these poems indicate Crane's attempt to acquire a stable "nuclear" self, not one that "would bear and *transfigure* the world's impinging chaos," as Frank has explained the aim of the mystic, but one that would simply "bear" it. In "The Broken Tower," Crane has provided us with what is perhaps the most revealing insight into the ultimate direction of his quest. First, he desires to find unity ("love") in the world around him:

> And so it was I entered the broken world
> To trace the visionary company of love, its voice
> An instant in the wind (I know not whither hurled)
> But not for long to hold each desperate choice.

But he feels a sense of failure in recreating, through his poetry, the logos of the absolute (Pocahontas, the Bridge):

> My word I poured. But was it cognate, scored
> Of that tribunal monarch of the air
> Whose thigh embronzes earth, strikes crystal Word
> In wounds pledged once to hope—cleft to despair?
>
> The steep encroachments of my blood left me
> No answer. . . .

Yet despite his doubt, he still imagines the possibility of achieving a nuclear self, a sense of inner repose, through a vision of the goddess:

> is it she
> Whose sweet mortality stirs latent power?—
> . . . .
> And builds, within, a tower that is not stone
> (Not stone can jacket heaven)—but slip
> Of pebbles—visible wings of silence sown
> In azure circles. . . .

The goddess here is akin to the one in "Voyages," which presents a similar experience of external chaos (the "broken tower" here is conceived of, obliquely, as a shipwreck) and internal resurrection:

> Waiting, afire, what name, unspoke,
> I cannot claim. . . .
> . . . .
> The solstice thunders, crept away,

> Like a cliff swinging or a sail
> Flung into April's inmost day—
>
> Creation's blithe and petalled word
> To the lounged goddess when she rose
> Conceding dialogue with eyes
> That smile unsearchable repose—

Here, again, is the attempt to apprehend the "crystal Word":

> The imaged Word, it is, that holds
> Hushed willows anchored in its glow.
> It is the unbetrayable reply
> Whose accent no farewell can know.   (VI)

But the point I am making is that in both "Voyages" and "The Broken Tower"—as in "Possessions"—the triumph of the poet, unlike that proposed in "Faustus and Helen" and *The Bridge* in virtually the same symbols, occurs on the merely personal and not on the social or cultural levels. To repeat, it is the passive triumph of stoicism, wherein the nuclear self does not seek to transfigure the world, but to renounce it. "That serenity that Prospero gains," Crane wrote in "To Shakespeare," "Is justice that has cancelled earthly chains." And in the seriocomic "Bacardi Spreads the Eagle's Wings," we find three Cubans, who, as their boat sinks, sit "like baking Buddhas":

> They're back now on that mulching job at Pepper's.
> —Yes, patent-leather shoes—hot enough to fry
> Anyone but these native high-steppers!

It may be primarily the rum that makes them Buddhas impervious to sea and sun—but in Crane's world, that scarcely makes any difference.

Characteristically, the quest for "selfhood" in Crane's poetry ends in self-annihilation. Although Frank's description implies that the two are the same, self-annihilation, for Crane, finally came to mean not the loss of personal identity by acquisition of an impersonal Dionysian role with tragic

significance for an entire culture, but merely a psychological
death by water:

> The sea raised up a campanile . . . The wind I heard
> Of brine partaking, whirling spout in shower
> Of column kiss—that breakers spouted, sheared
> Back into bosom—me—her, into natal power. . . .
>
> ("The Return")

And it was the fatal sea goddess, the personal alter ego of
the "socialized" Helen and Pocahontas, who exerted the final
influence on Crane.

8. EZRA POUND: FAC DEUM

It is a curious yet understandable phenomenon of literary history that Ezra Pound, one of the founders of the Imagist movement, was not really involved in the epistemological revolution that emerged from it—at least not until the writing of the *Cantos*, and then only in a manner that developed out of his own particular conception of experience. And one reason he was not so involved is that, whatever his use of natural images, Pound, unlike Williams, Moore, and Stevens, did not take the natural world as his starting point. For the most part, the emotions and attitudes that appear in *Personae* are, finally considered, not really unconventional. But if Pound did not contribute to a revolutionary nature poetry, he shared in the Aristotelian trend of thought that provided its rationale, and the development of his work reveals an aestheticism differing in subject matter but not in logic from that of the objectivists.

Pound's total involvement in the literary world is in itself a clue to the kind of poetry he wrote and to the poetic behind it for, in a sense, the world of letters was, to him, what the natural world was to the objectivist. To begin with, Pound, in characteristic "Aristotelian" fashion, is concerned with central "realities" in human experience and the need for an authentically "scientific" approach to those realities, an approach made through art:

> I have said that the arts give us our best data for determining what sort of creature man is. As our treatment of man must be determined by our knowledge or conception of what man is, the arts provide data for ethics.
> . . . the serious artist is scientific. . . . That is to say, a good biologist will make a reasonable number of observations of any given phenomenon before he draws a conclusion. . . . The results of each observation must be precise and no single observation must in itself be taken

as determining a general law. . . . The serious artist is
scientific in that he presents the image of his desire, of
his hate, of his indifference as precisely that, as precisely
the image of his own desire, hate or indifference. The
more precise his record the more lasting and unassailable
his work of art.[1]

And finally, revealingly, he writes that art "exists as the trees
exist, you can admire, you can sit in the shade, you can pick
bananas, you can cut firewood, you can do as you jolly well
please." Plainly visible in this statement is the dual focus of
interest that has determined the nature of Pound's poetry,
for if Pound is concerned with the universal states of mind
("desire, hate, indifference"), he is also concerned with the
"art" that expresses them—not simply with expressing his
own states but with investigating those states in other poets.
And in this latter instance, it is the work of art that becomes
the *ding-an-sich*, the essential reality to be revealed. In other
words, Pound, not just in the above statement, but in his
entire mode of commentary on other writers, seems to have
envisioned himself as the Aristotelian critic par excellence,
making the juxtapositions, providing the categories, and determining the principles, in the style of a biologist, of the
realities of literary history, and thereby of reality.[2] As poet,
the Aristotelian critic creates the persona, the "living image"
of the poet wherein his "true emotion" is resurrected. Thus
as early as 1908, when accused by Williams of being too
personal in his poetry, Pound could reply,

To me the short so-called dramatic lyric—at any rate
the sort of thing I do—is the poetic part of a drama the
rest of which . . . is left to the reader's imagination or
implied or set in a short note. I catch the character I hap-
pen to be interested in at the moment he interests me,
usually a moment of song, self-analysis, or sudden under-
standing or revelation. . . . I paint my man as I *conceive*
him.[3]

He then asks, "Why write what I can translate out of
Renaissance Latin or crib from the sainted dead?" and goes

on to list the "facts" that he and "9,000,000 other poets have spieled endlessly"—such as "Spring is a pleasant season," "Men love women," and so forth. One can detect here the historical bias that was to reach its fullest metaphysical expression in the *Cantos*, the notion that a single poetic sensibility is manifested throughout all epochs, that "discoveries" are made in one age that provide criteria for all ages, and that it is the function of the poet to resurrect these discoveries, a resurrection made possible only when the idiom of the interpreter is "vital" to his own era. Conversely, one of the primary functions of criticism, we learn in a later essay, is "excernment":

> The general ordering and weeding out of what has actually been performed. The elimination of repetitions. The work analogous to that which a good hanging committee or a curator would perform in a National Gallery or in a biological museum;
> The ordering of knowledge so that the next man (or generation) can most readily find the live part of it, and waste the least possible time among obsolete issues.[4]

Pound's well-known pronouncements on the true language of poetry really take on their fullest meaning in this context. Since the "touchstone of art is precision," "Good writing is writing that is perfectly controlled, the writer says just what he means. He says it with complete clarity and simplicity. He uses the smallest possible number of words." Pound's entire theory of language is epitomized in his imperative, "Go in fear of abstractions." Only in concrete language is authentic emotion able to be expressed; decorative and abstract language result only in vapidity.[5] Whatever the persuasiveness of this argument in itself, one must keep in mind that it is still part of a larger rationale, what amounts to a doctrine of essences in which the poet-interpreter becomes the very figure of insight, on the one hand seeing into the reality of experience, on the other into the reality of the feelings of those who perceived that reality before him.

It need hardly be said that *Personae* is, partly, the poetic

equivalent of Pound's prose works on the poets he has taken
to be authentic: Catullus, Propertius, the troubadours, Cavalcanti, Villon, and the rest of the now-familiar list. Aside
from metrical experiments, the aim in these interpretive
poems, as in the whole course of Pound's later translations,
is expression in a dramatic language, either lyrical or collo-
quial, that will have an immediate impact upon the reader.
Such an impact is the result of the poet's attempt to be as
precise as possible on the three levels of poetic discourse
that Pound labels "logopoeia" (actually, connotation),
"phanopoeia" (visual or imagistic quality), and "melopoeia"
(musical or rhythmic quality). Pound's reasoning seems to
lead to the conclusion that the total impression is ideally
the same as that which he described for an "Image," "an
intellectual and emotional complex" presented in an instant
of time and giving a "sense of sudden liberation; that sense
of freedom from time and space limits; that sense of sudden
growth, which we experience in the presence of the greatest
work of art." [6]

The recreated poets themselves are those who, in Pound's
estimation, were able to combine keenness of insight and
clarity of presentation—psychological perceptivity and tech-
nical mastery. In drawing up a "new table of values," Pound
insists on the recognition that "poets like Villon, Sappho,
and Catullus differ from poets like Milton, Tasso and
Camoens, and that size is no more a criterion of writing
than it is of painting." [7] Of Cavalcanti he writes:

> Than Guido Cavalcanti no psychologist of the emo-
> tions is more keen in his understanding, more precise in
> his expression; we have in him no rhetoric, but always a
> true description, whether it be of pain itself, or of the
> apathy that comes when the emotions and possibilities
> of emotion are exhausted. . . .[8]

Of Villon:

> [He] has the stubborn persistency of one whose gaze
> cannot be deflected from the actual fact before him: what
> he sees, he writes. . . .

Villon holds his unique place in literature because he
is the only poet without illusions. . . . [He] never lies
to himself; he does not know much but what he knows
he knows: man is an animal, certain things he can feel;
there is much misery, man has a soul about which he
knows little or nothing.[9]

All great poets are characterized by "precision of statement,
particularization." [10] Their personae provide "biological speci-
mens," ones that are living because of the special talent of
the "biologist."

But the problem of Pound's scienticism does not end here
and even though one is stating the obvious in saying that the
personae speak for Pound as well as he for them, such a
statement is necessary. Only rarely in his criticism does Pound
discuss psychological or philosophical problems divorced from
those of technique, but in two such places, both on the subject of love, he implies a great deal about the pattern of feelings and attitudes expressed in the collection. If one looks
closely at the argument in "Psychology and the Troubadours,"
a chapter added to the second edition of *The Spirit of Romance*, one can discern its objectivist logic, its attempt to
establish the scientific validity of a metaphysical vision, by
proposing a basis for it in immediate experience and precise
perception:

I believe in a sort of permanent basis in humanity,
that is to say, I believe that Greek myth arose when some-
one having passed through a delightful psychic experience
tried to communicate it to others. . . . Certain it is that
these myths are only intelligible in a vivid and glittering
sense to those people to whom they occur. . . . These
things are for them *real*.[11]

Pound asks whether or not the love expressed in troubadour
poetry did not "take on mediumistic properties":

Stimulated by color or quality of emotion, did that
"color" take on forms interpretive of divine order? Did

it lead to "exteriorization of the sensibility" and interpretation of the cosmos by feeling?

For our basis in nature we rest on the indisputable and very scientific fact that there are in the "normal course of things" certain times . . . when a man feels his immortality upon him.[12]

The figure of the Lady becomes for the troubadour the tangible and real object through which he can attain a sense of divine mystery otherwise lost:

> Richard St. Victor has left us one very beautiful passage on the splendours of paradise.
>
> They are ineffable and innumerable and no man having beheld them can fittingly narrate them or even remember them exactly. Nevertheless by naming over all the beautiful things we know, we may draw upon the mind some vestige of heavenly splendour.
>
> I suggest that the troubadour . . . progresses from correlating all these details for purpose of comparison, and lumps the matter. The Lady contains the catalogue [that is, of all beautiful things in nature], is more complete. She serves as a sort of *mantram*.[13]

In short, the troubadours achieved a balance between the real and the spiritual, they "transferred something of the manner, and something of the spirit, to the beauty of life as they found it"; they were "souls who belonged by reason of their refinement not in heaven but somewhat above mortal turmoil . . . [in] some middle way." [14]

Of interest in this argument is not the ideas per se on the troubadours, ideas that are, essentially, of little originality; rather it is his own involvement in the process that Pound is at such pains to present objectively. In the course of the discussion, Pound, still in the guise of biologist-metaphysician, introduces the notion of a "life-force," manifested in the fluid-force" of the cosmos and the "germinal-force" of nature. Man, we learn, is a "mechanism . . . rather like an electric appliance" and, in matters of consciousness, has either a reflective mind (in the sense that it reflects "sundry patches of the macrocosmos" and is a *"phantastikon"*) or a germinal one, "close on the vital universe." The Greeks represented the ideal consciousness, but at least the "reliqua" of it appeared in Provence, wherein the troubadours attempted to reach "the whole and the flowing" through sex.

This pseudo-Bergsonian doctrine reappears, in an extreme form, in Pound's postscript to his translation of De Gourmont's *Natural Philosophy of Love;* here he argues that the very basis of thought is sexual, the brain being "a sort of great clot of genital fluid held in suspense or reserve." Again we encounter a pseudobiological vocabulary that defines a process in which "life-sap" under "spermatozoic pressure" "up-shoots" into the brain which "out-spurts" images and ideas.[15] None of this kind of thing is expressed directly in *Personae,* but it does at least make clear that Pound himself was seeking what he thought was a "middle way" between mysticism and scientific method and that, in a very specific sense, he regarded himself as a neo-troubadour (or neo-Hellenist), not simply a poet-interpreter who resurrected the past, but one who created his own vision in its mold.

The analogy that Pound might have detected between himself, as an exiled poet with a new, misunderstood art, and such innovator-pariahs as Sappho or the neo-Hellenistic Catullus and Propertius, the wandering troubadours, François Villon, or even the author of "The Seafarer," seems obvious enough. The strength of the latter two in relishing their outcast positions—as perhaps that shown in the antisocial feelings of Bertrans de Born ("Sestina: Altaforte")— appeals to a side of Pound's sensibility that will be discussed at length. But can one really call Pound a love poet in the tradition that he seems to have chosen for himself? The very composition of *Personae* suggests the absence of a corporal Lesbia, Cynthia, or Maent and one soon has the impression that the Lady appearing in both the adaptations and the originals is simply a metaphor upon which a lyrical experience is created virtually ex nihilo, an image functioning in much the same way as the actual lady did, ultimately, for her poet lovers, but without any literal or physical meaning and without the complex sexual emotions associated with a woman who was real before she became idealized. In the notes to his translation of Catullus, Jack Lindsay suggests that Clodia (Lesbia) finally became for Catullus the very image of the Muse-goddess; "The poet's creative impulse was felt as the need to unite with Sappho-Clodia, the spring and liberation of all lyricism. By mating with Clodia he would become the inspired poet of his dreams." [16]

This is the notion Pound seems to have had in mind when, in the postscript just discussed, he speaks of ideal creativity as a result of "the balance of the ejector [male] and retentive media [female]" and suggests that the clue to the whole twelfth-century love cult as well as to those following it lies in Propertius' line "*Ingenium nobis ipsa puella fecit*"—My genius is no more than a girl," as he translates it in "Homage to Propertius," or, in the words of another translator, "My lady's self the fount of all my wit." Accordingly, we find him saying in the introduction to the Cavalcanti poems,

> The equations of alchemy were apt to be written as women's names and the women so named endowed with the magical powers of the compounds. *La virtù* is the potency, the efficient property of a substance or person. Thus modern science shows us radium with a noble virtue of energy. Each thing or person was held to send forth magnetisms of certain effect. . . .
>
> It is a spiritual chemistry, and modern science and modern mysticism are both set to confirm it. [17]

To call the Lady a metaphor, in Pound's poetry, a metaphor that appears to have the same significance as has the real lady for Catullus, is to return to the notion that the early Pound inhabits a chiefly literary universe; the poet who conjures the Lady out of his own soul, the image of the *mantram* that Pound tells us she was for the troubadours, really wears only one mask, that of Narcissus or his close relation, Pygmalion:

> How have I laboured?
> How have I not laboured
> To bring her soul to birth,
> To give these elements a name and a centre!
> She is as beautiful as the sunlight, and as fluid.
> She has no name, and no place.
> How have I laboured to bring her soul into separation;
> To give her a name and her being!   ("Ortus")

> But my soul sent a woman, a woman of the
>   wonder-folk,
> A woman as fire upon the pine woods
>   crying 'Song, a song.'   ("Praise of Ysolt")

> O you away high there,
>   you that lean
> From amber lattices upon the cobalt night,
> I am below amid the pine trees,
> Amid the little pine trees, hear me!   ("Au Jardin")[18]

In this last poem, the poet sees himself as a jester in a garden seeking out a fairy lady that he loved "Over beyond the moon." Each of these poems is, in its own way, almost the incantation of a poet figure seeking the love that means creativity and artistic fulfillment. The idea of "creating" the Lady, such as we find in "Ortus," is appropriate to the condition of the modern artist and in discovering Bertrans de Born fashioning his own ideal lady out of the best parts of others—though in a wholly different context —Pound perhaps felt that he was indeed resurrecting a persona and not merely a character. The whole tone of "Na Audiart" is, again, incantatory:

> Bertrans, master of his lays,
> Bertrans of Aultaforte thy praise
> Sets forth, and though thou hate me well,

Yea though thou wish me ill,
                    Audiart, Audiart.
Thy loveliness is here writ till,
                    Audiart,
Oh, till thou come again.

In seeking to create moments of illumination based upon
the traditional love situation, Pound is seeking to give an
aura of mystery to a psychological state—if not a sense of
actual love, then of the vitalistic "urge" to creativity that
perhaps lies behind such love. He is correspondingly attracted
to the idea of metamorphosis, in the style of Daphne, for
herein lies the mythic objectification of the pure vitalistic
experience:

The tree has entered my hands,
The sap has ascended my arms,
The tree has grown in my breast—
. . . .
And all this is folly to the world.   ("A Girl")

Apparently Pound could not resist the ironic comment of
the last line, a comment that puts the illumination into
moral perspective. The metamorphosis is an appropriate symbol for the aesthetic experience in general, the state of mind
by which the poet can identify himself or again by his
"refinement" can rise "somewhat above mortal toil." All
these attitudes and feelings are elaborated in "La Fraisne,"
the narrator of which Pound, defending himself against
Williams' charges, called "half or whole mad." But the
madness of the speaker is very much like that of the poet-
as-Daphne: an old man, he has gone into the forest and
taken a dogwood tree as his bride:

I have put aside all folly and all grief.
I wrapped my tears in an ellum leaf
And left them under a stone
And now men call me mad . . .
Because my bride

Is a pool of the wood. . . .
        my bride hath toward me a great love
That is sweeter than the love of women
That plague and burn and drive one away.

The experience here is clearly analogous to that of the poet figure, but one need not rely solely on internal evidence to prove the point. For, contradicting his remarks to Williams, Pound added a note on "La Fraisne" to *Umbra* (1920) in which he quotes Janus of Basil:

When the soul is exhausted of fire, then doth the spirit return unto its primal nature and there is upon it a peace great and of the woodland. . . .
Then becometh it kin to the faun and dryad, a woodland dweller amid the rocks and streams. . . .

Pound says that he chose the theme because he himself felt in such a mood, "divided between myself corporeal and a self aetherial, 'a dweller by streams and in woodland,' eternal because simple in elements . . . being freed of the weight of a soul 'capable of salvation or damnation.' " By reducing his own soul to a "simplex naturae," he is "at peace and trans-sentient as a wood pool." [19] The division here between the self corporeal and the self aetherial has behind it the characteristic preoccupation with the "middle way" between actuality and mystery that we have been discussing. That serenity stands at the apex of the vitalistic or creative experience is a theme that recurs generally throughout much romantic literature and becomes one of the identifying traits of the moment of illumination in the *Cantos*, as for example:

And we have heard the fauns chiding Proteus
        in the smell of the hay under the olive-trees
And the frogs singing against the fauns
        in the half-light.   (Canto 2)

Or:

Panisks, and from the oak, dryas,
And from the apple, maelid,

> Through all the wood, and the leaves are full of voices,
> A-whisper. . . .   (Canto 3)

This kind of poetry is really no more an authentic nature poetry than is the kind of poetry about the Lady an authentic love poetry. In both instances the central images are just that—images or projections of the imagination about which an essentially narcissistic poetic experience is conjured. The means of conjuration is language, which, rather than expressing a state, actually creates it. One recalls here an image in Cavalcanti which had a special interest for Pound, the "emanation" or "potency" that springs from the Lady's lips:

> I seem to see a lady wonderful
> Spring forth between her lips, one whom no sense
> Can fully tell the mind of, and one whence
> Another, in beauty, springeth marvellous,
> From whom a star goes forth. . . .[20]

The next stanza continues:

> There where this Lady's loveliness appeareth,
> Is heard a voice which goes before her ways
> And seems to sing her name with such sweet
>   praise. . . .

And in similar fashion, the "potency" of the poet, who is his own Lady, springs forth from his lips—the "virtù" manifested in language, the "philosopher stone" of the poet with which he practices alchemy. All Pound's love or nature poems are, in a sense, chants for the "transmutation of metals," the metal in reality being his own state of mind. Thus "The Alchemist":

> O Queen of Cypress,
> Out of Erebus, the flat-lying breadth,
> Breath that is stretched out beneath the world:
> Out of Erebus, out of the flat waste of air, lying
>   beneath the world;

> Out of the brown leaf-brown colourless
>   Bring the imperceptible cool. . . .
>   Quiet this metal!

Contained here is Pound's entire literary microcosm: the metamorphosis, the goddess, the magic breath, the serenity that represents the escape from Hell. To repeat, the poet contains all these elements within himself: he is both alchemist and metal; he creates the goddess in the act of invoking her through song and finds rejuvenation in the very utterance of language.

Pound's preoccupation with his own identity as a poet in an unsympathetic environment complements that with creating the moment of illumination in *Personae*. The many pseudotraditional poems in which the author addresses his own work in moods ranging from despair to defiance are indeed only part of the tendency that culminated in the kind of ironic statement that characterizes *Hugh Selwyn Mauberley* (1919–1920). An uneasiness exists even in *Homage to Sextus Propertius*, written two years earlier, in which the lyric poetry of love is defended against the public poetry of heroism. Propertius, who has been dabbling in the encomium of heroes, is warned off by Apollo:

> 'You idiot . . .
> Who has ordered a book about heroes?
>
>   'You need, Propertius, not think
>   'About acquiring that sort of a reputation. . . .
>   'No keel will sink with your genius
>   'Let another oar churn the water'. . . .
>   (p. 220)

Propertius commits himself to love poetry, if not to fidelity to his mistress Cynthia; he asserts that his "genius is no more than a girl," and he finds ample subject matter in her person:

> If she with ivory fingers drive a tune through the lyre,
>   We look at the process.

> How easy the moving fingers; if hair is mussed on her
>   forehead
> If she goes in a gleam of Cos, in a slither of dyed stuff,
> There is a volume in the matter. . . .
> And whatever she does or says
>   We shall spin long yarns out of nothing.   (p. 226)

Altering the original, Pound accordingly puts into Propertius' mouth what seems to be an ironic imitation of the war poetry he has foresworn:

> Now for a large-mouthed product.
> Thus:
> 'The Euphrates denies its protection to the Parthian
>   and apologizes for Crassus' . . .
> And so forth, Augustus. . . .   (p. 225)

The passage continues in this vein. As a Poundian hero, Propertius is a justification; on the other hand, Pound was not insensible to the dangers of devoting one's self to love poetry alone and there is more than idle scorn in Calliope's remarks during Propertius' baptism as a poet:

> 'Content ever to move with white swans!
> 'Nor will the noise of high horses ever lead you to
>   battle. . . .
> 'Obviously crowned lovers at unknown doors,
> 'Night dogs, the marks of a drunken scurry,
> 'These are your images, and from you the sorcerizing
>   of shut-in young ladies,
> 'The wounding of austere men by chicane.'   (p. 221)

The poet of love—the lyric poet—escapes the vapidity of public oratory, but he accordingly cuts himself off from social life and has for an audience only himself and his mistress, both unstable entities, to say the least.[21]

The position of Mauberley is that of Propertius made explicit and comprehended in terms of the moral conditions of life in modern society. In his virtually definitive study of *Mauberley*, John Espey sees a distinction between Ezra

Pound's image of himself as a poet and the figure that lends
his name to the title.[22] It is not until halfway through the
poem, in the section also named after him, that Mauberley
disengages himself, "always in contrast to the active Odysseus-
poet of the first section." Mauberley is a minor artist, writes
Espey, "unable to create a tradition of his own . . . but he
has not compromised with the age." Accordingly, the initial
poems represent Pound's own struggles; the apparently self-
directed irony in the first poem, "E. P. Ode Pour L'Election
de Son Sepulchre," Espey implies, is actually Pound's presentation of his critic's view of his career:[23]

> Unaffected by the 'march of events',
> He passed from men's memory in *l'an trentiesme*
> *De son eage*; the case presents
> No adjunct to the Muses' diadem.   (p. 197)

As convincing as this argument is, an ambiguity in the relation of Pound and Mauberley does remain, an ambiguity
that possibly has no solution because Pound's attitude itself
is dichotomous. His opinion in the alternatives of observing
"the mottoes on sun dials" and "the elegance of Circe's hair"
is clear enough, but the question is, having chosen the latter,
is one left with an ideal? Espey sees the preference for Circe's
hair as a love of "beauty for itself however dangerous." On
the other hand it is possible that Circe, who turns men into
swine, is not identifiable with the Venus of the *Cantos*, but
rather is the kind of beauty pursued by the hedonist, the
same kind pursued by Mauberley himself:

> For three years . . .
> He drank ambrosia,
> All passes, ANANGKE prevails,
> Came end, at last, to that Arcadia.   (p. 209)

And his own epitaph is,

> 'I was
> And I no more exist;
> Here drifted
> An hedonist.'

What I am suggesting here is simply that Pound perhaps
saw himself as he saw Mauberley or even Propertius: as the
authentic poet driven into a kind of impotence by being cut
off from the world. The statement that the case presents no
adjunct to the Muse's diadem is in one sense Pound's judgment of himself as well as it is, in another sense, that of his
critics. Neither is this apparently equivocal conception really
clarified in later sections. In the "Siena" poem, for example,
Espey writes that "here the two poets who stand out against
the background of diffuse mediocrity are Ernest Dowson and
Lionel Johnson, who shared Catholicism, alcoholism, and a
veneration for Propertius." [24] Yet could not both these men,
as well as Victor Gustave Plarr (the Monsieur Verog "Among
the pickled foetuses and bottled bones," who talks to the
poets of the nineties), themselves have said "Siena mi fe;
disfecimi Maremma"—for they themselves have been un-
made by England? Finally, Espey interprets the "Envoi" as
sounding "throughout the suggestion of active passion as
earnest against the destruction of time" and adds that it
represents an ironic triumph "in answer to the critical dis-
missal of Pound in the *Ode*." Still, it can be argued that the
envoi is a love poem in the tradition of the personae, not a
new epic statement, and that the vision of immortality seems
to be conditional rather than accomplished:

> *Go, dumb-born book,*
> *Tell her that sang me once that song of Lawes:*
> *Hadst thou but song*
> *As thou hast subjects known,*
> *Then were there cause in thee that should condone*
> *Even my faults that heavy upon me lie,*
> *And build her glories their longevity.*

The envoi is a wish for immortality, but the poet still fears
that in fact he is without "song" and sees his book as "dumb-
born" (an observation obviously not in Waller's "Go, Lovely
Rose"). If the poet could sing, his faults would be con-
doned and he'd build immortality for beauty—but that is
precisely the issue that the sequence is exploring.

I am aware that all the arguments presented to suggest the identity of, or at least the close resemblance between, Pound and Mauberley, are inconclusive. But my original point was merely that an ambiguity exists and that Pound, at best, vacillated between the ironic and heroic views of the poet and his capacity to deal with social reality. We have noticed this ambivalence in Williams, Stevens, and Crane, and we shall find it again (I state the obvious) in Eliot. It is a response to a central aestheticist problem: the consequences of aestheticism when it is conceived of as mere hedonism, and, as such, fails to provide a positive social vision.

Taken as a whole, the poems in *Personae* reveal Pound's impulse to realism on the one hand and to a form of subjectivism or idealism on the other. His concern for technique, for adaptation of foreign or historically remote material, and his reliance on universal emotions expressed through personae rather than on personal emotions expressed directly, are all part of the antiromantic values lauded by Hulme. Nonetheless, as we have seen, a self-image is implicit, and if mere self-expression is avoided, there is still apparent a kind of solipsism in which a world conjured up out of the literary imagination exists apart from the actual world. The social vision in the *Cantos,* in a sense a positive response to the dangers revealed in *Mauberley,* actually did nothing more than magnify Pound's conception of reality while preserving its basic paradoxes.

2

In technique, subject, and rationale, the *Cantos* are an almost perfect manifestation of realist poetics. The use of personae from all levels of society and from a multitude of cultures, and the extensive introduction of historical, political, economic, and mythological material are part of a single-minded attempt to present a revisionist philosophy of history and to provide metaphysical revelation in general. Furthermore, there is much in Pound's thought that is reminiscent of classical humanism. For example, in the course of his explication of the *Cantos*, Clark Emery discusses Pound's adherence, on the one hand, to Neoplatonism, with its conception of a Permanent behind the flux of reality, of a divine light, so to speak; and, on the other hand, to the theory of action, represented by the expression, "directio voluntatis," in which the poet directs a "fluid force against circumstance" in the world of men.[25] He cites Pound's distinction between undesirable and desirable mystical states, the former being that in which a man is "on fire with God" in a diffuse fanaticism, and the latter that in which he engages in "ecstatic-beneficent-and-benevolent" contemplation of "the divine splendour with good will to others." This state, Pound tells us,

> is a dynamism. It has, time and again, driven men to great living, it has given them courage to go on for decades in the face of public stupidity. It is paradisical and a reward in itself seeking naught further . . . perhaps because a feeling of certitude inheres in the state of feeling itself. The glory of life exists without further proof. . . .[26]

Whereas in the improper state of mind one indulges in vague fantasies of infinity that have no relation to human life, in the proper, one is in constant quest of a scientific exactitude and sharpness of form that complements his inspiration.

Insofar as they represent coherent conceptions, the notion of "ideas-into-action" and that of "directio voluntatis" seem to be part of the classical aestheticist antiabstractionism advocated by Hulme. But, more, they seem to imply a whole classical ethos. To put ideas into action through a force of will is to avoid the extremes of both abstractionism and mere expediency. The implication is that one has a conception of an ideal or universal and is able to act in accordance with it. "Directio voluntatis" thus presupposes a rational moral faculty that acts as a guide—the "right reason," for example, of classical humanism, with which one apprehends the universal order. It was the classical element in Confucianism, an ethical theory based on the interrelation of the universal (the divine) and the particular (the state, the man) by means of a moral force that provided the basis of ideal action, that appealed most to Pound. Accordingly, the theory of education as "rectification" of character, inherent in Pound's idea of "Kulchur," has a classical-Confucian proto-type in the idea of a disciplining of the passions (those ele-ments in the personality leading to egoism, prejudice, and delusion) by strengthening the reason-judgment (that ele-ment that insures action in accordance with universality and order).[27]

The so-called ideogrammic method, which provides the formal principle of the *Cantos*, is a product of both classical and aestheticist thinking. It is classical insofar as it is meant to be the language by which moral rectification is achieved ("truth," the "New Learning," drilled into the "encrusted" mind of the reader).[28] It is aestheticistic insofar as it repre-sents a "rectified" language in itself, a form of *cheng ming*. The notion that the Chinese character is inherently vivid and concrete because it is a pictograph or ideograph, a representa-tion close to the object it signifies, is, as is well-enough known, Ernest Fenollosa's contribution to Pound's theory. One can appreciate that, whatever the degree of its authen-ticity, this conception is merely an elaboration of Pound's early Bergsonian view of the "Image" and Hulme's notion of the metaphor.

As an interpretation of history, the *Cantos* are, broadly speaking, in the tradition of the German *kulturphilosophien*, those a priori conceptions in which an Idea unfolds or recurs. I make this point even though it is central to Pound's logic that idea is posterior to fact, for the results are the same: a dogmatic assertion of the "meaning" of history. Pound, no less than Friedrich Schlegel, or, for that matter, Karl Marx, claims scientific validity for a vision that is, finally, moral. The supporting theory of *kulturmorphologie* (that externals in a society are symptomatic of basic cultural phenomena) that Pound borrows from the German anthro-pologist, Frobenius—it could also have been Taine—is char-acteristic of the organicism upon which much speculative history is based.

Pound's general thesis that history is a conflict between the forces of creativity and order, on all levels of experience, and the forces of disruption, embodied in the "usurers," is comprehensible enough as a social vision. Although his revisionistic interpretation of such figures as Sigismundo Malatesta, Niccòlo d'Este, or Benito Mussolini may consciously or not ignore or explain away the disquieting features in their actions, it is still part of a fairly conventional moral conception. Indeed, ethical requirements usually take precedence, in the *Cantos,* over the aesthetic. By virtue of its "dramatization" through "ideogram," a state document, a letter, or a memoir, thematically valuable for its ethical implications, is presented as a form of poetry.

Again, all these considerations attest to the "realism" of the *Cantos,* but the matter does not end here. To begin with, for all the apparent impersonality of presentation, the personality of the author has scarcely been effaced; if the ideogrammic method is, supposedly, a mode of objective revelation, it is also the unmistakable voice of its creator. One is not simply aware, for example, of historical personages "brought to life," but of Pound in the very act of attempting to bring them to life with his own breath, so to speak, and in his own sometimes effective, sometimes banal, idiom. These figures are in fact "personae," masks through which the poet speaks, rather than fully realized dramatic characters. Furthermore, the *Cantos* are not only a pastiche of Pound's reading; they are virtually a mirror of Pound in the act of reading (just as a passage in Canto 23 is a transcription of Pound in the act of translating). Thus, if they are a "realistic" interpretation of history, they are also the projection of a specific mentality simultaneously experiencing, interpreting, and transforming historical material. Similarly, if the ideogrammic method is often reducible to a rational logic, it is also merely the correlative of an associationist mind, with its particular collection of habits, impulses, and preoccupations, as often eccentric and obscure as universal and clear. The theoretical justification for this phenomenon in which psychological process becomes part of the form of a work is that the poet, as "genius," is capable of direct insight into reality, and an insight into his process of insight is Insight itself.[29] In any event, the *Cantos* are paradoxical: at once coherent and incoherent, they present a vision that is much too general to be dismissed as mere subjective utterance, and at the same time are too solipsistic to represent a traditional philosophy of history.

We might now look at the question of the self-image of the poet in the *Cantos* and the quest that is the explicit subjective aspect of Pound's historical vision. To put the matter melodramatically, the creator not only creates out of himself but places himself in his creation; the persona, wearing a mask identical to the face of the author, recapitulates, in his quest, the seemingly endless process of interpretation made by his original. Although the image of the poet is constantly lost in mythical and historical personae —heroes who do or do not succeed in making effective their wills for good—it emerges from time to time as a separate identity engaged in a perpetual struggle to envision and maintain a partly mystical moral and aesthetic ideal. One may even go so far as to say poetic identity depends not upon the actual realization of poetic values but upon the capacity to conceive and keep faith in them, conception and faith being the sole fixed elements in an internal and external world characterized by process and flux. What characterizes the poetic sensibility is, as will be taken up in detail presently, the acceptance of the principle, annunciated by Tiresias in Canto 1, that one must "pass through spiteful Neptune, over dark seas." This principle is, in its own way, the equivalent of Nietzsche's "acceptance of tragedy through destruction," adopted by Crane. "Periplus," sea voyage, is the only possible context for a vast psychodrama, the hero (the basic "self") of which emerges as a poet in a constant state of "becoming," undergoing a tragic suffering as he seeks to create himself in the image of God: " 'Fac deum,' " sings Circe in Canto 47. " 'Est factus' / ver novum! / ver novum!'

/ Thus made the spring." Such is the ideal in a world in which spring can be only one season long and the poet, finally, only a man.

Although the Homeric-Ovidian world, such as is the setting of the first two cantos, was not ruled by the principle of social responsibility (Pound has so noted in *Guide to Kulchur*), it was in a sense ideal, both because the gods were manifest in the human world and were not mere Platonic abstractions, so that man and deity were intimately involved, and because the will to action and the sense of self-reliance took form and had scope within this context. Characteristic of Odysseus, with whom the poet is identified, is that he is at once a believer and a man of action—neither a pure abstractionist nor a disoriented man of will. His strength, then, comes not from his directing his own will against destiny (essential reality), but from his ability to obey the will of the gods or to survive when his crew has disregarded it. Typical, for example, is his willingness to visit Hades, as he is warned he must, a willingness that is no matter of course:

> "When the men had all come, I said to them, 'No doubt you think we are going straight home; but Circê has marked out another road for us, to the house of Hadês and awful Persephoneia.'
>
> "When I said this it fairly broke their [the crew's] hearts; they sat down where they were, and groaned and tore their hair. But it did them no good to lament." [30]

And one will recall, as another example, his refusal in the face of all pressure to allow his starving crew to kill Helios' cattle, because Tiresias had warned him against it.

What is important about the translation of the *Nekuia*, with which the *Cantos* begins, aside from any allegorical reading, is that it presents a vision of conformity to the rites and, thereby, of desired harmony with the forces of the universe. In quest of revelation, Odysseus has the strength to "beat off" his own mother who must not drink the sacrificial blood before Tiresias; and such strength, both of devotion and willpower, is essential to any man fated to cross dark seas "through spiteful Neptune." (This concern for the rites, incidentally, is part of the appeal of Confucian thought for Pound. I have argued elsewhere that Pound set out to translate the *Shih Ching*, the vast collection of Chou Dynasty songs and odes, because they concretely represented, in part, the devotional life of ancient China.[31] In the Confucian reading, these songs have a single moral theme: adherence to the rites is the principal manner of attuning oneself to the will of heaven. Performance of the rites actually began with the ruler, on whose self-cultivation and attunement with heaven the moral well-being of the society depended. By virtue of his position, the ruler exerted a moral force or "wind" that was benevolent when he performed the rites and achieved internal discipline, and malevolent when he did not. Thus in Chinese thought, as in Pound's, a dual moral responsibility, submission to the Way and exercise of one's own will in accordance with it, is incumbent upon the hero.)

But there are further possibilities in Pound's identification of the poet figure with Odysseus. Forrest Read, for example, has given the Homeric characters that appear in Canto 39 an almost allegorical significance:

> I would suggest [he writes] that Elpenor and Eurilochus embody alternatives Odysseus may choose as he stands before Circe, who tells him he must go to Hades to seek directions home from the shade Tiresias. Passive Elpenor (man-destroying passion) and aggressive Eurilochus (man-destroying intellect) are shown as aspects of Odysseus' own nature from whom he learns . . . to strike the middle way.[32]

Read goes on to develop the not-entirely-convincing thesis that the "structure of the *Cantos* is what the narrator sees, as Odysseus before him, in Hades." If approached in the same semiallegorical way that Read has approached Canto 39, Canto 1 suggests, primarily, the need of the poet to bury his alter ego, Mauberley, here represented by Elpenor, as part of his acquisition of the new role defined by Tiresias.

(Mauberley's epitaph, " 'I was / And I no more exist; / Here
drifted / An hedonist,' " is equally applicable to Elpenor who
has fallen off Circe's roof because of "ill fate and abundant
wine.")

Furthermore, Tiresias' prophecy itself—"Odysseus shall return over spiteful Neptune, over dark seas, / Lose all com-
panions"—is relevant to the fate of the poet insofar as it is
a foreshadowing of the idea of the periplus ("periplum") or
sea voyage associated with both the mysteries and the world
of action. Mentioned first in connection with the voyages of
exploration and foundation of the Carthaginian, Hanno, in
Canto 40, the term eventually takes on apocalyptic connotations, as in Canto 74:

> between NEKUIA where are Alcmene and Tyro
>   and the Charybdis of action
>   to the solitude of Mt. Taishan. . . .
> under the gray cliff in periplum[33]

I quote this passage out of context but it nonetheless suggests
the prophetic quest and the dire consequences of its under-
taking that the poet, as Odysseus, must endure. Nekuia is
revelation; history and action are violence; Taishan is the
final serenity beyond time, the psychological fulfillment of
the poet who has maintained vision despite his inability to
make it manifest. As expressed in the *Pisan Cantos,* of
which this quotation is a part, that vision involves faith
that resurrection of the ruined world (of Pound in particular,
and of society in general, at the end of World War II) will
be possible:

> [Odysseus]
> a man on whom the sun has gone down. . . .
> nor shall diamond die in the avalanche
>   be torn from its setting
> first must destroy himself ere others destroy him.
> 4 times was the city rebuilded, Hooo Fasa . . .
> now in the mind indestructible. . . .

As early as the adaptation of Hanno's voyages, the ideal was envisioned as being beyond the vicissitudes of periplum:

Their men clomb up the crags,
Rained stone, but we took three women [gorillas]
who bit, scratched. . . .
Killed, flayed, brought back their pelts into
    Carthage. . . .
Out of which things seeking an exit
To the high air, to the stratosphere, to the imperial
calm, to the empyrean, to the baily of the four towers
the NOUS, the ineffable crystal. . . .   (Canto 40)

In at least three other instances we learn that the sun makes a periplum, but this added dimension to the image is not wholly irrelevant. For example, in Canto 23, in a passage that is intended to represent Pound in the act of translating, painfully but precisely, the minor Greek poet Stesichorus, the setting sun is described as "going toward the low fords of ocean" to the "depth of black night" where he joins "his mother, his faithful wife, and his dear children." This periplum is reminiscent of Odysseus' and, as a matter of fact, Odysseus' feigned insanity is alluded to a few lines below ("The idiot / Odysseus furrowed in the sand"). One will recall that he feigned insanity by plowing the seashore precisely because he did not want to leave his family. It is true the sun meets his family *in* dark night, not by passing through dark night, as the poet-Odysseus explicitly does in the *Pisan Cantos* ("magna NUX animae"), but I don't think the association suffers because of it. Two other references to the sun's making a periplum appear in Canto 76: in the first, mythical and historical heroes appear to the poet and announce, "The sun in his great periplum / leads in his fleet here / . . . under our craggy cliffs"; in the second, we find "mouth, is the sun that is god's mouth / or in another connection (periplum)," and the Chinese character for mouth beside this statement. The former seems to be uttered in the same spirit as Tiresias' prophecy, a statement of the poet's fate that recalls the passage, quoted above, about passing through the Charybdis

of action "under the gray cliffs in periplum." The latter, with
its reference to "god's mouth," recalls the passage in Canto
74 about the "literary man" ("ouan jin"), identified with the
African rain god, Wanjina, and with the mouthless Aus-
tralian figures, or wondjina:[34]

> [Odysseus]
> "I am noman, my name is noman"
> But Wanjina is, shall we say, Ouan Jin
> or the man with an education
> And whose mouth was removed by his father
> > because he made too many *things*. . . .
> Ouan Jin spoke and thereby created the named
> > thereby making clutter
> the bane of men moving . . .
> > in principio verbum
> > paraclete or the verbum perfectum: sinceritas. . . .

That the poet speaks Logos (with the mouth of God), and
that his mouth is "removed" by a society that cannot abide
his Word (Sincerity) is, one need hardly repeat, the story of
the *Cantos* in general and the *Pisan Cantos* in particular:
the periplums of the sun, Odysseus, and the poet represent
the single periplum of tragedy. In the prophecy of Tiresias
that defines the struggles of Odysseus lies the indication of
the state of mind that the poet himself will finally reach:

> the sphere moving crystal, fluid,
> > none therein carrying rancour . . .
> πολλά παθεὶν [polla pathein]
> > nothing matters but the quality
> of the affection—
> in the end—that has carved the trace in the mind
> dove sta memoria   (Canto 76/35)

Polla pathein (according to the *Index*[35] "to experience or
suffer much," used in connection with Odysseus' sufferings

on the sea) has carved a trace in the poet's mind through
memory; yet it is this very memory that gives him a sense
of serenity, as a passage in Canto 74 would indicate:

> Serenely in the crystal jet
> > as the bright ball that the fountain tosses. . . .
> How soft the wind under Taishan
> > where the sea is remembered
> > out of hell, the pit
> > out of dust and glare evil.

The forecasting of Odysseus' fate and, by implication, the
fate of the poet, appears as early as Canto 2—that is, if one
can persuade himself to see in this section anything more
than the picture of a world of metamorphoses through which
gods mingle with human beings. The reference to Helen,
with whom "doom goes . . . in walking," is obvious enough,
and Tyro, depicted in the canto at the moment of union
with Poseidon, will tell her story to Odysseus in Hades. Both
these "ideograms" have, perhaps, a symbolic meaning, which
we shall look at presently, but the account of Dionysus'
revenge on the crew that unwittingly kidnapped him is particularly interesting in this respect. We find that only Acoetes,
the pilot who sensed the god's identity, is saved from being
changed into a fish:

> And I worship.
> I have seen what I have seen. . . .
> > And you, Pentheus,
> Had as well listen to Tiresias, and to Cadmus,
> > or your luck will go out of you.
> Fish scales over groin muscles.

In one sense, Acoetes is a persona of Odysseus, who, because
he does listen to Tiresias, and because he does worship, is the
one man who returns to Ithaca. Finally, the vision of tranquillity with which the canto concludes as it summarizes some
of the preceding action forecasts the arrival at Mt. Taishan
or Ithaca:

> Lithe turning of water,
>> sinews of Poseidon. . . .
>> glass wave over Tyro,
> Close cover, unstillness . . .
> Then quiet water . . .
>> pallor of Hesperus . . .
>> wave, colour of grape's pulp. . . .
>
> . . . .
> And we have heard the fauns chiding Proteus. . . .

The introduction of Helen, "destroyer of men, ships, and cities," even though she has the "face of a god," is part of the theme of the "dreadful" goddess that recurs throughout the *Cantos* and defines the tragic character of Odysseus' quest.[36] Aphrodite, "Cythera selva," who, in the poem, is clearly not just the goddess of love, represents the direful, apocalyptic nature of relations with deity in Odysseus' world and the direful, apocalyptic nature of the pursuit of order, truth, and beauty in Pound's. In particular, the demonic alter ego of Aphrodite is Circe, against whose "dreadful drugs" Odysseus must find protection in the herb "moly":

> To the cave art thou called, Odysseus,
> By Molü hast thou respite for a little,
> By Molü art thou freed from the one bed
>> that thou may'st return to another. . . .
>
> (Canto 47)

This passage appears in the canto on the fertility rites to Adonis and suggests that with moly the image of the malevolent Circe is, for Odysseus, transformed into that of the benevolent Aphrodite. Similarly in Canto 39, we find Circe demonic ("Lions loggy with Circe's tisane / Girls leery with Circe's tisane") and Circe apocalyptic ("Ad Orcum autem quisquam / . . . Been to hell in a boat yet?"). The lines from Catullus that follow are immediately relevant:

> Sumus in fide
> Puellaeque canamus
> sub nocte. . . .

(translated by the *Index:* "We have the protection . . . / . . .
and girls let us sing ((the praise of)) . . . / beneath the
night"). Protected by moly, Odysseus, rather than having to
enter the pigsty ("nec in harum ingressus sum"), finds himself in a relation with a goddess of love and fertility. Circe's
song, which originally attracted the crewmen to her house
("KALON AOIDIAEI," the beauty of her singing), becomes
associated, at the end of the canto, with a spring fertility
chant and bridal hymn, connected with the worship of
Jupiter, at Terracina or Circeo (Land of Circe):

> Unceasing the measure . . .
>   with the Goddess' eyes to seaward
> By Circeo, by Terracina. . . .
> With one measure, unceasing:
>   "Fac deum!" "Est factus."
> Ver novum!
>   ver novum!
> Thus made the spring. . . .

And in Canto 74, we find that the goddess with her "eyes to
seaward" is in fact Aphrodite, and Terracina somehow associated with her birth from the sea:

> as by Terracina rose from the sea Zephyr behind her
>   and from her manner of walking
>   as had Anchises . . .
>   till the stone eyes look again seaward. . . .

While perhaps recalling the union of Alcmene with Jupiter
("His rod hath made god in my belly"), the bridal song in
Canto 39 summons up a vision of union with deity in general,
of propagation, fertility, and renewal. The analogue to Odysseus' union with Circe-Aphrodite is that of Anchises and
Aphrodite, alluded to, significantly enough, in the context of
the rites of Adonis in Canto 23.[37] Anchises hears Greek
voices, lamenting the death of Adonis, coming from an
island (Cyprus?):

"Tet, tet...
   what is it?" said Anchises.
"Tethnéké," said the helmsmen, "I think they
"Are howling because Adonis died virgin."
"Huh! tet..." said Anchises,
   "well, they've made a bloody mess of that city."

There follows a vision of Anchises' own union with Aphrodite,
who lies about her background:

"King Otreus, of Phrygia,
"That king is my father."
            and saw then, as of waves taking form,
   As the sea, hard, a glitter of crystal,
   And the waves rising but formed, holding their form.
   No light reaching through them.

Union with deity, the apocalyptic moment, has, as its final
meaning, the creation of an ideal art out of divine inspiration.
The mythological analogues are not simply metaphors of this
act but lend it the connotations of mystery, divinity, and
fertility associated with the essential process of life:

   Form, forms and renewals, gods held in the air

   . . . .
   "as the sculptor sees the form in the air . . .
   "as glass seen under water,
   "King Otreus, my father...
   and saw the waves taking form as crystal. . . .
                                          (Canto 25/119)

   But to return to our original point, moly or the word of
Tiresias—talisman or revelation—is necessary to Odysseus and
to the poet. What is implied here, for the latter, is insight
into the tragic conditions of the struggle for efficacious poetic
expression and the "protection" against despair that such insight affords. It is because he did not have such protection
that Mauberley "drifted an hedonist," the spiritual hedonism
of fin de siècle aestheticism rendering him no less impotent
than actual hedonism. The proper attitude in the quest is
suggested by the motto in the chambers of Isabella d'Este,

Nec Spe Nec Metu ("Neither hope nor fear"), alluded to at
the end of Canto 2. The theme is taken up again in Canto 25
in the passage on Sulpicia, a Roman poetess, who, idealized
by Pound, tells her lover, "Pone metum / Metum nec deus
laudit," "Lay aside fear, / Nor does God praise fear." The
tragic attitude involves an appreciation of the dualistic nature
of the universe—that if the song of the sirens is "ligur"
(sharp and clear), as is the song of Circe, then so is the music
of Shun, "the sharp song with sun under its radiance," heard
by Confucius (Canto 74); that if the poet-revolutionary,
"tovarisch," is at one moment seen as springing eternally, in
sterility, from the seeds sown by Cadmus, as an armed soldier
(Canto 27), he is also capable of being seen as an Adonis,
sown fruitfully in the earth (Canto 47); finally, that if one
guise of Aphrodite is Circe, the other is Kuonon (Kuan Yin)
the Chinese goddess of mercy invoked in the *Pisan Cantos*.

The prevailing theme of the *Pisan Cantos* is that *"le
paradis n'est pas artificiel,"* a notion that, as employed by
Pound, represents a reassertion of belief in the Nature of
Greek mythology, all the stronger because of his personal
circumstances. Presided over by Gea and Kuan Yin, it is a
world in which mythological figures continue to express
themselves to the poet as ants, butterflies, katydids, and
spiders ("Arachne, che mi porta fortuna, go spin on that tent
rope"). Here, the talisman against despair is offered by Kuan
Yin:

> Kuanon, this stone bringeth sleep;
>   offered the wine bowl
>   grass nowhere out of place. . . .
>
> by thy herbs menthe thyme and basilicum,
>   from whom and to whom,
>   will never be more now than at present
> being given a new green katydid of a Sunday. . . .
>   (74/13)

The final union with deity is thus conceived of as the
"cunnubiam terrae," the poet's union with Earth (Gea) that

represents personal salvation in the midst of personal ruin:

> fluid ΧΘΟΝΟΣ o'erflowed me
> lay in the fluid ΧΘΟΝΟΣ:
>   that lie
> under the air's solidity
>   drunk with ΙΧΩΡ of ΧΘΟΝΙΟΣ
>   fluid ΧΘΟΝΟΣ strong as the undertow
>   of the wave receding. . . .   (82/104)

But the personal salvation here envisioned is neither permanent nor definitive; the poet continues to inhabit the human world and must thereby "live in that further terror," a terror, personal and symbolic, that he is fated to resist eternally in the endless periplum of the artistic mind.

9. T. S. ELIOT: FAC HOMINEM

The terms in which T. S. Eliot defined the ideal poetic process in one of his earliest and best known essays will not sound exotic to anyone acquainted with the anti-subjective rationale that provides the basis of aestheticist thought. The poet, we find, is engaged in a "continual surrender of himself as he is at the moment to something which is more valuable. The progress of an artist is a continual self-sacrifice, a continual extinction of personality. . . . It is in this depersonalization that art may be said to approach the condition of science."[1] In elaborating this conception, Eliot establishes the psychology that underlies much of his poetic:

> When the two gases previously mentioned are mixed in the presence of a filament of platinum, they form sulphurous acid. This combination takes place only if the platinum is present; nevertheless the newly formed acid contains no trace of platinum, and the platinum itself is apparently unaffected. . . . The mind of the poet is the shred of platinum. It may partly or exclusively operate upon the experience of the man himself; but, the more perfect the artist, the more completely separate in him will be the man who suffers and the mind which creates; the more perfectly will the mind digest and transmute the passions which are its material. . . .
>
> The poet's mind is in fact a receptacle for seizing and storing up numberless feelings, phrases, images, which remain there until all the particles which can unite to form a new compound are present together.[2]

The ironic detachment characteristic of Eliot's earlier poetry and its background in the work of Laforgue, Corbière, Gautier, and the symbolists, as well as the English metaphysical poets, has been discussed in detail by the critics. One can see clearly that ironic detachment is an attitude

appropriate to Eliot's theory of depersonalization, and, further, that it represents his solution to the same problem that
led to objectivism: the quest for a truth, a bare reality, un-
tainted by romantic or other sentimental feeling. Correspondingly, we find Eliot saying that poetry is not a "turning loose
of emotion, but an escape from emotion" by a man who has
emotions and knows what it means to want to escape from
them. Such escape is escape from the self into the "community," Eliot writes in another essay; "a common inheritance
and a common cause unite artists consciously or uncon-
sciously. . . . Between the true artists of any time there is, I
believe, an unconscious community." [3] Participation in this
community is made possible not only by the negative depersonalization but by the positive "historical sense," the notion
with which "Tradition and the Individual Talent" opens.
This sense "of the timeless as well as of the temporal and of
the timeless and of the temporal together, is what makes a
writer traditional," and, in effect, gives him the external allegiance "that men cannot get on without." If it is the mind as
"catalyst" that makes it possible for the poet to detach himself from his own chaotic feelings—or transform them into
something "rich and strange"—it is the mind as historical
sensibility that makes it possible for such transformed emotions to be of universal importance.

What is curious about this argument, aside from its relations to Eliot's technique and whatever accuracy it might
have as a general hypothesis, is its relevance to the moral
and psychological problems of the characters that constitute
Eliot's microcosm, a world in which, as in that of Stevens,
the central conflict really involves the ability of the mind to
resist an external pressure. It is now common knowledge that
Eliot was much taken by the Laforguian Pierrot, and the
ironic attitude of that clown, at the time he was writing
"Portrait of a Lady," "Prufrock," and "La Figlia." But one
must keep in mind that the "*dandy de la lune*" is basically
passive and wholly subject to lunar influences, seen in terms
of *Notre Dame*, the whimsical moon-lady. Accordingly, in an
early poem, Eliot, following Laforgue, actually conceives of

the pierrot as a "marionette." For all his sensitivity, the pierrot has no existence outside the lunar, and all his sharp comment to or about the Lady he is condemned to worship is evidence rather than denial of this fact.

It is precisely because of their passivity that Eliot's characters, like the lunar clowns, take their identity only from the world, the specific world, in which they find themselves. That is, like the effete clowns, they have a feminine sensitivity and are devoid of the active imagination that would make it possible for them to be more than the creatures of their environment, to assume a "masculine" or "creative" role and thereby acquire an authentic "identity." Speaking of "authentic identity," I am not certain that an existential vocabulary is entirely out of place in a consideration of the moral problems of Eliot's universe. Particularly pertinent is Sartre's idea that "we reach ourselves in the presence of others, and the others are just as real to us as our own selves"; "in order to get at any truth about myself," he writes, "I must have contact with another person. The other is as indispensable to my own existence, as well as to my knowledge about myself." [4] The definition of the internal by the external—realism—is also, as we recall, one of the distinguishing aspects of Stevens' world:

> I am what is around me
>
> Women understand this.
> One is not duchess
> A hundred yards from a carriage.   ("Theory")

Considered in moral rather than metaphysical terms, the problem becomes one of existence in Hell or in a lunar wasteland.

In his study of Eliot's sources and meaning, Grover Smith suggests that the debt is partly to Bergson, whom Eliot had been reading at the time. "The perceiver," he explains,

> by coming into contact with the material world, absorbs images into his consciousness, where they persist as memories. In the aggregate, memories thus form a *durée*, con-

sidered by Bergson to be creative, since . . . they affect the perception of things in the perceiver's future. Eliot's poem ["Rhapsody on a Windy Night"] . . . holds up to view a set of images so disagreeable . . . that an optimism like Bergson's must appear implausible. . . .[5]

Yet whether one accepts Bergson as an "influence" or not is really a matter of indifference. The important element in the first collection is the power of the object over the sensitive but passive mind, the power to determine the nature of that mind, the point being that all that sets the poetic sensibility apart from the world is the "awareness" of its own impotence and of the moral implications of that impotence.[6]

In "Rhapsody on a Windy Night," we are presented with the figure of the driven man whose mind *is* the wind that aimlessly blows through it the images of a sordid world, or the moon in whose light he must view the streets about him:

> Whispering lunar incantations
> Dissolve the floors of memory
> And all its clear relations
> Its divisions and precisions. . . .[7]

That is, the moon is destroying that part of the memory over which the speaker has rational control (conscious memory) and is summoning up the chaotic fragments of his unconscious, "As a madman shakes a dead geranium." Yet exactly what is his unconscious, if not a receptacle or mirror of the objects of a wasteland:

> The memory throws up high and dry
> A crowd of twisted things;
> A twisted branch upon the beach. . . .
> A broken spring in a factory yard. . . .

Similarly, the living things he remembers are but the images of himself—a child and a crab:

> I could see nothing behind that child's eye. . . .
> An old crab with barnacles on his back,
> Gripped the end of a stick which I held him.

He remembers what the moon remembers, and in the wasteland,

> The moon has lost her memory. . . .
> Her hand twists a paper rose. . . .
> The reminiscence comes
> Of sunless dry geraniums
> And dust in crevices . . .
> And female smells in shuttered rooms. . . .

The disintegration of the memory into a collection of fragments is the disintegration of a mind under the spell of a
"lunar incantation" by which a deadly external world pervades and redefines in its own image the internal world of
insufficient strength to resist it. Thus in "Preludes":

> You dozed, and watched the night revealing
> The thousand sordid images
> Of which your soul was constituted. . . .

In this kind of a world, existence does in fact precede essence.
The pierrot-like essence that the speaker does have, or fancies
himself to have, "some infinitely gentle / Infinitely suffering
thing," is mutilated and reshaped by the world:

> His soul stretched tight across the skies . . .
> Or trampled by insistent feet. . . .
> The conscience of a blackened street
> Impatient to assume the world.

The "Portrait of a Lady" is the portrait of a moon-lady,
one who twists lilac stalks as in "Rhapsody" she twisted a
paper rose and, along with it, the narrator's sensibility. The
power of the lady to derange the Prufrockian speaker or to
overwhelm what "self-possession" he is able to summon is,
one need hardly say, a recurrence in the genteel world of the
problem that confronted the poet in the common. There is a
double irony in her comment that Chopin's soul "Should be
resurrected only among friends . . . / who will not touch the
bloom / That is rubbed and questioned in the concert room."

The fate of Chopin, whether in the concert hall or drawing room, is the fate of Michelangelo and of Prufrock.

The speaker meets the smile of the Gioconda ("grown old") with the smile of Pierrot, and it is his only defense. Yet whatever his attempts at irony, he goes on drinking tea and continues to make his visits, for essentially his world is the sterile world she has created and he does not escape it by leaving her presence:

> You will see me any morning in the park
> Reading the comics and the sporting page.
> Particularly I remark
> An English countess goes upon the stage.
> A Greek was murdered at a Polish dance. . . .

We recall, too, that the lady and the speaker were brought together because "all were sure our feelings would relate / So closely." And, in a sense, the lady is right, except that the speaker has the sensitivity to appreciate the worth of those feelings even if he is powerless to escape from them. Similarly, his identity is the identity of Proteus, that of a man who must prepare a face to meet the faces that he meets—the *face* that he meets:

> And I must borrow every changing shape
> To find expression . . . dance, dance
> Like a dancing bear,
> Cry like a parrot, chatter like an ape.

The final irony of his situation is that even the death of the lady will not release him from himself; for if she should die, he would merely be left

> Not knowing what to feel or if I understand
> Or whether wise or foolish, tardy or too soon . . .
> Would she not have the advantage, after all. . . .
> And should I have the right to smile?

In the Prufrockian world, the women in fact have the ability to murder and create, as we already know well enough:

>The eyes that fix you in a formulated phrase,
>And when I am formulated, sprawling on a pin,
>When I am pinned and wriggling on the wall,
>Then how should I begin
>To spit out all the butt-ends of my days and ways?
>   And how should I presume?

When one has only the butt-ends of days and ways to spit out, how should one presume indeed?

In her role as "the eternal humorist, / The eternal enemy of the absolute," the lady of the moon is the antimuse who renders the poet impotent and allows him to express only the "music which we seize to body forth our own vacuity" ("Conversation Galante"). The final lines of this poem summarize the entire Prufrockian problem:

>Giving our vagrant moods the slightest twist!
>With your air indifferent and imperious
>At a stroke our mad poetics to confute. . . .

Poems like "The *Boston Evening Transcript*," "Aunt Helen," and even the symbolistic "Hysteria" adhere to the same logic as that characterizing the longer works. The narrator might make an implied judgment:

>The readers of the *Boston Evening Transcript*
>Sway in the wind like a field of ripe corn.

But he, too, is a man who mounts the steps to the lady's house "on hands and knees," himself a reader of the comics and sporting page, himself a man swaying in the wind:

>I mount the steps and ring the bell, turning
>Wearily . . .
>And I say, "Cousin Harriet, here is the *Boston Evening
>   Transcript*."

The automatic response, uttered wearily, is the definition of an entire mind and an entire world. Similarly, the one striking image of "Hysteria" is that of the speaker being devoured by the laughter of the lady: "I was drawn in by short gasps, inhaled at each momentary recovery, lost finally in the dark caverns of her throat, bruised by the ripple of unseen muscles." Smith asserts that the man, rather than the woman, is hysterical and cites the concluding lines in evidence: "I decided that if the shaking of her breasts could be stopped, some of the fragments of the afternoon might be collected, and I concentrated my attention with careful subtlety to this end." Smith, I think, is right if one remembers that the hysteria is like that of the pierrot who musters all his sophisticated irony to protect himself against the moon-lady. On the other hand, the fragments of the afternoon that he is trying to collect are, again, the fragments of his own soul, and the only way they can be collected is through an effort at a self-possession that can be fragile at best.

Only in this context does the laughter of a "Mr. Apollinax" become wholly meaningful, a laughter that contrasts with the hysteria of the lady and the smile, which "falls heavily among the bric-a-brac," of "Prufrock." Significantly, he is referred to in the epigraph of the poem to which he lends his name as a "novelty," and that is precisely what he is in the genteel world. Conversely, one might ask what it takes to be novel, and therefore independent, in Prufrock's world:

> In the palace of Mrs. Phlaccus, at Professor Channing-
> Cheetah's
> He laughed like an irresponsible foetus.
> His laughter was submarine and profound
> Like the old man of the sea's. . . .
> I looked for the head of Mr. Apollinax rolling under a
> chair. . . .

Smith notes that the poem depicts Bertrand Russell, but adds that the subject is mythologized to the point of absurdity.[8] This, it seems to me, is exactly Eliot's point, for only the absurd, nonhuman figure is proof against the world represented by Mrs. Phlaccus, proof because he cannot be "formulated" by them:

"He is a charming man"—"But after all what did he
    mean?"—
"His pointed ears. . . . He must be unbalanced."

But it is in "La Figlia Che Piange," despite its apparent
thematic deviation from the poetry that precedes it in the
collection, that we find a response to the Prufrockian problem. To again cite Smith, a plausible view of this poem is
the identification of the speaker with the lover under the
assumption that he is imagining a leave-taking with "la
figlia." [9] On the other hand, what seems to be most striking
about the piece is the speaker's assertion of an aesthetic
element over all other elements—specifically, the emotional
distress—inherent in the scene. For the speaker, all that
really matters is the "gesture and pose" of the weeping girl,
not her feelings:

Clasp your flowers to you with a pained surprise—
Fling them to the ground and turn
With a fugitive resentment in your eyes:
But weave, weave the sunlight in your hair.

The irony is that it is the very grief of the girl that gives her
the pose appreciated by the speaker:

Her hair over her arms and her arms full of flowers.
And I wonder how they should have been together!
I should have lost a gesture and a pose.

Whether or not the speaker is distinct from the lover, I am
not prepared to argue; in any event, he is attempting to
"escape from emotion"—either his own directly or his sympathy for the girl's—into an artistic, or imagistic, realm. For
the poetic sensibility in Eliot's world, the aesthetic moment,
divested of all conventional emotion and placed beyond introspection, is the only possible escape from a vapid environment, and, interestingly enough, even this form of response
is passive. That he can see beauty in a distressing scene indicates a detachment that disturbs the speaker himself and

gives rise to cogitations that "still amaze / The troubled midnight and the noon's repose."

"Gerontion," which appeared in the 1920 collection, represents the final extension of the passive but aware mind, the "dull head among windy spaces" controlled not merely by physical images of a wasteland, but by historical and religious fragments that it can neither unify nor comprehend. The old man is aware that, in the Prufrockian world, "Christ the tiger" (as Prufrock himself) is devoured not so much as a eucharist perhaps but in the same fashion that a Michelangelo is "devoured" by tea-drinking women:

> To be eaten, to be divided, to be drunk
> Among whispers; by Mr. Silvero
> With caressing hands. . . .
>
> By Hakagawa, bowing among the Titians;
> By Madame de Tornquist. . . .

Similarly, as the speaker in "Rhapsody on a Windy Night," the old man has no real memory, if only for the reason that he has no history that can be meaningful to him; "I have no ghosts," he says, and after "such knowledge," such awareness, "what forgiveness," salvation, is possible? His statement on the meaninglessness of history is merely a generalization from his own biography, just as his biography is a recapitulation of history. Ironically, the old man seems to be carrying out Prufrock's perpetual dialogue with a woman, in the endless attempt of the sensitive mind to explain its paralysis:

> I would meet you upon this honestly.
> I that was near your heart was removed therefrom
> To lose beauty in terror, terror in inquisition.
> I have lost my passion. . . .
> I have lost my sight, smell, hearing, taste and touch:
> How should I use them for your closer contact?

It is also possible that he is speaking to a Christ who has become a devourer himself—who has become, in fact, the women who have eaten him. In any event, the old man, in-

habiting a windy house and a windy world, cannot contemplate but with a windy mind:

> De Bailhache, Fresca, Mrs. Cammel, whirled
> Beyond the circuit of the shuddering Bear
> In fractured atoms. . . .
> > an old man driven by the Trades
> To a sleepy corner.

To return to Eliot's poetic and the genesis of this discussion: the argument that the poet's mind is a receptacle for
seizing and storing feelings, that it is a "catalyst," that the
poet himself is engaged in a process of depersonalization, an
attempt to escape from emotions ("by a man who has emotions and knows what it means to want to escape from
them") is, in a sense, the description of a Prufrock who has
succeeded. In effect, the only difference between Eliot's
description of the poet in "Tradition and the Individual
Talent" and the characters in his universe is that the true
poet is in possession of a strip of platinum (whatever that
platinum stands for), and, second, that he dwells in an ideal
environment constituted by the "tradition" and the "community" of writers rather than in a purely windy, history-less
realm governed by moon-ladies. The external maintains its
priority in both worlds. That is why it is not surprising to
find Eliot saying some five years before his conversion,
"Those of us who find ourselves supporting what Mr. [John
Middleton] Murry calls Classicism believe that men cannot
get on without giving allegiance to something outside themselves." [10] And correspondingly he expresses suspicion of the
"inner voice"; "Those of us who are Inner Deaf Mutes are,
however, sometimes compensated by a humble conscience,
which, though without oracular expertness, counsels us to do
the best we can. . . ." [11] It is true that Eliot is talking about
the responsibilities of the critic here, but such comments are
wholly applicable to the poet and to man in general. Neither
is it surprising to find Eliot making the characteristically
objectivist remark that a "critic must have a very highly developed sense of fact," the complete development of which

represents "the very pinnacle of civilization." All that I have
been trying to demonstrate here is that Eliot's orientation
was, in essence, similar to that of his more explicitly aestheticist contemporaries and that his subsequent attempts to write
"epic" poetry proceeded from a similar epistemological background, specific differences in attitudes, feelings, and techniques notwithstanding.

2

Hugh Kenner has read Eliot's note on Tiresias, "the most
important personage" in *The Waste Land,* as "an after-
thought, a token placation of . . . the ghost of Bradley."
Although Kenner draws the refreshing conclusion that "we
shall do well to discard the notes as much as possible" and
that the intention of the poem is "graspable without source-
hunting," [12] it is precisely the conception of Tiresias as a
single "important personage" fragmented into many personages that is one of the chief points of continuity between
the moral epistemology of *The Waste Land* and the earlier
poems. Thus while I find myself out of sympathy with the
"source-hunting" and the labored attempts to establish specific identities that mark Grover Smith's study, I agree with
the general conclusion that behind the many characters there
lies one personality struggling to attain salvation, and that
his failure is owing, in large part, to himself. Tiresias is never
really manifest because his identity is determined by the
characters that exist around him. What distinguishes him
from the rest of his world—as what distinguishes Prufrock—
is an "awareness" of his condition, one that leads to restless-
ness, fear, and a desire to talk without having the words to
do so. The real meaning of salvation for the poet figure in
The Waste Land, no less than for Prufrock, is the attainment of a genuine "self," one that is not subject to the
aimless winds that have "determined" the passive sensibilities of Prufrock and Gerontion. The embodiment in myth of
poetic awareness, the possibilities of the imagination, is a
Parsifal whose Holy Grail and cure for the Fisher King, repre-

senting sterility shared with a world, is the key to selfhood, the positive sensibility that ideally is able to transcend its environment through the directives, Give, Sympathize, Control. And with selfhood comes the cure for poetic aphasia, wherein lies personal fulfillment and social redemption. In short, the desired transformation of Tiresias from a Hollow Man into a Prophet, from voiceless or cacophony-voiced poet into annunciator of the Word, is the central issue that gives meaning to all the other sterility-fertility symbolism in the poem.

Considered in terms of Bradley's theory of "psychic totality" (a possibility that Hugh Kenner, in his comments on Bradley and Eliot, does not pursue),[13] the various characters of *The Waste Land*, conversely, take meaning as extensions of the poet. Smith says, for example, that the image of Marie remembering her childhood is a memory of Tiresias and that the two memories are involved. I agree, but the matter can be stated more distinctly. For, in effect, Marie's experience as an obviously restless and neurasthenic adult who has a fragmentary recollection of an intense childhood moment, the real meaning of which neither she nor the reader is able to grasp, is the experience of Tiresias, who "mixes memory and desire," but, like Gerontion, is unable to reconstruct a past and therefore must inhabit a windblown present. Because Tiresias' memory (consciousness) is only a "heap of broken images" (as Marie's recollections of a childhood moment), the poetry he would create is broken as, in fact, the form of *The Waste Land* suggests. The brokenness of poetic utterance, in its turn, is a manifestation of the loss of God.

Concerning the hyacinth-garden episode, Smith argues that the girl is a "grail-bearer" and that "Tiresias as the quester has omitted to ask the indispensable question of the Grail initiation"—he has merely "stood agape while she, bearing the sexual symbol . . . has awaited the word he cannot utter." [14] Cleanth Brooks, on the other hand, sees the experience as "the ecstasy of love." [15] That the passage has been interpreted as a moment of failure by some critics and as an ideal moment by others attests to its fragmentary and ambiguous character. And the ambiguity is really unresolvable, as is that in the Marie episode. The child's moment on a toboggan, the lover's moment after a visit to a garden, are moments out of time that the dissociated sensibility cannot reconcile with life in time, a mixture of memory and desire, a "handful of dust," a "heap of broken images" that results only in "fear." [16]

To continue this line of reasoning, the spectacle of Madame Sosotris' telling the poet his fortune finally reduces itself to the poet's trying to forecast his own fate. If Tiresias is unable to apprehend his past, he is no more able to comprehend his future, or to answer the central question of the poem: will rebirth follow death, will the dismembered god be reintegrated, will cacophony become the Word? Thus, in a sense, the tarot cards are themselves no better than a heap of broken images, since the one card (The Hanged Man) is missing that will explain all the other cards in the poet's life, the Phoenician Sailor (commerce), Belladonna, the lady of situations (the women of Prufrock), the Wheel (of "fortune," aimlessness, people "walking round in a ring"), the one-eyed merchant (Eugenides, the Phoenician Sailor, again). Each of these cards has an "apocalyptic" as well as a "demonic" face: the Sailor may be transformed into a Ferdinand or an Alphonso who undergoes rebirth into "something rich and strange," Belladonna may be transformed into Mary, and the Wheel may contain a still point at its center. But the problem is that Tiresias cannot tell which side will apply to his own fate, and even after hearing what the thunder said, he remains uncertain of his role: "I sat upon the shore / Fishing, with the arid plain behind me / Shall I at least set my lands in order?" Madame Sosostris in fact identifies the Phoenician Sailor with Alphonso ("Those are pearls that were his eyes. Look!") but the "Death By Water" section, another ambiguous prophecy, is as pessimistic as it is potentially optimistic: "O you who turn the wheel and look to windward, / Consider Phlebas, who was once handsome and tall as you."

Concerning the theme of sexual violation, Smith notes that

"the real victim is the quester . . . it is he who has been silenced and . . . spiritually mutilated. He is both Tereus and Philomel and she is a projection of his suffering upon the people of the waste land." [17] I am not certain I understand what Smith means by his last sentence, but I think his identification of Tereus and Philomel in the figure of Tiresias is a key point. That the poet has had his tongue cut out by a world in which he had a part is clear enough; similarly the violation of all the women in *The Waste Land* involves not simply lust, on the literal level, but the destruction of poetic communication, on the symbolic. Tiresias is the typist as much as he is the "young man carbuncular"; he is similarly the Thames maidens, who in their modern version of "Weialala" sing "jug, jug to dirty ears." Like Tiresias, the maidens are silent:

> "After the event
> He wept. He promised 'a new start.'
> I made no comment. What should I resent?"

Or else they can make nothing of their experience (as the poet cannot comprehend his own):

> "On Margate Sands.
> I can connect
> Nothing with nothing.
> The broken fingernails of dirty hands."

Accordingly, in "The Game of Chess," Tereus is transformed into the lady of situations who demands expression from a husband (or better consort) whom she has emasculated in characteristic Prufrockian style: "Speak to me. Why do you never speak. Speak. / 'What are you thinking of? What thinking? What?'" The answer provided is that of the Fisher King, not of Parsifal: "I think we are in rats' alley / Where the dead men lost their bones." And to the question, "Is there nothing in your head?," the reply is a demonic ragtime song from a poet whose headpiece is filled with straw. What seems to have taken place in the first part of "A Game of Chess," as implied in the Prufrock poems, is a characteristic

reversal of sexual roles in which the woman becomes the
jaded aggressor and the man the passive "violated" eunuch.
In the pub sequence, which occupies the second part of the
poem, it seems clear that we are not simply being presented
with the misfortunes of Lil and Albert (as Smith observes)
but with a specific betrayal, that by the narrator who has
seduced Albert and is now about to relate the affair:

> He's been in the army four years, he wants a good
>   time,
> And if you don't give it him, there's others will, I
>   said.
> Oh is there she said. Something o' that, I said.
> Then I'll know who to thank, she said, and give me a
>   straight look.

Lil, like Philomel, is the victim of a world in which lust
prevails; kept in perpetual pregnancy by her husband, she is
forced into abortion, and, having thereupon lost her appeal,
is betrayed by her calloused friend: "Well, if Albert won't
leave you alone, there it is, I said, / What you get married for
if you don't want children?" But the final irony of this section is that the episode should be related at all in the spirit
of a boast and with full insensitivity of the narrator to its
moral implications. For if Tiresias is Lil (Philomel) he is
also the narrator (Tereus), who can "connect nothing with
nothing."

The confusion of the sexes, both literal and symbolic, in
Tiresias, all the more supports the idea that the action of
The Waste Land is for the most part a kind of psychodrama
in which the poet, if he is in quest of anything, is in quest
of a soul. Even as late as the final section we find restated
the overwhelming question, at once in the context of the
journey to Emmaus and of the Shackleton expedition to the
North Pole:

> Who is the third who walks always beside you . . .
> I do not know whether a man or a woman
> —But who is that on the other side of you?

What is particularly prophetic about this passage is the implication that if the poet can recognize Christ, he can recognize himself. The final image of the woman is associated with the landscape on the approach to the Chapel Perilous, but in terms of the poem itself it represents the ultimate emptiness of the poet's mind, the failure of his memory, and the degeneration of his speech:

> A woman drew her long black hair out tight
> And fiddled whisper music on those strings . . .
> And upside down in air were towers
> Tolling reminiscent bells, that kept the hours
> And voices singing out of empty cisterns and exhausted
>   wells.

And the chapel itself, like the mind of Gerontion and Tiresias, is "empty, only the wind's home."

There is nothing in the experience of Tiresias to suggest that he is in fact capable of transcending the conditions of life in a wasteland. Implicit in "Gerontion" and explicit in "Ash-Wednesday" and "Burnt Norton" is the thesis that reason alone leads only to rationalization and that the merely rational man cannot escape the monotony and meaninglessness of life in time. That rain should finally come to the Waste Land and a kind of logos be revealed is, in a sense, gratuitous—or, better, an act of grace. But what is as important as the existence of an Answer is the ability of the poet to apprehend it when it is revealed to him. The problem is whether the words of the Thunder, *Datta, Dayadvham, Damyata*, do not then remain Sanskrit, an incomprehensible manifestation akin to the intense but incomprehensible visions of mermaids, hyacinths, church ornaments, and rose gardens. For the pre-Christian Tiresias, speaking for the pre-Christian Eliot, the revelation seems to be merely an ideal but confusing imperative, a heap of broken images to shore against a heap of broken images. In the *Quartets* the poet continues to live "among the breakage" and only periodically experiences aesthetic moments, but a Christian path, involving faith, love, and purification, gives his life *a* meaning, if not the *full* meaning that he seeks. In *The Waste Land,* revelation is merely an "aethereal rumour" and the poet a broken, disoriented man only momentarily revived, essentially a madman shaking a dead geranium, a figure "breeding lilacs out of the dead land." In the *Quartets,* revelation becomes the incarnate Word and the poet a penitent seeking to unstop his ears.

3

In contrasting John Donne with Lancelot Andrewes, Bishop of Winchester under Elizabeth, Eliot wrote,

> Donne is a 'personality' in a sense in which Andrewes is not: his sermons, one feels, are a 'means of self-expression.' He is constantly finding an object which will be adequate to his feelings; Andrewes is wholly absorbed in the object and therefore responds with the adequate emotion. Andrewes has *goût pour la vie spirituelle,* which is not native to Donne.[18]

That the terms of this contrast are not arbitrary but spring from a poetic and a theory of consciousness will be apparent, again, to anyone familiar with "Tradition and the Individual Talent." Since, for Eliot, "personality" was synonymous with romantic egoism and the doctrine of inner light by which it justified itself, "depersonalization," the continual self-surrender to "something more valuable," was the mode of the ideal poet. Absorption in the object represented a detachment from self that was the sole means to precision and objective creativity. Hence Andrewes is depicted as being at once a more devout believer (for being primarily concerned with the object of belief, not with his own feelings in regard to it) and more creative (for the resulting precision of which he was capable). Raised to a mystical level with the aid of the vision of St. John of the Cross, the theory of depersonalization, as applied to both believer and poet, provides the philosophical and moral basis of the *Four Quartets.*[19]

It is not surprising to find in the writings of St. John of

the Cross the conception of the mind as a tabula rasa and
the belief that detachment from self means detachment from
the worldly objects to which the mind, through desire, is
enslaved. The ideal mental state, preparatory to union of
the soul with God, the ultimate Object (one might say),
was absolute emptiness; devoid of volition and affection, the
soul found "its only support in dark faith." One can appreciate the appeal, both emotional and logical, that this
argument would have for the creator of the passive Prufrock
and the "active" Sweeney, one restless in the sense of psychological enslavement by the superficial women that define
his world, the other insensitive in his lust. In a world in
which the external defines the internal, salvation, if possible,
lies precisely in emanant deity: the difference between Prufrockian depersonalization and ideal depersonalization is a
matter of the object to which the self has surrendered and
the demands made upon the self in the course of its surrender. In the former, such surrender is a matter of impotence; in the latter, extreme discipline; in one, the suffering is sterile, in the other, redemptive. The burden of the
Quartets is to endow the sensitive man with an authentic
being (apparent beinglessness, selflessness in God) while
purging him of apparent being (actual beinglessness, determination by worldly objects). To use Eliot's chief metaphor,
the goal is to transcend the wind, to reach the eye of the
hurricane, to find the still point of the turning world. From
a psychological point of view, it is to achieve the serenity of
Atlantis and Mt. Taishan.

In connection with the ontological problem, the *Quartets*
is concerned with three other interrelated questions: the
metaphysical problem of time, the epistemological problem
of knowledge, and the moral problem of salvation. We have
already seen that these problems were no less the concern
of Crane, Pound, and Williams, who attempted to provide
their own non-Christian solutions. Similarly, the formal characteristics of Eliot's vision are identical to those apparent in
The Bridge, the *Cantos*, and *Paterson*. Crucial in Eliot is
not merely that a distinction exists between time and eternity,

but that the ideal is the "intersection" of the two.[20] That is, chronos is man's fate; in the quest for union with deity, man retains his own nature:

> only in time can the moment in the rose-garden . . .
> Be remembered; involved with the past and the future.
> Only through time time is conquered.   ("Burnt Norton")

What is noteworthy about this conception, aside from its specifically Christian assumptions, is that it is part of the antiromantic bias of the objectivist position. Accordingly, its implications are felt both in the epistemological and moral problems. If only through time, time is conquered, what are the modes available in time for achieving this goal? Knowledge derived from experience through reason is mere knowledge in chronos that "imposes a pattern, and falsifies," leaving men "on the edge of a grimpen, where is no secure foothold, / And menaced by monsters, fancy lights. . . ." This is the secular knowledge of Gerontion and the speaker in "East Coker," who returns to his ancestral home only to have a vision of the endless cycle of life and death. The past is "unredeemable," for men live in a present that allows but "little consciousness" and, conversely, men live in such a present because they cannot redeem the past:

> Distracted from distraction by distraction
> Filled with fancies and empty of meaning
> Tumid apathy with no concentration
> Men and bits of paper, whirled by the cold wind
> That blows before and after time. . . .
>
>   ("Burnt Norton")

The ultimate release from chronos, achievable by man living in chronos, is "an occupation for the saint," and involves "cleansing the affection from the temporal," a "life-time's death in love, / Ardour and selflessness and self-sur-render." The knowledge of the saint, we learn from John of the Cross, begins in discursive meditation and ends in what is called infused contemplation, the final concentration upon God. One is reminded here of the passage from Richard of

St. Victor on the "gradation of processes," quoted by Pound
in *The Guide to Kulchur*: "(1) the aimless flitting of the
mind, (2) the systematic circling around the object, (3)
contemplation, the identification of the consciousness WITH
the object." [21] Central to Eliot, as to Pound, is the "gradation of process," which precludes mere flight from reality
and provides for the "intersection" of human meditation
and divine grace. For Eliot and John of the Cross, man is
obliged to pursue discursive meditation until it is exhausted,
the moment of its exhaustion bringing despair yet also sig-
naling the readiness of the penitent to pass to a higher
spiritual state. Motivated by its love for God (*eros*), the
soul ascends to the best of its ability; on the other hand, its
elevation is finally made possible by God's love (*agape*). In
this Christian version of the tragic principle in the neo-epic
in general, fulfillment depends, therefore, upon one's capacity
to suffer, as measured by the profundity of faith, and upon
divine grace. To undergo the Dark Night, without which
knowledge and salvation are impossible, one yields oneself up
to Christ the surgeon, "to be redeemed from fire [of worldly
passion] by fire [of purgation]":

> Who then devised the torment? Love.
> Love is the unfamiliar Name
> Behind the hands that wove
> The intolerable shirt of flame
> Which human power cannot remove.
>
> ("Little Gidding")

The point, however, is that knowledge of God conditions
knowledge in time. If man ascends to God by repudiating
the demands of the flesh, God descends to man through
Incarnation. The appearance of the Logos in history, of *kairos*
in chronos, is the intersection of the divine with the human.
In such a context, the "timeless moment" becomes not mere
contingency, as in *The Waste Land*, but is envisioned as
part of a "pattern." "History may be servitude, / History may
be freedom." In the former, the pattern is imposed by mere
reason and "confirms a prison"; in the latter, memory is used

> For liberation—not less of love but expanding
> Of love beyond desire, and so liberation
> From the future as well as the past. . . .
>
> ("Little Gidding")

Both the secular man and the saint live in an eternal present,
but whereas the one is surrounded by the gloom of a time-
kept city, the other is invested with the "invisible Light" of
God (*The Rock*) or redemptive Darkness; for the one, the
present allows little consciousness; for the other, for whom
it contains eternity, it allows ultimate consciousness.

The chief concern of the *Quartets* is with the poet, who
cannot remain secular but does not have the capacity to become a saint:

> For most of us, there is only the unattended
> Moment, the moment in and out of time,
> The distraction fit, lost in a shaft of sunlight . . .
>   music heard so deeply
> That it is not heard at all, but you are the music
> While the music lasts.   ("The Dry Salvages")

The sequence concludes:

> And right action is freedom
> From past and future also.
> For most of us, this is the aim
> Never here to be realised;
> Who are only undefeated
> Because we have gone on trying. . . .

Until he can emulate the saint, all that is possible to the
poet is the aesthetic moment, the vision of the rose garden
that he must quickly leave because he "cannot bear very
much reality"—not the ultimate "zero summer," but "mid-
winter spring," a "shaft of sunlight" amid the frost of
chronos. And if he lives with such moments, he also lives
with the "moments of agony" that mark his condemnation
to life in time and the "primitive terror" of his original sin:

> the agony abides.
> Time the destroyer is time the preserver,
> Like the river with its cargo of dead Negroes. . . .
> The bitter apple and the bite in the apple.
>
> ("The Dry Salvages")

Hence, the advice of Krishna to "fare forward" ("And do not think of the fruits of action") is the only meaningful advice the poet, a fisherman with "years of living among the breakage," can follow. (It is also the only advice meaningful to Faust, Odysseus, and Paterson.)

The struggle for apprehension of the Word has its counterpart, as most critics of the *Quartets* have realized, in the struggle of the poet for articulation, poetic precision. Again, what is available is the ideal; just as there is no hope of perfectly emulating the saint, so there is no hope of perfectly emulating the great writer:

> And what there is to conquer
> By strength and submission, has already been
>   discovered
> Once or twice, or several times, by men whom one
>   cannot hope
> To emulate—but there is no competition—
> There is only the fight to recover what has been lost
> And found and lost again and again. . . .
>
> ("East Coker")

Even though "Little Gidding," the last quartet, concludes with a passage in which spiritual and poetic salvation is imagined, one can hardly say that the quest is completed; indeed, after a vision of ideal articulation, the poet announces, "We shall not cease from exploration." But what is definitive is the optimistic assertion, "All shall be well," an explicit avowal of the assumption that lies beneath the imperative, "Fare forward."

To state the obvious, the musical analogy, cited by the title and apparent in the form, is wholly relevant to the theme. Insofar as "only by form, the pattern, / Can words or

music reach the stillness," the quartet mode into which the
words of the poet are shaped suggests at least an approach
to the "meaning" fated always to be missed. The title of
the sequence itself represents an act of affirmation.

The vision of an ultimate metaphysical unity, a pattern
larger than the self that gives the self an authentic identity,
has, we find in Eliot's essays, a social and cultural counterpart. The idea of a Christian society is, in effect, the ideal
of a unified Christian milieu, an order that contrasts with
the social fragmentation that Eliot associates with democratic
liberalism. Speaking of the "Community of Christians," the
articulate element of the ideal society, Eliot writes:

> It will be their identity of belief and aspiration, their
> background of a common system of education and a com-
> mon culture, which will enable them to influence and be
> influenced by each other, and collectively to form the
> conscious mind and the conscience of the nation.[22]

In *Four Quartets*, "the detail of the pattern is movement";
the boarhound pursues the boar, but pursuit is "reconciled
among the stars." In the social universe, "a constant struggle
between the centripetal and the centrifugal forces is desirable. . . . Christendom should be one. . . . But within that
unity there should be an endless conflict of ideas." [23] In an
ordered society, the turning world has a still point; in a dis-
organized society, the turning world is merely the turning
world.

Characteristically, Eliot provides an ideal and, as he says,
not a blueprint. As in the *Quartets*, the issue is not so much
the achievement of the ideal as it is the recognition of the
need to achieve one. "We have to remember that the Kingdom of Christ on earth will never be realised . . . that whatever reform or revolution we carry out will always be a sordid
travesty of what human society should be." He cites with
approval a statement that concludes:

> Realistically viewed the task [of constructing a Christian
> society] is so far beyond the present capacity of our British

Christianity that I write as a fool. But if the will were there, I believe that the first steps to be taken are fairly clear. The presupposition of all else, however, is the recognition that nothing short of a really heroic effort will avail to save mankind from its present evils. . . .[24]

Again, as in the *Quartets*, the ideal is unrealizable; what saves men, at least in part, is their *will* to realize it, along with "the grace of God without which human operations are vain." If the Kingdom of Christ on earth will never be realized, "it is always being realised," and "the world is never left wholly without glory." Salvation for the mystic and for the Christian man in society begins in the faith in salvation and with the "heroic effort" to achieve it.

10. POSTSCRIPT: CHARLES OLSON AND ROBERT DUNCAN; THE MYSTIQUE OF SPEECH AND RHYTHM

In an essay called "The Poem as a Field of Action" Williams argued that, in a relativist world, "the only reality we can know is MEASURE." The poet must seek "a new measure or a new way of measuring that will be commensurate with the social economic world in which we are living as contrasted with the past. It is in many ways a different world from the past calling for a different measure." Thus Williams tries to relate metric to the "reality" defined by modern science:

> . . . we as loose, dissociated (linguistically), yawping speakers of a new language, are privileged . . . to sense and so to seek to discover that possible thing which is disturbing the metrical table of values—as unknown elements would disturb Mendelyeev's [sic] table of the periodicity of atomic weights and so lead to discoveries.[1]

The point of this argument is that such "discoveries" arise from "speech." "It is there in the mouths of the living, that the language is changing and giving new means for expanded possibilities in literary expression and, I add, basic structure —the most important of all." What Williams means by "structure" is implied in "Against the Weather," in which it is argued that "a work of art is important only as evidence, in its structure, of a new world which it has been created to affirm. . . . A life that is here and now is timeless. That is the universal I am seeking: to embody that in a work of art, a new world that is always 'real.' " In other words, as a so-called field of action, the poem is a verbal equivalent of a "sensual reality," its measure (structure) establishing the equivalence.

This statement represents what might be considered the prosodic version of the idealization of language: a "rhythm mystique" that is comparable to the mystique of perception, the belief in the power of language to create "phrase objects" through visual image or, again, provide a vision of essential reality. Pound, whose theory of the ideogram is perhaps the most explicit formulation of the perception mystique, is no less preoccupied with metric, not simply as an attribute of poetry, but as the determining element. Thus he argues, in "A Retrospect,"

> I am constantly contending that it took two centuries of Provence and one of Tuscany to develop the media of Dante's masterwork, that it took the latinists of the Renaissance, and the Pleiade, and his own age of painted speech to prepare Shakespeare his tools. It is tremendously important that great poetry be written, it makes no jot of difference who writes it. The experimental demonstrations of one man may save the time of many. . . .[2]

While there is scarcely anything mystical in this argument, there is at least an assumption that poetry is almost wholly a function of metric and that personal elements are manifested in an "absolute rhythm" by which a man's "sincerity" can be tested.

With all its whimsies, obscurities, and affectations, Charles Olson's essay, "Projective Verse," a characteristic statement of the avant-garde of the fifties, apparently had enough meaning to Williams for him to include a part of it in his autobiography, and for good reason. Olson's pseudoscience, his notion of the poem as a "high-energy construct" and an "energy-discharge" is, considered in the light of some of Williams' metaphors, not really bizarre. More important than the metaphor, however, is its signification, for by energy

Olson means "speech-force," and, at the outset, he argues that if poetry is to be of "use," it must "catch up and put itself into certain laws and possibilities of the breath, of the breathing of the man who writes as well as of his listenings." [3] We are told that "breath is man's special qualification as an animal. Sound is a dimension he has extended. Language is one of his proudest acts." This notion is but part of a larger view of reality, one that is sufficiently objectivistic for Olson to call "Objectism." As in objectivism itself, the first principle is a denial of romantic egoism, "the getting rid of the lyrical interference of the individual as ego, of the subject and his soul," for the soul is a "peculiar presumption" by which Western man has cut himself off from nature. To deny the ego, however, is not to deny an intuitive "inwardness" by which man, a participant in the "larger force" of reality, realizes himself as a natural object and therefore obtains "the secrets objects share." Such is the "projective act" of poetry, in which the artist, hearing nature through himself, "takes up speech in all its fullness" and causes "the thing he makes . . . to take its place alongside the things of nature." The principle involved here seems reminiscent of Hazlitt's doctrine of sympathetic identification as well as of Sartre's conception of the "phrase-object." [4]

Olson presents a notion of prosody based on this vision. Apparently in the mystical state of sympathy, man "hears" with his head ("the play of the mind," "the dance of the intellect") and speaks with his heart. "From the union of the mind and the ear" the syllable is born; from the "breathing of the man who writes, at the moment he writes," the "line is born." Olson believes that the syllable, a "root element of words, is the root element of speech, and hence of consciousness and thought"; the line, its "twin," is the metric, the chief element in the actual writing of the poem, and is related, supposedly, not to the mind but to the heart. Whether these distinctions seem nonsensical and confused is not the issue; what is important is that they are the results of a view in which sound becomes the single basis of speech, and speech of poetry, in the context of a mystical conception of reality.

It is not surprising to discover that this notion of "breath" has an implicit forerunner in *Paterson*, in which the central dramatic and moral problem is the struggle of the sleeping hero to awaken, of the poet to find his idiom. His breath, "Stale as a whale's breath: breath! / Breath!," Paterson "neither moves nor rouses and is seldom seen." He is, however, capable of isolated moments of achievement:

> Only of late, late! begun to know, to
> know clearly (as through clear ice) whence
> I draw my breath or how to employ it
> clearly—if not well. . . .

Since, in this vision, the life of Paterson the city, society in general, depends upon the breath of Paterson the poet, "speech-force" and "life force" are identified. Because for Williams there are "no ideas but in things," Paterson's crisis is comprehensible partly in terms of Olson's belief that the mind projects itself into its environment—becomes an object to share the "secrets" of all objects.

The *Maximus Poems*, Olson's major work to date, presents a vision of history obviously modeled on that in the *Cantos* and a vision of place (the fishing port of Gloucester, Massachusetts) modeled on that in *Paterson*. Like the structure of its prototypes, the repetitive form of this neo-epic has its "epistemology" and rhythm mystique: "ONE PERCEPTION MUST IMMEDIATELY AND DIRECTLY LEAD TO A FURTHER PERCEPTION . . . get on with it, keep moving, keep in, speed, the nerves, their speed, the perceptions theirs, the acts, the split second acts, the whole business, keep it moving as fast as you can, citizen." [5] Whatever this assertion means, it seems to be Olson's version of Pound's ideogrammic method, implying, as it does, a value of spontaneous, inconsecutive presentation.

Olson accordingly reexpresses Pound's conception of the

need for precision in language, *verita,* and the corruption of
language through advertising and other manifestations of
economic exploitation. We are told that under "pejorocracy"
(plutocracy) "even sound is neoned in," and all that is heard
is "mu-sick," whereas in the ideal society ("polis"), the
word is "meant to mean not a single thing the least more
than what it does mean . . . not at all to sell anything to
anyone." Again, as in Pound, the ideal of "precise language"
results in an objectivist poetic: "I distinguish / between
chanting, / and letting the song lie / in the thing itself,"
announces Maximus. A principal metaphor for speaking
true, creating poetry, is that of building a nest or constructing
a vessel:

> in! in! the bow-sprit, bird, the beak
> in, the bend is, in, goes in, the form
> that which you make, what holds, which is
> the law of the object, strut after strut, what you are,
>   what you must be, what
> the force can throw up, can right now hereinafter erect,
> the mast, the mast, the tender
> mast![6]   (p. 4)

Written in a rhythm that Olson might consider "percussive,"
this passage reveals a moral view akin to Pound's conception
that "sincerity" is the foundation of ideal art.

The direction of this aestheticist logic is, again, toward
idealization of the object and of the language by which it
is recreated or apprehended as things-in-themselves. "I measure my song, / measure the sources of my song, / measure
me, measure / my forces," says Maximus. And since, if we
apply Olson's view of the proper relation of man and nature,
subject and object are unified through sympathetic identification, the measure of one's forces and the measure of reality
are the same. Ideal poetry becomes one of "those self-acts
which have no end no more than their own," self-acts in
which "self-things" are apprehended:

```
these things
which don't carry their end any further than
their reality in
themselves. . . .                                    (p. 42)
```

This view has as its complement a Poundian interpretation of history and a corresponding obsession on the part of Olson with direct, concrete, and accurate relation: "to get down, right in the midst of / the deeds, to tell / what this one did, how / in the fray, he made this play, did grapple / with that one, how / his eye flashed / to celebrate / (beauty will not wait) / men, / and girls" (p. 98). Again, the proper language for this narrative is that which is most "sincere"—closest to reality, to idiomatic speech. Given the speech-nature mystique presented in "Projective Verse," one can appreciate all the more the whole moral context of the *Maximus Poems*. Just as Pound's vision of "paideuma" is ultimately characterized in Arcadian terms, as the ideals of Williams and Crane are characterized in terms of a nature myth, so we find Olson speaking of "polis," Plato's ideal state (specifically the spiritual essence of Gloucester, presently degraded), in terms of pastoral images, such as the "tansy," a local flower. The heroes, the so-called root-men, of "polis" are the men who lived close to nature and faced its perils with equanimity and purpose: explorers, map-makers, founders of colonies, settlers, and fishermen (all in contrast to "owners" and exploiters). But the point is that the technique appropriate to revealing natural-historical truth is purported to be itself natural, and a natural technique involves the "breath" of the poet, speech force, personal idiom, and, inevitably, personal experience. The practical manifestation of this poetic is no different from what it is in the *Cantos*. There is an intermingling of historical and personal material, of document and "memoir," according to what is virtually an associationist logic taken to be closer to the way of things than is conventional form. There is also, correspondingly, the same proliferation of minutiae, the "correct" presentation of which is part of a moral-aesthetic imperative. Olson's

editor calls Maximus "the man in the Word," an accurate
enough epithet if it is taken to suggest poetic-colloquial
revelation of nature, history, and self—or, conversely, the
expansion of personal speech to universal logos.

Another version of speech mysticism appears in Robert
Duncan, a onetime associate of Olson. In "Pages from a
Notebook," Duncan propounds the ideal of living "in the
swarm of human speech. This is not to seek perfection but
to draw honey or poetry out of all things. . . . It is, whatever our mastery, the use we make of speech that betrays to
ourselves and to our hunters (our readers) the spore of what
we are becoming." [7] Duncan shares with Mallarmé a vision
of an eternal world accessible, if at all, only through poetic
language. He shares with Hart Crane a Dionysian vision of
poetic language as a transconceptual rhythm or force that
reflects the forces of nature or life: "the force that words
obey in song / the rose and artichoke obey / in their unfold-
ing toward their form." Elsewhere we find:

> Lovely their feet pound the green solid meadow.
>   The dancers
> mimic flowers—root stem stamen and petal
>   our words are,
> our articulations, our
>   measures.
> It is the joy that exceeds pleasure.   ("The Dance")[8]

The "green solid meadow" is, of course, something more
than a meadow, as an earlier poem indicates:

> Often I am permitted to return to a meadow
> as if it were a given property of the mind
> that certain bounds hold against chaos,
>
> that is a place of first permission,
> everlasting omen of what is.
>
>   ("Often I Am Permitted to
>   Return to a Meadow")[9]

A series of poems entitled "The Structure of Rime" provide
a number of metaphysical variations on this theme. Written

in a hallucinatory Rimbaudian idiom, these poems reflect a
struggle to achieve what might be called a cosmic identity
through the Word:

> I ask the unyielding Sentence that shows Itself forth in
>   the language as I make it,
>
> Speak! For I name myself your master, who come to
>   serve.
> Writing is first a search in obedience.[10]

That is, "obedience" to the laws of life and eternity that
define the "bounds . . . against chaos." As for Mallarmé,
language is *le Verbe*, Logos, the means for apprehending
absolute reality: "There is a woman who resembles the sentence. She has a place in memory that moves language. Her
voice comes across the waters from a shore I don't know to
a shore I know, and is translated into words belonging to
the poem." [11] The poet learns that he must "suffer the sentence / a law of words moving / seeking their right period."
    The conception of speech as a mode of crystallizing the
nameless, invisible world in the human consciousness might
appear in so bizarre a poem as "An Owl Is an Only Bird
of Poetry," in which Duncan provides diagrams, in theo-
sophical fashion, for the vowels, associated with an occult
Holy Ghost, and the consonants, associated with a church
and with space and time.[12] Or it might provide the source
of tension in the more traditional poem, called "Doves,"
which is prefaced with an excerpt from a statement by
Norman Pearson on aphasia suffered by H.D.:

> She raises the bedroom window
> to let in the air and pearl-grey
>   light of morning
> where the first world stript of its names extends,
> where initial things go,
> beckoning dove-sounds recur
>   taking what we know of them

> from the soul leaps to the tongue's tip
>   as if to tell
>   what secret
> in the word for it.[13]

The intimation persists, but the "secret" cannot be formulated. The dove has flown and "the nets of words" in which man catches "the designs of the stars" are gone. What remains are "voices in the wind verging into leaf sound," not the "Tree's Talking." The poem concludes with the speaker's apparently feeling that he has suffered a similar deprivation: it is not that he has been rendered speechless, but that what seems to be a mystical syntax has gone out of his utterance: "O fateful thread! / Sentence that thru my song most moved! / Now from your courses the flame has fled / making but words of what I loved." The astral world is revealed in words, but words alone do not capture the astral world.

But Duncan's work reaches its highest pitch in orphic poems, wherein sex, music, and cosmos fuse into a mystical trinity. In "A Set of Romantic Hymns," [14] for example, the speaker is again plagued by the nightingale: "Sweet tones! Vibrant wing! / Towards-melody-shimmering lure / I d leap once more / to catch." This intimation, compared to a dazzling display of jewels, becomes a "clamor of bell tongues" that "breaks from Time's keep / Eternity—a flash!" But the music that the poet would "leap" to catch is music created "from the flesh" that "strikes images upon the Orphic lyre" —the "lure" is "muscular," a male lover:

> The Lover's thighs
> your thighs perform
> melodic torsos
> in one form
> (nipples are notes).

In this "secret trust," "life springs," and so does poetry, in a mystical moment that cannot be repeated:

> Never again this one life, this
> universe bent to this lyre

> he would make in the language
> for music's sake.

> Never again just this derivation
> from manhood, these numbers,
> this dwelling in the shape of things.

The sex-music experience is perilous because the trust is inevitably broken and the poet fated to suffer, as we discover in Duncan's translation, "Cyparissus," in which the hero unwittingly kills a beast lover:

> Apollo's art
> . . . from the lyre
> sends notes to pierce the human soul
> from which the life of music flows. . . .[15]

The orphic element in Duncan's poetry presupposes a belief in the kind of communication that, related to a mystical life force, transcends conventional language in the same way that music "transcends" words. One recalls Hart Crane's intention for the second part of "For the Marriage of Faustus and Helen": to "invent an idiom for the proper transposition of jazz into words," or, conversely, to find an idiom that had the musical qualities appropriate to a Dionysian experience. Important here is the assumption of an elemental sound or rhythm, prior to the language of significance, and quintessential to what is taken to be true poetry. Accordingly, in a poem called "An A Muse Ment," Duncan speaks of a "deconstruction—, for the reading of words" and of "lists of imaginary sounds I mean sound signs I mean things de signed in themselves." Such imaginary sounds, we are told in a pun, are the true "signs of life" and come (it is not surprising) from "the breath, pulse, / the constant / sluffing off of old stuff." [16]

This logic, it need hardly be asserted, provides the principal rationale for Beat poetry, as, in fact, for the whole Beat idiom in general. Allen Ginsberg announces in the "Notes for *Howl* and Other Poems" that his inspiration was "Hebraic-Melvillian bardic breath." [17] *Howl*, we are told, is a "huge, sad comedy of wild phrasing, meaningless images for the beauty of abstract poetry of mind running along making awkward combinations like Charlie Chaplin's walk, long saxophone-like chorus lines I knew Kerouac would hear *sound* of." Ginsberg asserts that he is exploiting Whitman's technique by seeking a "new speech-rhythm prosody to *build up* large organic structures," and that *Howl* is "my own heightened conversation, not cooler average-dailytalk short breath." It is precisely this notion of a rhythm, "transconceptual and non-verbal," that provides one of the main lines of continuity between the beat as individual, the beat as poet, and the beat as mystic. "Cooler average dailytalk short breath" differs quantitatively, not qualitatively, from the "heightened conversation" that establishes the poetic rhythm, just as poetic rhythm merges into "Angelical Ravings" that as the "music of the Spheres" reveals the ineffable "secrets of the imagination." *Howl* mentions "a lost battalion of platonic conversationalists" who talked steadily for seventy hours. The continuity of conversational, poetic, and mystic speech is, to repeat, one of the essential parts of a monistic attitude toward experience in which the profane and the sacred, the banal and the ecstatic, the sordid and the spiritual, are fused.

As it appears in Beat poetry, the rhythm mystique is the extreme primitivistic extension of linguistic romanticism. The idealization of language, in either its oral or visual aspect, need not inevitably take a primitivistic direction, although it clearly has a tendency toward some form of mystification— if not subrational, then, as in Eliot's *Quartets*, superrational. As we have noted, even Pound, who is perhaps the most rationalistic of modern poets, views rhythm and ideogram as both a "force" and as the direct expression of an ideal moral-psychological state.

A common logic and a common set of problems underlie the various conceptions of reality in modern American poetry. Antipathy to personal sentiment or conventional emotion, faith in an essential or ultimate reality, a belief in language as a mode of revelation, all constitute a "realist" poetic. Because this view assumes that apprehension of reality is attainable through a special intuition, the relation between subjective and objective elements, between transformation and revelation, between poetic psychology and philosophy of history, remains problematic. A general unity of orientation, however, scarcely means a specific uniformity of vision. To emotional primitivists like Fletcher, Cummings, and Crane, intuition is not what it is to ascetics like H.D. and Eliot. Marianne Moore's analytical apprehension of the "unparticularity" is not the same as Stevens' abstractionist apprehension of the "para-thing." Aesthetic perception, bizarre in poets like Williams or Stevens, is traditional in poets like Pound and Eliot. For Pound, the world of reason coexists with the world of mystery; for Eliot, the two worlds are discontinuous. There is perhaps no end to the number of distinctions one can make. But my point is that it is precisely the existence of a *common* logic that makes the formulation of such distinctions possible.

NOTES

NOTES TO CHAPTER 1

1. "Preface des poèmes antiques," in *Oeuvres de Leconte de Lisle: Derniers poèmes* (Librairie Alphonse Lemaire, Paris, 1942), p. 216.

2. *Criticism; The Major Texts* (Harcourt, Brace and World, New York and Burlingame, 1952), p. 272.

3. See *Literature Considered as Philosophy: The French Example* (Collier Books, New York, 1962).

4. *Pour un nouveau roman* (Gallimard, Paris, 1963). See particularly, "Nature, humanisme, tragédie."

5. In *The Philosophy of Schopenhauer* (Modern Library ed., Random House, New York, 1956), pp. 146–147.

6. Reprinted as part of *Speculations*, ed. by Herbert Read (Harvest ed., Harcourt Brace, New York, n.d.), pp. 143–169.

7. *Ibid.*, pp. 75–109. Quotation is on p. 86.

8. Reprinted as *Literature and Existentialism*, trans. by Bernard Frechtman (Citadel Press, New York, 1964), pp. 12–13.

9. "The Angelic Imagination," in *The Man of Letters in the Modern World, Selected Essays, 1928–1955* (Meridian Books, New York, 1960), p. 117. For an interesting theory of Hulme's conception of language, see Murray Krieger, *The New Apologists for Poetry* (Indiana Univ. Press, Bloomington, 1963), chap. 1.

10. An excellent discussion of Mallarmés aesthetic theories appears in Guy Delfel, *L'Esthetique de Stephane Mallarmé* (Flammarion, Paris, 1951). A standard English work on symbolist aesthetic theories is, of course, A. G. Lehmann's *The Symbolist Aesthetic in France* (Oxford, 1950).

11. See *The Continuity of American Poetry* (Princeton Univ. Press, Princeton, 1963). This work, partly monumental, partly a tour de force, has been attacked by René Wellek who argues that Pearce "uses cultural anthropology and existential terms for what, in the upshot, seems a high-minded romantic nationalism." ("Philosophy and Postwar American Criticism," reprinted in *Concepts of Criticism* [Yale Univ. Press, New Haven, 1964], p. 335.) One cannot deny, however, that Pearce has provided a number of authentic illuminations on a variety of poets.

12. I have discussed this point at length in *Hart Crane's Sanskrit Charge: A Study of the Bridge* (Cornell Univ. Press, Ithaca, 1960). I have offered a detailed consideration of Con-

fucian poetics and the theory of *cheng ming* in *The Confucian Odes of Ezra Pound: A Critical Appraisal* (Univ. of California Press, Berkeley and Los Angeles, 1963).

NOTES TO CHAPTER 2

1. Cited by S. Foster Damon in *Amy Lowell: A Chronicle* (Houghton Mifflin, Boston, 1953), p. 351.

2. Pierre Martino, *Parnasse et symbolisme* (1850–1900) (A. Colin, Paris, 1925).

3. In *Literary History of the United States*, Spiller, *et al.* (Macmillan, New York, 1953), pp. 1187–1188. Stanley K. Coffman's *Imagism: A Chapter for the History of Modern Poetry* remains the most detailed historical study in English of the movement (Univ. of Oklahoma Press, Norman, 1951).

4. *Oeuvres de Leconte de Lisle: Derniers poèmes* (Librairie Alphonse Lemaire, Paris, 1942), p. 217.

5. Reprinted as part of "A Retrospect" in *Literary Essays of Ezra Pound*, ed. by T. S. Eliot (Faber, London, 1954), p. 4.

6. *L'Influence du symbolisme Français sur la poésie Americaine* (1910–20) (Librarie Ancienne Honoré Champion, Paris, 1929), pp. 97–98.

7. Introduction to *The Complete Poems of Richard Aldington* (Allan Wingate, London, 1948), p. 16.

8. *Oeuvres de Leconte de Lisle: Poèmes antiques* (Librairie Alphonse Lemaire, Paris, 1948), p. 292.

9. *Ibid., Poèmes tragiques* (1952), p. 61.

10. *Goblins and Pagodas* (Houghton Mifflin, Boston and New York, 1916), pp. xvi–xvii.

11. I have quoted from the original version (later revised) which appeared in *Irradiations—Sand and Spray* (Houghton Mifflin, Boston, 1915).

12. *From Classic to Romantic: Premises of Taste in Eighteenth Century England* (Harper Torchbook ed., Harper, 1961), p. 132.

13. *Life Is My Song: The Autobiography of John Gould Fletcher* (Farrar and Rinehart, New York and Toronto, 1937), pp. 68–69.

14. *Selected Poems* (Farrar and Rinehart, 1938), pp. 56, 58. This convenient volume contains all that Fletcher wished to save

from his earlier works. As noted above, however, some of the poems have been revised.

15. *Ibid.*, pp. 148–150.

16. *Ibid.*, p. 44.

17. *The Burning Mountain* (Dutton, New York, 1946), p. 11. The poem is dated June, 1933, and hence postdates *The Bridge* (1930).

18. *Complete Poems*, p. 133.

19. *Cadences* (Poetry Book Shop, London, n.d.), p. 7.

20. *Ibid.*, p. 4.

21. *Ibid.*, p. 5.

22. *Life Is My Song*, pp. 213–214.

23. "The Black Rock" and "Elegy on Tintern Abbey" in *Selected Poems*, pp. 142, 211.

24. *Life Is My Song*, p. 371.

25. "Christmas Tree," *South Star* (Macmillan, New York, 1941), p. 61.

26. In *The Collected Poems of H.D.* (Liveright, New York, 1925): "Sea Rose," p. 3; "Sea Lily," p. 17; "Sea Iris," p. 53; "Sea Violet," p. 36; "Sheltered Garden," p. 25.

27. *Collected Poems*, p. 6.

28. *The Classical World of H.D.* (Univ. of Nebraska Press, Lincoln, 1962).

29. *Collected Poems*, p. 205.

30. *The Walls Do Not Fall* (Oxford Univ. Press, London and New York, 1944).

31. *Tribute to the Angels* (Oxford Univ. Press, London and New York, 1945).

32. *The Flowering of the Rod* (Oxford Univ. Press, London and New York, 1946).

33. *Helen in Egypt* (Grove Press, New York, 1961). For Swann's comments, see chap. xi; for Horace Gregory's, see introduction to the above edition.

34. Swann anticipates this argument, but does not really answer it. See *op. cit.*, p. 177.

35. *Ibid.*, p. 180.

36. Page references to the poem are thus cited.

37. See Damon, *op. cit.*, pp. 343, 360.

38. *The Complete Poetical Works of Amy Lowell* (Houghton Mifflin, Boston, 1955), p. 27. All citations are from this

edition. Since the work contains an index of titles, I have hence-
forth not provided page references.

NOTES TO CHAPTER 3

1. In "Marianne Moore," *The Selected Essays of William
Carlos Williams* (Random House, New York, 1954), p. 122.
2. *Selected Essays,* p. 5.
3. Cf. Coleridge in "On the Principles of Genial Criticism":
"So far is the Beautiful from depending wholly on association,
that it is frequently produced by the mere removal of association."
4. *The Autobiography of William Carlos Williams* (Random House, New York, 1951), p. 265.
5. *Selected Essays,* p. 257.
6. Williams' theory of the poem as object is in accord with
the fundamental principles of the Objectivist Movement, so
called, of which Louis Zukofsky was the leading spokesman.
Zukofsky outlined an Objectivist program in the February, 1931,
issue of *Poetry,* of which he was the guest editor. In an essay
not distinguished by clarity, he argued that "objectification" was
attained when the reader was "satisfied completely as to the
appearance of the art form as an object. That is: distinct from
print which records action and existence and incites the mind to
further suggestion, there exists . . . writing . . . which is an
object or affects the mind as such" (XXXVII, 274). Commenting on their own poems, Parker Tyler and Charles Henri Ford
pursued a logic analogous to Williams': "The poem is a gratuitous and arbitrary organism designed to contravene the hypothesis of continuous experience through time and space. It must
consciously eliminate the assumption of a continuous or historical type of experience by the projection of a system of
correlated images having an inevitable dramatic pause. The
images of these poems are not representative because neither a
duplication nor yet an embellishment of actual experience is
desired; all that is desired is an experience which is not subject
to the continuous or historical premise; the poem is an object"
(p. 287). Tyler and Ford appear to be talking about the
transconceptual experience, a recurrent subject in modern poetics.
Concerning the poem as object, one also recalls Gautier's

"sculptor-poet," who makes verbal enamels and cameos. John Espey has traced this tradition in regard to Ezra Pound (*Ezra Pound's Mauberley: A Study in Composition* [Faber, London, 1955], chap. 2), and Donald Davie has elaborated upon the thesis in *Ezra Pound: Poet as Sculptor* (Oxford Univ. Press, New York, 1964), *passim*.

7. In *The Collected Earlier Poems of William Carlos Williams* (New Directions, Norfolk, 1951), p. 55. Hereafter cited as CEP; since this edition has an index to titles, no page references will be given.

8. In *The Collected Later Poems of William Carlos Williams* (New Directions, Norfolk, 1950), p. 65. Hereafter cited as CLP; since this edition also has an index to titles, no page references will be given.

9. *Selected Essays*, pp. 197–198.

10. *Ibid.*, p. 5.

11. In *Pictures from Brueghel* (New Directions, Norfolk, 1962), p. 108.

12. Admittedly, the point is debatable. Linda Wagner, in *The Poems of William Carlos Williams: A Critical Study* (Wesleyan Univ. Press, Middletown, 1964), sees a humanistic element in such portraits and she argues that "innate majesty and dignity are one with the natural in the poet's sight" (p. 22). The only difficulty with this view is that it fails to take into account the whole aesthetic impulse toward novelty and non-conventionality. I might add at this point that Mrs. Wagner presents a competent and balanced survey of Williams' work.

13. One recalls the stoicism of H.D. Tragic fatalism, as I hope to demonstrate, is explicit in *Paterson*.

14. The best introductory study of *Paterson* remains Sister M. Bernetta Quinn's. See *The Metamorphic Tradition in Modern Poetry* (Rutgers Univ. Press, New Brunswick, 1958). The most recent study, that of Linda Wagner, *op. cit.*, does not add very much, I fear, to Sister Quinn's interpretation.

15. *Paterson* (New Directions, Norfolk, 1963), p. 173. All citations are from this edition.

16. *Autobiography*, pp. 390–391.

17. See Vivienne Koch, *William Carlos Williams* (New Directions, Norfolk, 1950).

18. *Poetry and the Age* (Vintage, New York, 1962), p. 238.

19. *The Selected Letters of William Carlos Williams* (Mc-
Dowell, Oblensky, New York, 1957), p. 226.
20. *Pictures from Brueghel*, p. 66.
21. *Ibid.*, p. 140.
22. *Ibid.*, p. 90.
23. *Ibid.*, p. 86.

NOTES TO CHAPTER 4

1. Needless to say, the issue has been discussed extensively
and from numerous points of view. General introductions, such
as Frank Kermode's *Wallace Stevens* (Grove Press, New York,
1961), William Van O'Connor's *The Shaping Spirit: A Study
of Wallace Stevens* (Regnery, Chicago, 1950), and Robert Pack's
Wallace Stevens: An Approach to His Poetry and Thought
(Rutgers Univ. Press, New Brunswick, 1958), are, as intended,
only a first step toward comprehension of the subtleties of
Stevens. Joseph Riddel's *The Clairvoyant Eye: The Poetry and
Poetics of Wallace Stevens* (Louisiana State Univ. Press, Baton
Rouge, 1965) appeared while the present work was in press.
2. All quotations are from *The Collected Poems of Wallace
Stevens* (Knopf, New York, 1954). Since the edition contains
an index to titles, no page references will be given for shorter
poems.
3. *Adagia*, in *Opus Posthumous* (Knopf, New York, 1957),
p. 164.
4. *Ibid.*
5. *Ibid.*, pp. 162, 168.
6. In *The Necessary Angel: Essays on Reality and the
Imagination* (Knopf, New York, 1951).
7. *Ibid.*, p. 130.
8. Stevens' hat imagery is discussed by Marius Bewley in
"The Poetry of Wallace Stevens," *Partisan Review*, XVI, September, 1949; reprinted in *The Achievement of Wallace Stevens:
A Critical Anthology*, ed. by Ashley Brown and Robert S. Haller
(Lippincott, Philadelphia and New York, 1963). See pp. 142 ff.
9. I disagree with Roy Harvey Pearce, who argues that "the
poet progresses from romantic subjectivism, to crude realism, to
exotic realism, to a kind of local-colorism, to a disciplined,
mature realism" ("Wallace Stevens: The Life of the Imagina-

tion," PMLA, XLVI, no. 5, September, 1951; reprinted in *Wallace Stevens: A Critical Collection*, ed. by Marie Boroff [Twentieth Century Views, Prentice-Hall, Englewood Cliffs, 1963]. See p. 112.). Pearce says he is following Hi Simons' interpretation, but in fact Simons argues that the intellectual development of the poet ends in "petit-bourgeois realism," not, as Pearce says, in "imaginative realism." ("The Comedian as the Letter C: Its Sense and Its Significance," *Southern Review*, V, Winter, 1940; reprinted in *The Achievement of Wallace Stevens*. See p. 111.) I find Simons' study the most useful introduction to date. An interesting study of the comic elements of "The Comedian" appears in Daniel Fuchs' *Wallace Stevens: The Comic Spirit* (Duke Univ. Press, Durham, 1963).

10. *Collected Poems*, p. 40.
11. *Ibid.*, p. 41.
12. *Ibid.*, p. 45.
13. *Necessary Angel*, pp. 29–31.
14. *Opus Posthumous*, p. 225.
15. *Collected Poems*, p. 373.
16. *Ibid.*, pp. 403–404.
17. *Ibid.*, p. 471.
18. *Ibid.*, p. 468.
19. *Ibid.*, p. 392.
20. *Ibid.*, p. 451.
21. *Opus Posthumous*, p. 189.
22. *Collected Poems*, p. 466.
23. *Opus Posthumous*, p. 183.
24. *Collected Poems*, pp. 320–321.
25. Harold Bloom provides a detailed analysis of this poem in "*Notes Toward a Supreme Fiction*: A Commentary," in *Wallace Stevens: A Critical Collection*, pp. 76–95. The point of view is considerably different from my own.
26. *Collected Poems*, p. 381.
27. *Ibid.*, p. 383.
28. *Ibid.*, p. 385.
29. *Ibid.*, p. 388.
30. *Necessary Angel*, pp. 50–51.
31. *Collected Poems*, p. 264.
32. *Ibid.*, pp. 390–391.
33. *Ibid.*, pp. 381–382.
34. *Ibid.*, p. 382.

35. *Opus Posthumous*, p. 220.
36. *Collected Poems*, p. 406.
37. *Ibid.*, pp. 278, 279.
38. "Wallace Stevens: Some Relations Between Poetry and Painting," *Comparative Literature*, XI, Winter, 1959; reprinted in *The Achievement of Wallace Stevens*.

NOTES TO CHAPTER 5

1. *A Marianne Moore Reader* (Viking, New York, 1961), pp. 254–255.
2. *Collected Poems, Marianne Moore* (Faber, London, 1951), p. 63. All quotations, unless otherwise noted, are from this edition.
3. *A Grammar of Motives* (Meridian, Cleveland and New York, 1962), p. 486.
4. *Marianne Moore* (Twayne, New York, 1964), p. 19.
5. A discussion of Miss Moore's attitudes toward Hebrew poetry appears in R. P. Blackmur's "The Method of Marianne Moore" in *Language as Gesture*; reprinted in *Form and Value in Modern Poetry* (Anchor, Doubleday, Garden City, 1957).
6. Engel believes that Miss Moore is criticizing the Greeks, in this passage, for having "light, excessively sophisticated ideas." Thus, they are "grasshoppers, not mountain climbers" (p. 74). Such a reading seems compelling enough, but it does not account for "Emotionally sensitive, their hearts were hard" or " 'Happy souls in Hell,' enjoying mental difficulties." If their wisdom is remote from the practicality, as Engel says, of the wardens of the game preserve, it is, again, because they possessed "such power as Adam had and we are still devoid of." The resolution of this ambiguity perhaps lies in the notion that what modern man needs is the Greek spirit of investigation, based on an "inner happiness," but not the simplified Greek solutions to the complexities of the universe, emblemized in the modern world by the octopus of ice.
7. "Spiritual poise" is discussed at length by Charles Tomlinson in "Abundance Not Too Much: The Poetry of Marianne Moore," *Sewanee Review*, LXV, 677–687.
8. I am indebted to Engel for this information.

NOTES TO CHAPTER 6

1. *E. E. Cummings: A Miscellany*, ed. by George Firmage (Argophile, New York, 1958), p. 12.

2. (Harcourt, Brace, New York, 1938), no pagination.

3. *E. E. Cummings: A Miscellany*, p. 13.

4. Foreword to *Is 5* (Liveright, New York, 1926). Reprinted as part of *i: Six Nonlectures* (Atheneum, New York, 1962), p. 64.

5. I might acknowledge at this point two useful studies: Norman Friedman's *E. E. Cummings: The Art of His Poetry* (Johns Hopkins Press, Baltimore, 1960) and Barry Marks' *E. E. Cummings* (Twayne, New York, 1964).

6. *Nonlectures*, p. 81.

7. All quotations are from *E. E. Cummings, Poems, 1923–54* (Harcourt, Brace, New York, 1954), which supersedes *Collected Poems*.

8. *Nonlectures*, p. 65.

9. *Ibid.*, p. 82

10. Jean-Paul Sartre, *Literature and Existentialism* (Citadel Press, New York, 1949), p. 38.

11. *Le Rire*, translated as "Laughter" in *Comedy*, ed. by Wylie Sypher (Modern Library ed., Random House, New York, 1956), pp. 157–58.

NOTES TO CHAPTER 7

1. Introduction to *The Collected Poems of Hart Crane* (Liveright, New York, 1946), p. xiv.

2. *The Letters of Hart Crane*, ed. by Brom Weber (Hermitage, New York, 1952), p. 31.

3. The following discussion is based on my "Hart Crane's Early Poetry," *University of Kansas City Review*, XXVII, Spring, 1961.

4. Reprinted in Brom Weber, *Hart Crane: A Biographical and Critical Study* (Bodley, New York, 1948), p. 385.

5. *Letters*, p. 66.

6. *Collected Poems.* Unless otherwise noted, all quotations are from this edition. Since poems may be found conveniently, no page references are given.

7. "Modern Poetry," reprinted in *Collected Poems*. See pp. 177–178.

8. "General Aims and Theories," reprinted in Philip Horton's *Hart Crane: The Life of an American Poet* (W. W. Norton, New York, 1937), pp. 326–327.

9. I have discussed this point in detail in *Hart Crane's Sanskrit Charge: A Study of The Bridge* (Cornell Univ. Press, Ithaca, 1960).

10. I have noted in *Hart Crane's Sanskrit Charge* that "how much Crane actually read of Nietzsche, or how deeply, is unknown. Nietzsche was much admired in the twenties and it seems improbable that Crane would not have read Mencken's *The Philosophy of Nietzsche* which appeared as early as 1908."

11. *Letters*, p. 89.

12. *The Birth of Tragedy*, trans. by William Haussman, in *The Complete Works of Friedrich Nietzsche*, ed. by Oscar Levy (T. N. Foulis, Edinburgh, 1909), III, 28–29.

13. *Letters*, p. 121.

14. *Noa Noa* (Greenberg, New York, n.d.), pp. 48–49.

15. *Ibid.*, p. 51.

16. *Our America* (Boni and Liveright, New York, 1919), p. 9.

17. *Ibid.*, p. 10.

NOTES TO CHAPTER 8

1. "The Serious Artist," in *Literary Essays*, ed. by T. S. Eliot (Faber, London, 1954), p. 46.

2. See "The Teacher's Mission," in *Literary Essays*, pp. 58 ff.

3. *The Letters of Ezra Pound, 1907–1941*, ed. by D. D. Paige (Harcourt, Brace, New York, 1950), pp. 3–4.

4. "Date Line," in *Literary Essays*, p. 75.

5. This view is not, of course, original. Noel Stock attempts to trace its "tradition" in *Poet in Exile: Ezra Pound* (Barnes and Noble, New York, 1964), pp. 42–68.

6. "A Few Don'ts," reprinted as part of "A Retrospect," in *Literary Essays*, p. 4.

7. "The Renaissance" in *Literary Essays*, p. 215.

8. Reprinted in *The Translations of Ezra Pound*, ed. by Hugh Kenner (New Directions, New York, n.d.), pp. 18–19.

9. *The Spirit of Romance* (Dent, London, 1910), pp. 168–169.

10. *Literary Essays*, p. 215.

11. *The Spirit of Romance*, p. 92.

12. *Ibid.*

13. *Ibid.*

14. *Ibid.*

15. (Liveright, New York, 1942), pp. 295–311.

16. *Catullus: The Complete Poems* (Sylvan Press, London, 1942), Introduction.

17. *The Translations of Ezra Pound*, p. 18.

18. *Personae* (Faber, London, 1952). Since this edition has an index of titles, page references will be given only for quotations from longer poems.

19. *Umbra* (Mathews, London, 1920), p. 127.

20. "Ballata V," in *The Translations of Ezra Pound*, p. 107.

21. The best study of *Propertius* to date is J. P. Sullivan's *Ezra Pound and Sextus Propertius: A Study in Creative Translation* (Univ. of Texas Press, Austin, 1964).

22. *Ezra Pound's Mauberley: A Study in Composition* (Univ. of California Press, Berkeley and Los Angeles, 1955). This work is essential to any study of the poem. For an interesting argument relevant to the present discussion see William V. Spanos' "The Modulating Voice of Hugh Selwyn Mauberley," *Wisconsin Studies in Contemporary Literature*, Vol. VI, no. 1, Winter-Spring, 1965.

23. Espey, *op. cit.*, 98–99.

24. *Ibid.*, p. 92.

25. *Ideas into Action: A Study of Pound's Cantos* (Univ. of Miami Press, Coral Gables, 1958), chap. 1. Although this book is poorly organized, it is the most thorough study to date of the *Cantos*.

26. *Guide to Kulchur* (New Directions, Norfolk, n.d.), pp. 223–224.

27. I have presented a detailed version of this argument in *The Confucian Odes of Ezra Pound: A Critical Appraisal* (Univ. of California Press, Berkeley and Los Angeles, 1963), chap. 2. I might add that Pound's classical humanism has some interesting affinities with that of Matthew Arnold. Particularly relevant are Arnold's conception of Culture as "curiosity," the desire for "seeing things as they are," and his notion of the "application

234 NOTES TO PAGES 169–183

of ideas to life," a counterpart of ideas-into-action. The view that ideal knowledge is completed only by virtuous action is, of course, part of the whole classical rationale. Sidney's "Defence," one recalls, is based upon this point—the Aristotelian argument that "not *gnosis* but *praxis* must be the fruit."

28. Harold Watts discusses the canto as ideograph in *Ezra Pound and the Cantos* (Routledge and Kegan Paul, London, 1952).

29. Donald Davie, in *Ezra Pound: Poet as Sculptor* (Oxford Univ. Press, New York, 1964), presents an interesting discussion of another aspect of Pound's subjectivity, the conception of "forma" (form held in the mind just prior to expression) as an organizing principle of the *Cantos*.

30. The *Odyssey*, trans. by W. H. D. Rouse (Mentor, New American Library, New York, 1949), p. 115.

31. *The Confucian Odes of Ezra Pound.*

32. Forrest Read, "A Man of No Fortune" (*English Institute Essays*, 1953). Reprinted in *Ezra Pound: A Collection of Critical Essays*, ed. by Walter Sutton (Twentieth Century Views, Prentice-Hall, Englewood Cliffs, 1963), p. 65.

33. Quotations are from the New Directions edition of the *Cantos* (Norfolk, 1948).

34. For a discussion of the "Ouan jin-Wanjina-wondjina" associations, see Guy Davenport, "Pound and Frobenius," in *Motive in the Cantos of Ezra Pound*, ed. by Lewis Leary (Columbia Univ. Press, New York, 1954), p. 50.

35. *Index to the Cantos of Ezra Pound*, ed. by J. H. Edwards and W. Vasse (Univ. of California Press, Berkeley and Los Angeles, 1957). I must also acknowledge the useful *Analyst*, Nos. I–VIII, XIII, mimeographed publication of the Department of English, Northwestern University, no date.

36. A discussion of the goddess-destroyer image appears in George Dekker's *Sailing to Knowledge: A Study of the Cantos of Ezra Pound* (Routledge and Kegan Paul, London, 1963).

37. Dekker discusses the fertility theme in detail.

NOTES TO CHAPTER 9

1. "Tradition and the Individual Talent," in *Selected Essays* (Faber, London, 1961), p. 17.

2. *Ibid.*, pp. 18–19.

3. "The Function of Criticism," in *Selected Essays*, p. 24.

4. *Existentialism* (Philosophical Library, New York, 1947), p. 44.

5. *T. S. Eliot's Poetry and Plays: A Study in Sources and Meanings* (Univ. of Chicago Press, Chicago, 1956), pp. 22–23. Smith gives a Bergsonian reading to a number of the poems, but he is aware of the limitations of following Bergson too specifically.

6. From another point of view, Eliot's "realism" can be regarded, paradoxically, as a form of idealism, as indeed can any theory in which the distinction between subject and object is eliminated. Thus, in analyzing Eliot's indebtedness to the idealist F. H. Bradley, Hugh Kenner cites Eliot's paraphrase in his (Eliot's) dissertation on the philosopher that "in feeling, the subject and the object are one." Kenner goes on to discuss Bradley's theory that "all we do and suffer and are forms one psychic totality. It is experienced all together as a coexisting mass, not perceived as parted and joined even by relations of co-existence. It contains all relations, and distinctions, and every ideal object that at that moment exists in the soul." He later quotes Eliot as saying that "I, the objective world, and my feelings about it, are an indissoluble whole" (*The Invisible Poet: T. S. Eliot* [McDowell, Oblensky, New York, 1959], pp. 49, 61). The fact remains, however, that in the "psychic totality" involving a wasteland, the mind is inadequate to the task of imposing order and, accordingly, of acquiring an "identity."

7. Quotations are from *The Complete Poems and Plays* (Harcourt, Brace, New York, 1952).

8. Smith, *op. cit.*, p. 32.

9. *Ibid.*, pp. 27–28.

10. *Selected Essays*, p. 26.

11. *Ibid.*, p. 30.

12. Hugh Kenner, *op. cit.*, pp. 150–151.

13. See note 6.

14. Smith, *op. cit.*, p. 74. Similarly, George Williamson interprets the protagonist's failure of response as the "effect of the vision of the Grail upon the impure" (*A Reader's Guide to T. S. Eliot* [Noonday, New York, 1963], pp. 131–132).

15. *Modern Poetry and the Tradition* (Univ. of North Carolina Press, Chapel Hill, 1939).

16. This is not to preclude the possibility of a symbolic interpretation in accord with the theme of spiritual aphasia.

17. Smith, *op. cit.*, p. 80.

18. "Lancelot Andrewes," in *Selected Essays*, p. 351.

19. I have not discussed "Ash-Wednesday," since the problems considered recur more explicitly in *Four Quartets*.

20. The most thorough discussion of the problem of time in Eliot appears in Staffen Bergsten's *Time and Eternity: A Study in the Structure and Symbolism of T. S. Eliot's Four Quartets* (Svenska Bokforlaget, Stockholm, 1960).

21. *Guide to Kulchur* (New Directions, Norfolk, n.d.), p. 328.

22. *The Idea of a Christian Society*, in *Christianity and Culture* (Harcourt, Brace, New York, n.d.), p. 34.

23. *Notes Toward the Definition of Culture*, in *Christianity and Culture*, p. 157.

24. *Ibid.*, p. 68.

NOTES TO CHAPTER 10

1. *Selected Essays of William Carlos Williams* (Random House, New York, 1954), pp. 283, 286. For a specific discussion of Williams' material theories, see Linda Wagner, *The Poems of William Carlos Williams: A Critical Study* (Wesleyan Univ. Press, Middletown, 1964), chap. 5.

2. *Literary Essays*, ed. by T. S. Eliot (Faber, London, 1954), pp. 9–10.

3. "Projective Verse," in *The New American Poetry, 1945–1960*, ed. by Donald Allen (Grove Press, New York, 1960), pp. 386–397.

4. See Introduction to this work.

5. Allen, *op. cit.*, pp. 387–388.

6. Quotations are from the *Maximus Poems* (Jargon/Corinth Books, New York, 1960).

7. Reprinted in Allen, *op. cit.*, p. 400.

8. In *The Opening of the Field* (Grove Press, New York, 1960), p. 8.

9. *Ibid.*, p. 7.

10. *Ibid.*, p. 12.

11. *Ibid*

12. Allen, *op. cit.*, pp. 42–43.

13. *Roots and Branches: Poems by Robert Duncan* (Scribner's, New York, 1964), p. 86.

14. *Ibid.*, pp. 106–114.

15. *Ibid.*, p. 166.

16. *The Black Mountain Review*, Vol. I, no. 3, Fall, 1954, pp. 19–22.

17. Reprinted in Allen, *op. cit.*, pp. 414–418.

INDEX

Crape Myrtle," 110, 111; "The Mind Is an Enchanting Thing," 111; "The Hero," 111, 112; "Voracities and Verities," 112; "In the Days of Prismatic Colour," 112–113; "A Carriage from Sweden," 113; "Critics and Connoisseurs," 113; "The Icosasphere," 113–114; "An Octopus," 114–115, 116; "Nevertheless," 115; "Melancthon," 116–117; "The Jerboa," 117; "Spenser's Ireland," 117; "Too Much," 117; "Virginia Brittania," 117
Murry, John Middleton, 193

Nietzsche, Friedrich, 17, 23, 28, 43, 133, 137, 139, 140, 141, 143, 147, 171, 232

Objectivism (conception), 1–4, 6, 9, 47, 48–80 *passim*, 88, 108, 109, 119, 125, 133, 151, 184, 202, 210
Objectivism (Movement), 49, 226
O'Connor, William Van, 228
Olson, Charles, 9, 208–214

Pack, Robert, 228
Parnassus (Movement), 1, 11
Pearce, Roy Harvey, 5, 221, 223–229
Pearson, Norman, 215
Plarr, V. G., 166
Pound, Ezra, 9, 74–77, 122, 151–182, 201, 219; *poems cited:* Cantos, 5, 7, 8, 13, 40–41, 46, 151, 153, 161–162, 165, 167, 168–181, 201, 213; "Sestina: Altaforte," 157; *Homage to Sextus Propertius*, 158, 163–164; "Au Jardin," 159; "Ortus," 159; "Praise of Ysolt," 159; "Na Audiart," 159–160; "A Girl," 160; "La Fraisne," 160–161, "Ballata V," 162, "The Alchemist," 162–163; *Hugh Selwyn Mauberley (Life and Contacts)*, 163, 164–167, 173–174, 180; *prose works cited:* "A Few Don'ts," 11, 122, 154; "The Serious Artist," 151–152; *Letters*, 152–153; "Date Line," 153; introduction to Cavalcanti Poems, 154, 158; "The Renaissance," 154, 155; *The Spirit of Romance*, 154, 155, 156; postscript to the translation of de Gourmont's *Natural Philosophy of Love*, 157; introduction to *Umbra*, 161; *Guide to Kulchur*, 168, 172, 202–203; *conceptions: cheng ming*, 6, 169, 223–224, *directio voluntatis*, 168; ideas into action, 168; *kulchur*, 169; *kulturmorphologie*,